THIRTY YEARS IN A  RED HOUSE

For Elaine,

with best wishes.

Zhu Xiao Di

ZHU XIAO DI

FOREWORD BY ROSS TERRILL

THIRTY YEARS IN A RED HOUSE

A MEMOIR OF CHILDHOOD AND YOUTH IN COMMUNIST CHINA

UNIVERSITY OF

MASSACHUSETTS

PRESS

AMHERST

Printed in the United States of America
LC 97-15886
ISBN 1-55849-112-0 (cloth); 216-x (paper)
Designed by Richard Hendel
Set in Minion and Lithos types by Keystone Typesetting, Inc.
Printed and bound by Thomson-Shore, Inc.
Library of Congress
Cataloging-in-Publication Data
Zhu, Xiao Di, 1958–
Thirty years in a red house: a memoir of
childhood and youth in Communist China /
Zhu Xiao Di ; foreword by Ross Terrill.
   p. cm.
Includes index.
ISBN 1-55849-112-0 (cloth : alk. paper) — ISBN 1-55849-216-x (pbk. : alk. paper)
1. Zhu, Xiao Di, 1958– . 2. China—
History—Cultural Revolution, 1966–1969—
Personal narratives. I. Title.
DS778.7.Z48   1998
951.05'6—dc21
[B]   97-15886
  CIP
British Library Cataloguing in
Publication data are available.

This book is published with the support and
cooperation of the University of Massachusetts
Boston.

CONTENTS

CHAPTER EIGHT

FOREWORD

Sometimes one person's story, like a single ray that bursts from a mirror as a powerful wave of light, illuminates the life of an epoch and a nation. Such is the case with *Thirty Years in a Red House*. It is a book about Chinese Communist history. Yet, more profoundly, it describes survival in an alarming environment, and the hopes and aches of the human heart.

Zhu Xiao Di, born in 1958, grew up in a Nanjing family of idealistic, educated Communists. He developed a strong interest in books, ideas, and the English language. Inevitably, he and his family repeatedly collided with the juggernaut of Communist rule. Their fortunes waxed and waned with the degree of China's openness to the outside world.

Along the rocky road of the Zhu family's journey, we glimpse the "anti-rightist drive" of 1957 that ruined Zhu's uncle, Mao's Promethean efforts to clinch communism overnight in the Great Leap Forward of the late 1950s, and the combined purge and search for revolutionary immortality that was the Cultural Revolution of the 1960s. Although Japan's wartime activities in China appear rarely in Zhu Xiao Di's memoir and he does not draw the following comparison, one feels compelled to note the irony that the Chinese Communists rail against Japan for "not apologizing" for World War II but have never apologized to the Chinese people for their own elimination of innocent millions during Mao's class warfare and social engineering. Up and down China, with its 1.2 billion people and its forty cities with populations of more than a million, there is no monument to the victims of these gyrations.

The stratum that suffered more than any other were the people of education and culture—like Zhu's family. The Cultural Revolution was unleashed by Mao, yet it could only be a violent storm because enough people responded to Mao's call. Private values were so held back as to be a virtually nonexistent force against wayward public policy. Most Chinese believed that to take an individualistic stand was foolish. They had learned from experience, or it had been drilled into them, that the only way to survive was to go along with the tribe. We see all these accommodations in *Thirty Years in a Red House*. Yet we also see the Zhu family holding on to its integrity; and Zhu Xiao Di being raised as a boy of conscience and sensitivity. He learned to appreciate the ironies of history. His family largely protected itself from the corruptions of public life. Most of its members merely went through the motions of conformity without losing hold of their consciences.

Sometimes there is a moral shallowness to Chinese writing about the Mao era—a result of the toll totalitarianism takes on the morality of those it binds tight. Yet in *Thirty Years in a Red House* a certain purity prevails. The Zhus' ordeal is deeper than a story of interchangeable heroes and villains.

The narrator's father, Zhu Qiluan, was at various times underground Communist, teacher, journalist, government official, and college administrator. In this last role, Mr. Zhu received a letter from the son of a famous literary dissenter, Hu Feng, asking him to undo the injustice that had befallen him as the offspring of a writer who upset Mao. Mr. Zhu thought the younger Hu's argument was reasonable and asked an officer under him to restore the man's proper salary and benefits. The flunky reminded Mr. Zhu that the person was Hu Feng's son. "Yes, I know," said Mr. Zhu. Like a machine, the officer repeated, "He is Hu Feng's son." Mr. Zhu smiled. "I heard you. Please just do what I said. . . . Hu Feng is Hu Feng. His son is his son. They are not the same person." Mr. Zhu tried to uphold individualism in the midst of collectivist frenzy.

In *Thirty Years in a Red House* we learn less about the landscape of Mao's revolution than, say, in Nien Cheng's *Life and Death in Shanghai* or Liu Binyan's *A Higher Kind of Loyalty*. Zhu Xiao Di is not a dissident with a political program. He merely tells the story of himself and his family. But he does so with a beautiful sense of the interactions between private and public life, and a knowledge of Western literature and culture that gives his story a universal ring. The book is not unremittingly bleak; it has charm, a moral sense, and the human appeal of a family trying to uphold traditional values. It is a Nanjing "cultural" book, not a Beijing "political" book, and this gives it originality.

As you turn the pages of *Thirty Years in a Red House*, you come to like Zhu, to feel with him; when he is cheated by an unscrupulous rival from going to study in Australia, you feel angry! His mind is interesting; his angle of vision on China and life and literature is acute. After the book is read, the character of its author lingers in memory.

As communism is buried in the former Soviet Union and Eastern Europe, China stands as the last great bastion of the costly Marxist experiment. Can China throw off Communist dictatorship? This book gives us clues to the traditions, cultural traits, and social ways that have reinforced the Mao/Deng dictatorship, and which in the future could complicate China's post-Communist search for a political system at once modern and Chinese. It also displays the subtlety of some Chinese people's resistance to that dictatorship.

Zhu does not hide the keenness he felt to get away from China; in 1987 he came to Boston and began graduate studies, first at the University of Massachusetts, Boston and then at MIT. Yet in spirit he has not taken leave of China. Raised in a loyal Communist family, he has always cared a great deal about his motherland. Like many of the best of Deng Xiaoping's generation—and of generations in between Deng's and today's youth—Zhu went to the West to study and breathe a more invigorating air. It remains to be seen how many Chinese like Zhu for whom Tiananmen Square is a shadow will return to enrich China, and how many will stay in the West, flourishing as individuals, but lost to a China whose politics has made them orphans.

Ross Terrill
Boston, Massachusetts

ACKNOWLEDGMENTS

Even today I am still amazed that I could write this book in English, which is not my native language. I know that without the help of many people I could never have accomplished this endeavor.

First, I want to thank Helen Snively for her advice to get my story out without worrying too much about my English, and for her fascinating efficiency in polishing my English. Without her, I might still be working on the first chapter.

Next, I express my hearty thanks to Louisa Birch, who not only helped focus my story but also spent an incredible amount of time carefully editing my manuscript. Her comments gave me great encouragement and her input has greatly increased the quality of this book.

I also thank Nicholas Herman, who devoted his time and thought to improving my manuscript in a timely manner that one could hardly expect from anyone but perhaps the author himself. I am deeply grateful for his valuable suggestions and advice.

Also, I want to thank several of my former professors at the University of Massachusetts, Boston. Seymour Katz, professor of English literature and American civilization, not only took the time to read and edit my manuscript, but also gave me very constructive criticism as well as advice for revising. Kathleen Hartford, professor and chair of the department of political science and also my academic advisor, was one of the few who gave me the initial encouragement and support to start this project. Both Barry Bluestone of political economy and Irving Bartlett of the American civilization program gave me invaluable encouragement and help in getting this book published.

I also thank John Braun, professor emeritus of English at Lewis and Clark College in Portland, Oregon, although we have never met. His and his wife's enthusiasm in reading my manuscript and their understanding of the spirit of my book moved me deeply and convinced me that my story deserves a larger audience.

I have to thank the University of Massachusetts Press and its staff, particularly my editor, Paul Wright, not only for his usual editor's role, but also for his initiative in inviting the renowned Ross Terrill to write a foreword for my book. Of course, I must thank Mr. Terrill for his highly complimentary piece, although we have never met each other either.

Some people may have only read parts of my manuscript, but their encouragement and help are also invaluable to me. Therefore, I am grateful to Judith Shapiro in Washington, D.C., another supporter whom I have never met, Liu Xiaogan in Singapore, and Robert Elmore and Patti Grossman in Boston.

Above all, I have to thank my wife, Meirong. Without her consistent encouragement and enormous support, I could never have completed this book. She was my first and most committed reader. Her thoughts have greatly increased the strengths of my book. It is also remarkable that, although she could not speak a word of English when she married me, she helped me more than once to rephrase my text into more idiomatic English. Indeed, I could only find the time to write the book because Meirong so eagerly took over much of the responsibility—which should have been mine—for our energetic and talented son, Alexander, who taught himself how to read at the age of four and a half. Whatever value this book holds, great credit should go to Meirong. As she and I approached the publication of this book, a new joy came into our lives: our second son, Jefferson. We thank God for this new blessing.

Boston, Massachusetts
April 1997

THIRTY YEARS IN A   RED HOUSE

CHAPTER 1

A LONG-AWAITED SON

When I was born in 1958, my father was already forty-four years old. This was unusual in a society where most babies were born to parents in their twenties. Because I was born so late, my father was old enough to be my grandfather. In fact, to my friends, my father was more like a grandfather than a father. Because they related to their grandparents as I related to my father, it made me seem their parents' age. This unusual situation helped me mature at a young age and enabled me to experience the feelings of two generations, both my contemporaries and their parents.

In China, it was considered fortunate when someone over forty finally had a first son, because in this male-dominated society only sons carry on family lines. Even the 1949 Communist Revolution could not quite change this traditional view. My birth must have brought a special atmosphere of joy and excitement to the family.

I could have brought material fortune to my parents had I been born a few years earlier. During the first three years of Communist rule, government employees did not have salaries. This was because, in an ideal Communist society, each individual was supposed to contribute to society by working as hard and conscientiously as possible; in return, they would have the right to whatever they needed. After the 1949 Revolution, Chinese Communists tried to apply this theory to China. However, as a practical compromise, it was applied only to government employees. Instead of a salary, a public employee was given an allowance for pocket money while all of life's necessities—from food and clothes to soap—were allocated according to family size. Therefore, when a family had another child, it received more shares of allotted materials. However, by the time I was born, this policy had been changed. Like other workers, government employees now received salaries to support their families. Thus I was born a little too late to earn my own bread at birth.

The earlier work/compensation policy was also consistent with the policy of encouraging mothers to have more babies. As in the Soviet Union, a woman with more than five children would be highly honored as a "Heroic Mother." Thus, many of my parents' colleagues had four or five, even eight or ten children. Later on, when the policy was changed to control the population, those who had too many children were easily victimized. I remember people often joked about one of my neighbors who had eight children. His youngest daughters were less than a year apart and people often asked which girl was Number Seven and which was Number Eight. He always hesitated and often gave the wrong answer. Yet things looked quite different to a child. I always envied my playmates who had many siblings, especially older brothers. I felt vulnerable, for I had no older brother to back me up in a fight. Later I had a hard time surviving the political and social turmoil of the late 1960s because I had little sibling support.

I did have an elder sister. Before my mother became pregnant with me she had serious heart trouble and once was hospitalized. Her doctor told her that a patient with her kind of heart disease was not likely to live more than ten years. Indeed, she was the only survivor among dozens of hospital roommates. Half of them went into surgery and never returned; the other half were sent home as there was no cure, and within a few years they all died of heart troubles. My birth must have been a trial, for both my mother's body and my father's nerves.

At the time, my mother worked in a public high school and as a public employee had full health care provided by the government. It was this good, government-financed health care that enabled my mother and me to survive. I was born in the city hospital, which had been a church hospital, built by American missionaries early in the century. The doctors were well trained Western-style physicians. Because of my mother's complicated situation, three physicians stood by as a rescue team. They were Doctor Ma, a physician specializing in heart disease; Doctor Zhang, specializing in heart surgery; and Doctor Liu, the only male gynecologist I have ever heard of in China. I don't know exactly what happened in the delivery room, but my mother often told me, in a grateful voice, that had it not been for those doctors, neither of us would have lived.

While the public health care system seemed to work well, some other policies based on the same ideology caused great harm. In the year I was born, the Communist authorities decided to speed up the process of reorganizing millions of peasants into a collective farming system. They put hundreds of neighboring peasant families together as a work unit and forced everybody to share everything, including farm tools and food. Public cafeterias were set up and people ate for free. Everyone seemed happy and the enthusiasm soon created an illusion that such consumption was sustainable. The leaders in Beijing, who thought they had created a wonderland overnight, called it the "Great Leap Forward." Communism was believed to be the final stage of social evolution, when the world would become perfect. Now, that day was about to come because we were taking a great leap forward. That year, many parents named their newborn babies "Yue Jin," meaning the "Great Leap Forward."

My parents did not give me that name. Instead, they called me "Xiao Di." Unlike English, Chinese does not have special words for people's given names; parents just pick any word. A typical Chinese name consists of two or three words. The family name comes first, then one or two words as the given name. My name was chosen by my father. The first word was "Xiao," or "little." The second was "Di," the name of a rare flower, symbolizing friendly brotherhood, and the word is pronounced the same way as the word "younger brother."

For many years I disliked my name. First of all, it was hard to write the second word. In Chinese, words or characters are formed with strokes, and the number of strokes may vary from one to more than a dozen, although most have fewer than ten. But "Di" has twelve strokes! I always felt it was unfair when the kindergarten teachers praised others who could write their names. I said to myself, "Yes. But their names have many fewer strokes than mine." Second, my name sounded exactly like "little younger brother." This annoyed me as a child because it made me feel I would never grow up and people would always joke about me as their "little younger brother," even if I were seventy years old.

I did not fully change my feelings until I went to college. One day I had a bitter quarrel with my father over my name and he suddenly said, "Why can't you see the most obvious advantage of it? Di is so rarely used as a name that there will never be another person on this earth with the same name. Doesn't that give you a sense of being a special individual?" I understood his point finally. Later, when I began to publish articles in local newspapers and popular magazines, I came to see how right he was. I believe my unique name helped me to be recognized and remembered. I sometimes wondered how my father could have retained such a strong sense of the individual in his heart since he had joined the Communist movement as a teenager.

Perhaps another reason that my father picked "Di" for my name was that he wanted to see me have a brother. This occurred to me when a close friend wrote to me after he had attended my father's funeral:

> I was visiting your father at the hospital the other day when you called from America. He was so happy to receive your call. He had long lost his appetite. Yet after talking to you, he joyfully invited me to have lunch with him. At the lunch table, he asked about my brother and kept on saying what a pity it was that you did not have a brother.

My heart was touched as I read this paragraph, but a deeper chord was hit as I read the next part of the letter. Because it was just after the Tiananmen Incident that my father was ill, neither my mother nor my wife thought it was a good time for me to return to China to visit him. During the last days of his life, in his delirium, he told my mother several times that he heard I was coming home soon and he was going to see me again. I was a long-awaited son when I was born. Now I kept him waiting again, and missed my last chance to see him alive. When I read my friend's comments my heart was bleeding. He wrote:

> While I was attending his funeral and wept over his body, I was preoccupied by the following thought. The benign old man had devoted his life to a course which he thought would benefit all families of future generations. Yet, what a tragedy that even his own son could not come back to see him although he knew he was dying.

In his words, I could see a tragedy that was not just mine but that of the whole nation. My father's death helped me look more carefully at his life. As I reflected on his past, I felt I not only knew him better, but I also began to better understand the youth of his generation and the Communist Revolution as well.

FATHER AS A YOUNG REBEL

My father was born in the southern province of Anhui in 1914, three years after the last emperor was overthrown. The 1911 Revolution, led by Dr. Sun Yat-sen, ended thousands of years of dynasties and began China's modernization. My father was born into a family that followed the modernization trend. In a largely agricultural society, my grandfather successfully became a banker, working as a high-level manager for banks in different provinces throughout China. He enjoyed an upper-middle-class standard of living in a society of mass poverty.

My grandmother came from an educated, elite family; she was good at math and could use an abacus. Yet, like many women of the day, she was a housewife with bound feet, whose main duty was to bear and raise children. In a male-dominated society, my grandmother was considered to be very lucky because she had three sons and one daughter, my father being the eldest. The family did quite well until my grandfather died suddenly in 1923, when my father was only nine years old.

This was extremely hard for the family because Grandfather had been the sole wage earner. Although my grandmother was only forty years old, in a culture where women were not supposed to work and widows were not allowed to remarry, it was very difficult for her to survive and support four young children aged two to nine. I do not know exactly how she managed. What I do know is that with savings left by her husband and some help from her brother, an engineer working for a major railroad company, she managed to send my father to excellent private schools and to the Law and Business School at Beijing University. Beijing University was the best and one of the oldest universities in China, and this was a great accomplishment.

After Grandfather's death, the family moved to Nanjing to be close to relatives in their extended family for help and support. It was a time of civil war between warlords in China. My father grew up in an environment of mass poverty, injustice, war, and death, and always dreamed of living in a better place.

He studied very hard at school, hoping to escape his environment. In order to enter the State School of Nanjing, a school with an excellent reputation at the time, he had to pass a very selective exam. Only 5 percent of the applicants could pass the exam, and when his time came my father was among them. However, he soon began to realize that even this school could not quite satisfy his strong desire for more knowledge and his general social concerns.

My father's sympathy toward the Chinese Communist Party began in April 1927 after Chiang Kai-shek abruptly arrested nearly three thousand people and killed at least three hundred Communists in Shanghai. The crackdown on the Communist movement spread throughout the nation, and several faculty members in my father's junior high school were arrested in their classrooms. Others simply disappeared: there were rumors that they were Communists and had therefore been executed. The tension and terror were escalating, and when a rumor circulated that all the Communists had Western-style long hair, many people rushed to cut their hair to save their heads.

At the age of sixteen, my father entered Nankai High School, then one of the best in China. It was in Tianjin, a city near Beijing, more than five hundred miles away from his home city of Nanjing. He received not only a good education, but also an exposure to radical thinking and Communism. Many prominent Communists, including Zhou Enlai, the first premier of the People's Republic of China, were graduates of this school. At first, my father seemed to enjoy student life there. He loved sports and began to read a lot of literary works by contemporary Chinese writers such as Lu Xun. Most of these writers were liberal and progressive, and their works greatly appealed to the youths of the day. On his first summer vacation he brought home a suitcase full of such books. His enthusiasm was so great that even his younger brother was strongly influenced and dreamed of becoming a writer.

It seems natural that my father became a student activist. He was energetic, articulate, and extremely patriotic. He was also very handsome and elegant, liked by old and young, men and women, and looked very much like Zhou Enlai. All my life, I have heard how much my father looked like Zhou. In fact, in the early 1980s, a filmmaker came to our home to see if my father would star in a movie featuring Zhou. Since Zhou enjoyed enormous popularity in modern China, particularly in the 1970s and early 1980s, I was thrilled by this comparison.

My father might not have become involved in the Communist movement if the Japanese had not invaded China on September 18, 1931, and quickly occupied the three northeastern provinces. Like many educated youth of his day, he was deeply disappointed by the nonresistance policy of the Chinese government under Chiang Kai-shek, who held that Communism must be eliminated before he would fight the Japanese, because there should be only "*one* leader adhering to *one* ideology in *one* government of *one* nation." This seemed ridiculous and unacceptable to a patriotic youth like my father. Chiang's position generated more public sympathy and support for the Communist Party. As it promised to build a stronger, independent China with democracy and freedom, the Communist Party began to symbolize a brighter future for patriotic students, and they were eager to join it. My father was not only one of them but one of the pioneers; he joined the Chinese Communist Youth League in 1932.

That year, he founded the Nankai High School Student Federation and was elected its chairman. On the anniversary of the Japanese invasion, the Student Federation started a campaign to collect donations to resist the Japanese. The school authorities felt threatened by the growing popularity of the Student Federation, and on December 1, 1932, they decided to disband the Student Federation and expel thirty student leaders, including my father.

To implement the plan, the school called in armed city police. Right before he was forced to leave, my father rushed into the school sports ground, where there was a stage, and climbed upon it and shouted to the crowds of students coming to listen. "My fellow students," he said, "we are forced to leave the school today. But the fire of resisting the Japanese will never be extinguished! It will grow and grow. All those who do not want to be citizens of an enslaved nation unite! Let's keep on . . ." Before he could finish his speech he was pushed off the stage by the police and fell to the dusty ground. He was soon on his feet again and tried to finish his speech while the police attacked him again. All these things were witnessed by his guardian, my grandmother's brother, who had been summoned by the school authorities to take my father away. The following morning, my father's name appeared in the major newspaper in Tianjin in its report on the event in Nankai the day before.

My grandmother's brother did not want to be my father's guardian any more. He insisted that my grandmother go to Tianjin to take my father home. My father returned home as a hero in the eyes of his younger brothers and sister. He told them his exciting stories and they told him how their young hearts were depressed by what they saw every day. Instead of mobilizing resistance to the Japanese invasion and occupation, the government tried its best to suppress patriotic youths. During the day, pedestrians walked nervously in the streets; they stepped aside for sword-carrying officers who strode by ostentatiously. At night, gendarmes, wearing red badges on yellow woolen overcoats, stood at almost every street corner. Letters were often opened and examined by the government. Despite the risk, my uncle once wrote to his best friend: "Nanjing is a dark prison suffocating all revolutionaries. I can feel the heat is increasing and an explosion will soon come. I salute the tempest of revolution and open my arms to embrace its coming!" That was how this sixteen-year-old felt at the time. When my father came home, the brothers had long talks about the future of the nation and what a patriotic youth could do for his country. On one occasion, my father even revealed that he had secretly joined the Communist organization. Under his influence, both his younger brothers and his sister accepted Communist ideology and joined the Communist Party or the movement a few years later.

Soon after my father was expelled from Nankai High School, his mother sent him to Shanghai to finish school. A year later he entered the Law and Business School at Beijing University. There he had the chance to study classical philosophers such as Bacon, Kant, Descartes, Spinoza, and Hegel, and Communist theory. These writings reinforced the ideological belief he had developed from reading John Reed's *Ten Days That Shook the World*, which was later banned in the 1940s as Communist propaganda. He felt only socialism would help China overcome oppression, injustice, mass poverty, and the yoke of imperialism.

John Reed's book remained his favorite. In 1974, when I was sixteen years old and asked him what to read, it was his first recommendation, followed by Edgar Snow's *Red Star Over China*. Ironically, I could not find Reed's book anywhere, because it was banned by the government, for relations between China and the Soviet Union were terrible at the time.

At the Law and Business School of Beijing University, my father's major was economics. Soon, he again became a student leader and organized an underground student federation. He visited liberal-minded professors and tried to set up an alliance of progressive professors and students. He also contacted staff and campus policemen to get their sympathy and support. He called news conferences and presented student demands to reporters. He was also in charge of keeping contact with other student organizations at other schools and universities in Beijing. On December 9, 1935, a large student demonstration broke out in Beijing, appealing to the government to lead a nationwide resistance movement against the Japanese invasion and occupation and give up its policy of suppressing its political opponents, the Communist Party and the Red Army. The government brutally attacked the demonstrators and many of my father's classmates and friends were injured and jailed. However, the demonstration succeeded in awakening and mobilizing the entire society and psychologically preparing them for the resistance movement. My father was one of the chief organizers of this demonstration.

In modern Chinese history, this demonstration is remembered as the December 9th Student Movement. When I was in college in the early 1980s this movement was still an inspiration for current student movements and activities. The government watched college campuses in early December every year for fear of a new wave of demonstrations. To some extent, this worry was legitimate. After all, more than half a century ago it was the Communists who were on the streets as student demonstrators. They know how effective a student movement can be and how it can eventually lead to the overthrow of an unpopular government.

I still suspect that my father's unexpected death in 1990 was accelerated by the student demonstrations in 1989. Although history never repeats itself exactly, events can be very similar. Witnessing such similar social tragedies must have been deeply painful to an aged man with such wide, genuine social concerns. He certainly did not want to see the event turn out to be such a tragedy.

MY NANNY

Although my father was so important to me, the first person I remember is not him, but my nanny. She also worked as a housekeeper for my parents. Some may wonder how a Communist government official could hire a housekeeper. It is true that after the Communist takeover in 1949, some occupations were banned immediately. Although there were some debates within the Party about whether a Communist government official should hire a housekeeper, it was decided that housekeeping was a decent profession and it was permissible.

My parents hired a housekeeper because both of them were so busy with their jobs that they did not have time to take care of my sister. The first housekeeper they hired was a very capable person, and my mother was extremely satisfied with her. That was the first time in her life that she had hired someone. She was surprised when she was informed by the security agency that the woman had been a housekeeper for Madame Chiang, wife of Chiang Kai-shek. For security reasons, they asked my parents to fire her immediately. My mother soon found a new one, but even today she misses the dishes the first housekeeper cooked.

My nanny had worked for our family for two years before I was born. She came from the countryside at the age of seventeen, and was only ten years older than my sister. My sister was ten years older than I was and didn't play with me very often. My parents were also too busy to spend much time with me, so my nanny was the person I was closest to as a young child. In fact, I always called her "Aunt" instead of nanny, as if she were a member of my family.

In China, we do not use people's given names as often as in the West. In fact, about the only time we use a person's given name alone is to address them in a love letter. It is especially impolite to call someone who is older by his or her given or even full name. Instead, we often use the relationship as salutation, for example, Aunt, Elder Sister, and so on. This also reflects that our society is very family or group oriented; an individual is important only in terms of his or her relationship with others.

I often wondered how Aunt was related to the other members of my family and I asked her many questions about relationships:

"What is my sister to my father?"

"She is his daughter."

"Then what is my father to my sister?"

"He is her father."

"Who are you?"

"I am your *aunt*."

"And what is my father to you?"

". . ."

She always hesitated awhile and then repeated: "I am your *aunt*."

I liked this game and often asked questions about relations between members of my family. Her answers always stopped when I asked about her relation to members of my family other than me. This created a big question in my mind. It seemed to me that she was my aunt but she was nothing to anyone else. What a strange situation! But I preferred to think about it in a positive light: it seemed that she was only mine and no one else shared her with me!

Aunt was a very good cook and could make all kinds of dishes. I loved to watch her prepare and cook dinner. Most Chinese eat steamed bread instead of baked bread and I loved watching her make it: stirring the flour, making the dough, and steaming it in a big pot on the stove. Sometimes she would make a special loaf for me, making it look like a little fish. She used the edge of a bowl to carve a net of curved lines resembling the scales of a fish. Finally she put a brown bean on the head to look like an eye. It seemed so alive that I would play with it before eating it.

Aunt's family lived in a rural town not far from our city on the northern bank of the Yangtze River. We were on the south side and before the Yangtze River Bridge was built, it was very inconvenient and expensive to get to her home. She missed her family very much and often cried during the night. No one could hear her but me, as we slept in the same bedroom and bed. Furniture was very expensive. As a public official, my father had the right to rent a few pieces of furniture from the government, paying only a couple of yuan a month because the rent was subsidized. My father did not want to ask for more pieces of subsidized furniture, so I shared a single bed with Aunt until I was seven years old.

Aunt worked for us for room and board, and an 18 yuan monthly wage. This was comparable to a factory worker's wage of 30 yuan a month. The salaries of an average worker, 30 yuan a month, and my father, government official, 180 yuan a month, were actually within a tolerable range. The polarization between the rich and the poor had been much greater before the Communist Revolution in 1949. It was reported that a factory worker in Shanghai once said his best wish was that the new government would enable him to afford fried rice with eggs every day, and he felt happy under the new government because he was getting what he wanted. Unfortunately, poor political decisions made in 1958 soon interrupted this worker's happiness.

A famine came in the early 1960s, and millions of people died of hunger. It was partly due to natural disasters such as flood and drought, but it was in great part due to the government policy of transforming individual farms into collective farms in such a radical way, including the establishment of free cafeterias. The problem was further complicated by the disruption of the relationship between the Soviet Union and China. Instead of supporting China and giving it financial aid, the Soviet Union demanded that China repay everything she owed. Natural disasters made many areas in China unproductive. Productive areas had to give up huge portions of their produce to the Soviet Union as payment for the loans. As a result, each day we had less and less food to eat. Even in my family, the food shortage was a serious problem, especially food containing protein. Meat and eggs were almost impossible to find in the market. Often, the green stems and leaves of carrots were our main food.

On August 1, 1960, the central government decided to provide rationed food to its high-ranking officials and prominent intellectuals. Each month, a cabinet minister or a high-ranking professor at a university would be provided with four pounds of meat and three pounds of eggs. Two things surprised me when I recently discovered this piece of old news. First, after witnessing the increased privileges of the Communist elite in China during the 70s and 80s, as well as observing the polarization between the rich and the poor in the United States since I came here in 1987, I could hardly believe that, back in 1960, the Chinese Communist government only allowed its cabinet members to have three pounds of eggs more than an ordinary citizen. Second, I was amazed to learn that the allowance to the handful of cabinet ministers was also extended to a group of prominent intellectuals. What a great contrast to the anti-intellectual mood six years later! Admittedly it was under the influence of the Soviet Union that the Chinese Communist government gave such priority to intellectuals, but I think it was a good practice, as long as the limited privileges given to the selected few were reasonable and did not badly polarize the society. It was actually unfortunate that the policy was not continued very long in China.

During those hard times in the early 1960s, each month the government gave my father a little additional food, such as enriched flour, pasta, and brown beans. Most of this food was in our house for only a short time. Whenever someone working for him or my mother was ill, my parents would give extra food to the sick person. When Aunt brought a pound of pasta to the ill person, they were sometimes moved to tears. Aunt's heart was also touched. When she came home, her eyes were often still red from weeping.

My father was entitled to a couple of dozen eggs a month. He would not eat them, wanting to save them for other members of the family. My mother wanted him to eat them because she wanted to give him priority. As a result, no one would touch the eggs. Month by month they were saved up, and stored in a basket under a bed.

Out of her special love for me, Aunt occasionally boiled an egg secretly and buried it under the rice in my bowl. As an innocent child, I did not understand why she wanted to keep it a secret, so when I was surprised to find an egg in my rice bowl I would always cry out excitedly, "Hey! I found an egg in my rice!" She would be very embarrassed and her face would turn red, because she felt she was not authorized to do this. In my early memory, Aunt was the dearest person to me and I still cherish her memory. She remains our family friend, and the tie with her has helped us remain in touch with reality and ordinary life in China.

A NICE NEIGHBORHOOD

The first home I remember was a residential compound called the Public Education Village. Almost everyone working for the municipal government lived here, from the mayor to secretaries and security guards. It was adjacent to the government office center, separated by a creek crossed by three short bridges. Since most people would walk from home to office in about five minutes, many even had lunch at home. Other conveniences in the compound included a barber shop, a tailor, and a public bathhouse.

The sixty buildings in the compound were of three types: ten single family houses, forty apartment buildings, and ten buildings of studio apartments. Each apartment building had two stories and was painted pale yellow, about the color of cheesecake. Blue bricks showed through in places where the paint was worn. Each apartment building had eight units, four with two bedrooms and four with one bedroom.

Our apartment building was an exception. It was a three-story building with twelve units. Half had two bedrooms and half had three. It was not painted on the outside, and the bricks were red instead of blue. The color made it stand out among the other buildings. It had been built more recently, and represented a model for future apartment buildings.

The structural model for these buildings, including ours, was one the Soviets developed from public housing projects designed by Josef Hoffmann in Vienna in the early 1920s. Unlike other houses constructed before the Communist takeover, these new buildings had modern kitchens and bathroom facilities. For example, each unit in the new building had a bathtub, while those old buildings did not even have a toilet. As a child, I never felt our modern environment was Western; I thought it was all Chinese. It was only in 1990 that I understood its similarity to Western architecture when, as a graduate student in urban planning at MIT, I saw a slide presentation of a public housing project by the Austrian designer. The linkage further convinced me that the Communist Revolution in China was actually a part of China's modernization, which was to a great extent a process of Westernization.

Our apartment was a three-bedroom unit on the third floor at the east end that got plenty of sunlight during the day. My family moved into the compound in 1960 when I was two years old, because in October my father was appointed director of a department in the municipal government that was in charge of education, health care, cultural affairs, and media control, as well as sports activities. He became one of the eleven members of the standing committee of the Communist Party in Nanjing, overseeing everything going on in the city.

Almost all the houses in the cities were subsidized by the government. The houses in this compound were more substantially subsidized. My family paid only about eight yuan (five dollars) a month for our three-bedroom apartment. Thus my parents only spent 3 percent of their income on housing. Residents in other parts of the city might have to pay twice as much to live in a similar apartment. In fact, they might not be able to get such a big apartment. Space was allocated based on people's positions. People holding positions with more responsibilities would get a more spacious housing unit. The rationale was that public housing was a part of the working conditions for an employee, just like his office. In my father's case, this turned out to be true, for he often worked at home during weekends and evenings.

This coincided with the policy of wealth distribution in a socialist society. Each one was supposed to work as hard as possible, and in return, was rewarded according to his contributions. The differences in wealth between the rich and the poor were recognized as legitimate, but were meant to be controlled within a reasonably small range. A person with my father's responsibilities could have a three-bedroom unit while a receptionist or a security guard lived in a studio apartment. The difference was there, but the contrast was not much. Because people working in the same institute lived close to each other, the neighborhood actually contained people of very different social status. After the Communist takeover, many new neighborhoods were built in this way. This policy not only curbed the polarization of housing conditions between the rich and the poor, it also reduced some other social problems such as street crime and ghetto poverty. It was worthy of careful study as a housing model for other societies as well.

Because our unit was the highest spot in the compound, my little friends loved to come to play on our balcony and enjoy the great view. At the time, most children attended kindergarten for three years before beginning school at the age of seven. There was both a kindergarten and a primary school in our compound. The kindergarten was only about a three-minute walk from our home. I went to kindergarten a year later than most kids because my parents had a housekeeper, and they did not want me away from home at an early age.

Every morning Aunt walked me to kindergarten, and at noon she took me home for lunch and then back to kindergarten again in the afternoon. About half of the kids in my class had their lunch at school. It was more expensive to have lunch at school, so families avoided it if they could. The kids who stayed in the kindergarten had a nap after lunch before the rest of us came back at about 1:30 or 2:00. I always envied those who stayed because I thought it would be much more fun to have a little communal nap.

In the afternoon, before 5:00 p.m., Aunt came to pick me up. On the way home I liked to ride on her back, but I was embarrassed when the other kids called me a baby. I encouraged her to come to class a little early before anyone else left. I walked the first few steps and once I made sure that no one could see us, she would squat down so I could climb on her back for a ride.

My parents never spoiled me. In fact, my father always tried to make me behave like an ordinary kid, not the son of an important official. My clothes were never expensive or fashionable, because my parents hated waste. I often wore my sister's outgrown clothes. Although Aunt altered those clothes a bit to make them fit me, they still looked somewhat girlish. Even some of the teachers in the kindergarten felt sorry for me, for they thought I was a nice-looking boy and would have been more attractive had I dressed like the other boys. However, each semester on the report card, they wrote comments like this: His dress reflects a simple and thrifty lifestyle, which we always encourage other children in our kindergarten to adopt.

It was true that a simple and thrifty lifestyle was encouraged for everyone, and especially for Communist government officials. It was considered sinful to waste, and officials were not allowed to live luxuriously. A Chinese tradition of egalitarian idealism made it legitimate to overthrow an extravagant and ruthless ruler. Having used this tradition to gain power, the Communists were conscious of it for many years. From childhood on, I was taught, both at home and in public, to live a simple and thrifty life. My parents always encouraged me to make friends and play with kids from different backgrounds who lived in our residential compound, such as the sons of barbers and tailors. Their families lived in the studio apartments at the back of the compound, where five buildings of studios were connected in a shape of a star. In fact, this was one of my favorite places to play hide-and-seek because we could get lost in the maze. Although as a child I never quite understood its social meanings, I certainly loved our neighborhood.

PREOCCUPIED PARENTS

As a young child, I did not have much chance to be with my parents or sister. The one I saw least was my mother. When I was three years old she began to manage a local opera group. The group gave performances almost every night, and Mother always stayed at the theater until the performance was over. By the time she came home, I was asleep.

There was a black-and-white photo of her on the desk in her bedroom. I remembered her face by looking at that picture more often than at her. She was a pretty woman and had some slightly Caucasian features. In modern Chinese society, people with Caucasian features are considered handsome or beautiful. A typical Asian face with small eyes, a flat nose, and darker skin is thought of as plain or ugly. My mother had very light skin, big eyes, and a very high, almost hawklike nose. Some of my little friends were scared of her when they came to play at my home. They thought she was a foreigner.

I saw my father only at meals. In the evening, he usually went out again with my sister. There were always invitations for first nights or other ceremonies and performances. As I was too young to sit quietly at those occasions, only my sister went with him. More often than not he would receive several invitations for the same date, and had to decide which one to attend. I often heard people say how disappointed they were that he did not show up because he had gone somewhere else. If he could not accept an invitation, he was invited again and again until he could attend.

When I was old enough to start going out, my father found a good solution to these time conflicts. He would go to the most important function and let Aunt, my sister, and me go to the other. He asked us to make some excuse so people would not be offended by his absence. Once at the theater, my sister and I would find the person who sent the invitation and tell him or her that our father wanted us to apologize for his absence.

I began to be such a messenger at age five. I loved this job and wanted to go more often. It felt unfair that my sister could go out almost every night. Sometimes I would openly protest: "How come my sister goes out so often? I haven't been to a movie or a play for years." Everybody would burst into laughter. They would say, "Oh, really? How old are you now? If you haven't seen a movie 'for years,' then you must have seen the last one before you were born."

Even on Sundays I didn't have much chance to be with my parents. Usually there were visitors at our house all day. In China, most families did not have telephones. People just stopped by and knocked at the door. You could get all kinds of visitors: friends, acquaintances, and strangers. Unlike many of the officials of his rank, my father never refused to see anyone who came to our door. As the word spread, even more people came to talk with him.

Most people came to talk about their problems. However, Chinese people usually do not pour out their complaints straightforwardly. So it was only after listening to them for a while that my father knew where the problem lay. An administrator might come because he did not get a promotion, which he thought he deserved. An actress might come because she did not get the chance to play a role for which she believed she was the best candidate. My father could not always intervene with the decisions his subordinates had made, but he would try his best to make the person feel a little more comfortable. They all trusted him and hoped for justice in the end.

Quite often Sunday was just like another work day for my father; he simply turned our house into his office. People working for him at the department came in groups to discuss various issues. In the early morning it might be the elementary school group talking about guaranteeing all school-age children access to school. Later in the morning a high school group might come to discuss the issue of competing with other cities for places in colleges. Few high school graduates could go to college because there were too few places for all who wanted to attend; graduates had to compete by taking an extremely selective exam. Even in China today this problem remains, and it is only getting worse. Naturally a school's quality and reputation depended on the number of graduates it sent to college. The same competition occurred between cities. In his position, my father had to address these issues.

In the afternoon, it might be other groups talking about how many shows could be put on or what sports teams might come to the city. The whole day went on like this; sometimes my father would ask the visitors to stay and have lunch so they could continue a discussion. As we had only a one-day weekend in China, the whole weekend was ruined.

Our apartment had only one living room and sometimes there would be too many people at the same time, or people from very different groups. Then my father had to ask some of them to wait in his bedroom. He talked with one person or group in one room while the others waited their turn in the other room. Father always offered each visitor a cup of tea. I loved bringing the tea to the guests because it gave me a chance to chat with people. When I was too young to do it well, Aunt came with me in case I spilled hot water. Sometimes Father would let me stay during the conversations. Although I did not quite understand what they were talking about, I certainly could tell how people respected and liked him.

The most exciting and memorable events at home in my childhood were the activities around the Chinese New Year. It was a major holiday in China and each family spent days and weeks preparing special food for the occasion. The celebration lasted at least a week and sometimes a whole month. For New Year's Eve, most families had an eight- to twelve-course dinner. My mother liked to invite her colleagues at the theater group for a New Year's dinner party. At first, this was for single people only, because they were alone during the holiday. As word spread about her successful annual party, more people wanted to come. By the third year she had to hold the party twice. On the first night all the actors and actresses came, and on the second night, playwrights, musicians, composers, conductors, and designers were invited. The joy these people shared was more than I can describe.

My love for my parents did not come directly from their love for me, but from observing how they were loved and respected by other people. Gradually I began to enjoy their popularity and feel very proud of it. I had reason to believe that I had the best parents in the world.

During those years, my father was often involved in diplomatic activities. In addition to his title as the director of the department, he held at least thirteen other official titles. One of them was Chairman of the Chinese Association for Friendships Abroad, Nanjing Chapter. This was a quasi-government agency that received all foreign visitors. Each week my father was the host at formal banquets for foreign delegations. Between 1960 and 1965, most of the delegations came from socialist countries such as the Soviet Union and nations in Eastern Europe. Others came from developing countries in Asia, Africa, and Latin America, and some were radical groups from Japan.

Once, I remember, there were about 300 Japanese youths visiting the city. It was a big event, officially called the "Great Celebration of the Friendship between Chinese and Japanese Youth." It was an effort to ease the general hatred against the Japanese who had occupied China during the 1930s and 1940s. Hatred was particularly strong in Nanjing, where the Japanese Army had indulged in massacres and mass rapes. On the evening of the Mid-Autumn Festival in 1964, the visiting Japanese youths and hundreds of Chinese people were invited to a big party at the city's largest park, Xuanwu Lake Park. Tables were set up along the side of the lake and people chatted with each other as they enjoyed special food such as autumn moon cakes under the beautiful light of the full moon.

My whole family went to the festival. My parents sat at the host table while my sister and I were at a table with three Japanese people and some officials working for my father. During the conversation one Japanese woman asked me: "What are you going to do when you grow up?" I said: "I am going to be a soldier in the Chinese People's Liberation Army." "Why?" she asked. "So I can fight the Japanese devils." Everybody was shocked and someone had to explain that I only meant those Japanese who had invaded China during World War II. Someone else added that I must have seen too many war movies. Anyway, I was the only one at the table who was not embarrassed.

The best accommodation for foreign visitors was the Nanjing Hotel. There were other activities at the hotel, including buffet dinners, bridge-playing, acrobatic performances, previews of new movies, and ballroom-dancing parties for high-ranking officials and their families on holidays. This kind of elite living eventually led to political and social disasters years later, although few questioned it at the time. I heard my parents discuss the issue at home: they were concerned about high-level government officials enjoying their lives so much while ordinary people still had a hard time making ends meet. But I do not think they ever mentioned these concerns in public; to do so would have been political suicide.

My father did not dance at all, nor did he play bridge or mah-jongg, although he did enjoy the Western-style food cooked on those occasions in the Nanjing Hotel. For the rest of the family, it was a great opportunity to enjoy new movies. As for my father, he came mainly to get his work done. This was the best place for him to get documents approved and signed by various officials. He could avoid making separate appointments, and efficiently bypass the bureaucracy.

Even if he had not wanted to work at the hotel, he could not have avoided it. Because he was in charge of media control, every night someone from the local newspaper showed him a sample of the following morning's paper and asked for his approval so it could go to press. Even on a holiday evening, when our family was at the Nanjing Hotel, my father was not spared his duty as the official censor. Today, a critic might say that much of his work was actually unnecessary and counterproductive, but we certainly cannot say that he neglected his responsibilities. He only did the best he could, leaving history as the final judge.

ONCE UPON A TIME

I don't remember how my mother's parents came into my life, but suddenly they were living with us in our apartment. I clearly remember my grandmother's bound feet. It was amazing to me that a grown-up could have such small and pointed feet. Under her socks she wrapped her feet with a long cloth band. Late every afternoon, after unwrapping the long cloth, she washed her feet. I was amazed by the length of the band. Once her foot appeared it was really terrifying. All her toes were bent over to one side and the shape of her foot looked awful. While I watched, she would tell me that this was the fault of the old society, meaning the time before the Communist Revolution and even before the 1911 Revolution, when women were forced to bind their feet. This ugly custom had been practiced in China for hundreds of years. Girls had their feet bound when they were only a couple of years old. It was believed that the smaller a woman's feet, the more beautiful she was.

Those who failed to bind their feet to the required size had a hard time finding a husband.

Grandpa told me many stories and he had many more to tell. Most of them came from two of the classic novels in Chinese literature: *The Three Kingdoms* and *Water Margin*. He told me many of the episodes several times. At kindergarten I could retell most of the episodes, which made me popular among my playmates. Whenever kids had an argument over who was telling the story correctly they would come to me for an answer; I became an authority. Because my grandparents were born when China still had an emperor, I often associated them with ancient history. When Grandpa started a story with "Once upon a time, there was an emperor . . . ," I often asked him if he had been born at the time. He would smile and then explain to me that the story took place more than a thousand years ago.

Grandpa taught me how to play Chinese chess, a game very similar to chess, which we called international chess. This gave me another boost in popularity among the other kids, because it was a game demanding intelligence, not as easy as the so-called Chinese checkers. As I taught them how to play, I set the rules. If I did not quite remember a rule, I would just invent one, and they would believe me. When I told them the correct rule after checking with my grandpa they would say, "How come you told us differently last time?" I would blush with embarrassment.

Even my father was surprised to find that I could play Chinese chess. I was only six years old then, and he decided to teach me how to read even before I went to school. He made about 300 cards with one Chinese character on each. Whenever he found some time he would teach me a few characters. By the time I went to school I had already learned how to read newspaper headlines. He was very proud of this achievement. Whether he was proud of me or of himself, I was not quite sure. Maybe both.

I would have loved to watch my father play Chinese chess with my grandpa, but they never did. Although my grandparents lived with us, most of the time they stayed in their bedroom. It seemed to me that my father did not want them to meet many of the visitors at our house. Somehow I sensed that it was not appropriate to tell people what my grandpa did for a living before the Revolution, but I was too young to understand why.

The ideological line of the Chinese Communist Party became more and more radical; by the mid-1960s it developed into a political frenzy that cost millions of lives. According to the radical thinking, it was glorious to be born into a family that was poor before the Communist Revolution, and disgraceful to have a parent who had been rich. Family background could ruin one's entire life—career, marriage, everything. In a sense my father's political future was already threatened because his late father had been a banker. He certainly would not want to be hurt again because of his father-in-law.

In fact, Grandpa wasn't very rich before the Revolution. He only had a very small shop in the biggest downtown shopping area in the city. At that time Nanjing was the capital of China. It was a consumer's city without much industry. Although retail space was expensive downtown, it was still profitable for my grandpa to rent a little space there.

After the Communist takeover in 1949, the government nationalized some large businesses and confiscated those that were largely in the control of the bureaucrats of the previous government. For a few years, however, small businesses like my grandpa's were allowed to continue. In fact, the new national flag was designed with a symbolic meaning: the big star symbolizes the Communist Party, and the four small ones surrounding it represent four major classes among the people. It may seem surprising today that the four classes recognized and represented on the red flag of Communist China were workers, peasants, the "petty bourgeois," and the "national bourgeois." The "petty bourgeois" referred to small businessmen and the more educated part of the population. The "national bourgeois" referred to those capitalists and big enterprise owners who were still allowed to run their businesses.

The government revised its policy four years later, and took all the businesses out of the hands of their owners or changed them into a public and private partnership where the owner became a co-manager. In either case, the owner would still get some of the profit. Once the new manager appointed by the government learned the skills to run the business, the owner was encouraged to retire. Usually he was given a lump sum payment instead of an annual pension. The owner might still get an annual share of the profits. This policy continued until the mid-1960s. In the case of my grandpa, he received a lump sum and retired in the late 1950s before he was sixty years old.

Grandpa seemed to be quite happy about those early years under the Communist government. At that time, the Communist Party was particularly careful about its relationship with businessmen. The Communist officials assigned to work with them were often thoughtful and responsible individuals. One of the officials Grandpa came to know then was named Zhang; twenty years later he became our downstairs neighbor. Zhang weighed over 200 pounds, an enormous size for a

Chinese man. An anecdote I heard many years later about Zhang illustrates how the Communist government in the early 1950s respected the business community. Once Zhang was holding a meeting with a group of local businessmen. During the meeting he began to feel the need to pass wind, which was considered very rude and uncivilized. Zhang felt that if he passed wind in front of these local businessmen, he would do great damage to the image of the Communist Party. So, he was determined to control himself, but holding in the gas for so long caused him great pain. When the meeting was over he had to be carried away and was hospitalized immediately! Today, such a story seems so bizarre that the storyteller might have to start it by saying, "Once upon a time...."

SEVEN "GRANDMAS" AND TEN "GRANDPAS"

Family means a great deal in the Chinese society, where each member of the family is responsible for the honor of everyone else. The concept of a family often extends beyond the nuclear family, to include all one's relatives. From early childhood I was very family conscious and knew the exact relationships between each member of my family.

As I recall, there were more relatives on my mother's side than on my father's. Mother's mother had six sisters and two brothers, and each of her siblings and their children stayed in contact with my family. On Sundays, and especially on holidays, our house was often crowded with relatives. Because each of the relatives might have a different occupation and belong to a different social class, a big family like mine was actually a miniature society in which all the social issues of the time could be reflected.

All my grandmother's younger sisters would call her by her place in the family, "Third Eldest Sister." It seemed that in the old days boys and girls were counted separately, although I have never quite understood why. And my grandmother would refer to her younger sisters as "Fifth Sister," "Sixth Sister," and so forth. Since all of these sisters were of the same generation as my grandma, I was supposed to call them "Fifth Grandma," or "Sixth Grandma."

Grandma's eldest sister died before I was born. She had only one daughter, and she died young also, leaving a daughter and a son. The daughter often came to visit us, and because she was of my generation I always called her "Elder Sister Xiuzhen," although she was more than twenty years older than I. In China it was polite to call a man of one's father's age "Uncle" and a woman of one's mother's age "Aunt." I often made a mistake by referring to Elder Sister Xiuzhen's husband as "Uncle." People would laugh and ask me, "How come the wife was your sister and the husband became your uncle?"

This couple had two sons, and the elder one was older than I. People often teased by asking these boys to call me "Uncle." Because I was close to their age, they always felt embarrassed and refused to call me "Uncle." China was a patriarchal society, and it was a shame and an insult to be forced to call someone "Uncle" or "Grandpa." In primary schools and even in some kindergartens, when boys fought, the winner would force the loser to call him "Uncle," "Grandpa," or even "Daddy," which gave him great psychological satisfaction.

One of Grandma's sisters was mentally disabled and lived in a special hospital for the mentally ill. In Chinese society, a mentally ill person was rarely given sympathy. People would refer to them as a mad man or woman, and show little respect. Parents often disciplined their children by threatening that, if the child did not behave, a mad man would come. I had never seen her before in my life and was really scared when this woman whom I was supposed to call "Fourth Grandma" escaped from her hospital and showed up at our door.

She wore shabby clothes that looked a little dirty to me. During her conversation with Grandma, she often broke into unnatural and unexpected laughter. After about half an hour Grandma gave her some pocket money and persuaded her to return to her hospital, and she finally left. I instantly felt great relief, but I was worried that she might not find her way back to her hospital, and could not sleep that night.

Not only was I expected to call my grandmother's sisters "grandmas," but also her cousins. They remained in constant contact with my family, and the concept of "my family" was thus extended even further. One day, a cousin of my grandmother came to visit us. I was asked to call this woman the "Fourth Grandma," too, because that was her placement among her siblings. Although this confused me, I was very glad that she came, because she then took me and my grandma out for afternoon tea. It was during a famine year, and most people were hungry. There were places where one could still buy what one wanted, although few people could afford to. Those who could were mostly former business owners who either got a huge lump sum at retirement or still received some profits. This cousin of my grandma seemed to be one of them. She bought us eight little steamed stuffed buns, which cost twenty-five times as much as they had before. After so many months of humble food, what a lovely change and luxury this was! The memory of those buns still makes my mouth water. My grandmother was happy, too. Even her daughter and son-in-law could not afford such a treat, although my father was a high-ranking official in the Communist government. As we walked home after we said good-bye to her cousin, she warned me not to tell anyone about the buns we had just eaten. I kept my promise.

If I have already confused you by having so many "grandmas," I must tell you that I had even more "grandpas." They were not the husbands of "grandmas" but the brothers and cousins of my mother's father.

I had ten grandpas, but I only met the fifth, ninth, and tenth. When they came to visit they called my grandpa Third Eldest Brother. At first I thought they were all brothers, but the "Tenth Grandpa" was, in fact, a cousin of my grandpa. All the male cousins were counted in sequential order. So it sounded as if their family had more male children than it actually had, for in Old China it was desirable for a family to have many male children. This was because males brought laborers into the family while female children only grew up to become laborers for their husbands' families.

"Fifth Grandpa" was the poorest of all and the only job he could find was folding paper boxes for a small factory. This was because his only son had been a pilot in the air force for the Nationalist government of Chiang Kai-shek and fled to Taiwan before the Communists took over; that disqualified the "Fifth Grandpa" from many jobs, although he was a good accountant.

As the parents of a "public enemy," my fifth grandpa and his wife had a hard time surviving in this new society. They lived with one of her nieces and did all the housekeeping in exchange for room and board. My mother used to give them ten to fifteen yuan on the three major holidays. Compared to their income, which was about twenty yuan (ten dollars) a month, the money from my mother was quite a help. My mother kept doing this until they were finally allowed, by both the Chinese and Taiwanese governments, to join their son in Taiwan in the mid-1980s. Ironically, now that they live with their son in Taiwan they are the richest of all our relatives, and their son sends money to my mother periodically.

What is even more interesting and ironic is that, today, Taiwan seems to have eliminated the mass poverty that my father and many others in his generation wanted to eliminate in China. History often develops in strange circles, and as the ancient Greek tragedies show, heroes sometimes hurt or even destroyed themselves trying to avoid an inevitable fate. They saw something they disliked and tried to change it, but got exactly what they did not want. Had they simply left well enough alone, they might have reached their goals.

CHAPTER 2

MY FIRST YEAR IN SCHOOL

I began elementary school in the fall of 1965 at age seven. It was a time when the entire nation was about to experience events unprecedented in human history. Yet, just like times of other dramatic historical upheavals, life went on as usual for the people whose existence was soon to be profoundly changed.

As was typical for children in the city, I attended a school very close to home, almost a part of our residential compound. The front gates were next door to each other, and the back door of the school opened to the sports ground inside our compound. My school was one of the best in the city and all the buildings were new. There were about 1,500 students. The campus was beautifully landscaped with a small pond with lotuses and other water flowers. There were also little fish swimming in the water. A short bridge crossed the pond and split it into two equal parts. On both sides of the bridge were glass-covered panels with photos and paintings hanging inside. The wooden part of the panel was painted light green, perfectly matching the color of the lotuses in the pond. At the end of the bridge, a pavement flanked by roses and other flowers led to the front building, where my classroom was located. There were five other buildings and a playground in the school.

There were about twenty-five boys and twenty-five girls in my class, coming from a broader neighborhood, not just my residential compound. Some of their parents worked in a nearby university, the Nanjing Institute of Technology, which had its own residential compound. Others came from a residential compound next door. Their fathers had served as officers in Chiang Kai-shek's army, and during the civil war between Chiang and the Communists these men decided to abandon the old regime and joined the Communist force, which got more support from the general population. Now they worked as faculty members in the new Army Academy, which had its own residential compound. Like ours, all these residential compounds of large institutes had a mix of residents of different social status. Because the heads of household worked in the same institute, families living next to each other knew each other well. This was often very appealing, because people living and working together did not feel isolated in the neighborhood. If other aspects of the social system had worked out well, this might have become a very attractive housing model for modern society.

On our first day of school, each of us only knew a few others in the class, because the rest of the class came from a different neighborhood. Before we got to know each other well, the teacher announced that we were to elect a student monitor as a leader. She said the main responsibility of this position was to assist the teacher in organizing and managing the class. Then she began to explain what kind of a person should be elected to this position. The person should love our country and the people, study hard, and follow all the rules and regulations. The candidate had to live a simple lifestyle, love physical labor, and keep personal belongings clean and neat. The person had to be nice to everyone and respect teachers and the elderly. As we did not know each other yet, she said, it would make no sense to hold an election this semester. Instead, for the moment she would appoint one of us to the position on a trial base. A real election would be held at the beginning of each of the next semesters. Then she announced that I would be the monitor. I wasn't prepared for this and felt my throat choke up. She asked the class to support my nomination by clapping. Of course, the class did as she asked, and I became the class monitor.

Although we didn't have a real election, I was still impressed by the democratic process introduced to us. I felt we were treated with trust and respect, and it was definitely different from the kindergarten days.

It made me feel grown up. I excitedly reported my first day at school at the dinner table. I talked a lot about the voting system and both my father and sister smiled at me, but I could see that they were proud. I knew my mother would feel the same if she were at home, but she had left for her night work at the theater and wouldn't be back until midnight.

My father explained to me that later in my life I would participate in more elections. "Our country is a socialist nation," he said, "and each citizen has rights and responsibilities. When you become eighteen years old you will become eligible to vote for the president of China. Right now you are too young to understand all this, but someday you will know what I'm talking about. As a grade school student, your main task is to study. One has to acquire knowledge and learn the skills needed in order to serve one's country and the people." I nodded my head vigorously to show I understood what he had said, although it turned out that within a year his words would no longer explain the situation and he himself wouldn't be able to understand it. A political storm and social upheaval would sweep through China, not only driving the president of China out of power but causing the entire society to fall into frantic confusion. At the time, neither I nor my father knew that we were already on the eve of that terrible disaster.

My father was optimistic about the nation's future, but he certainly did not think ours was a perfect society. Even I was soon to see its undesirable side. On the first day of school our teacher assigned each boy in our class to sit with a girl. I was assigned to sit with a girl whose family name was Li. She had seven younger sisters and brothers. I asked her what her father did, but she never gave me a straight answer. I knew Li's family was very poor, because she could not afford to pay her tuition and fees, which were only five yuan and two yuan respectively a semester, not more than three dollars.

After looking at what Li wore, I began to understand what shabby meant. I never wore fancy clothes and felt quite proud of my simple and "revolutionary" lifestyle, because this was the way we were supposed to live. In those days, one always tried to be "revolutionary." Ironically, when the word "revolutionary" was used in China it meant the opposite of what it means in the West. Instead of pertaining to radical change, the word implied conformity with the authority or being "politically correct." I remember that each time my sister got a new dress she would worry whether it was too colorful and beautiful to be "revolutionary." She would cry after wearing it for the first time if others commented that her dress was too beautiful, because then it became "bourgeois," not "revolutionary." However, it was for an entirely different reason that Li always wore such shabby clothes.

A special event helped me realize how poor Li really was. It was the first cultural shock in my life. During the season of the Chinese New Year, most families in southeastern China made special food from powdered rice. As we could only buy hulled rice in the market, we had to grind or mill it into powder. There was one mill to do this processing in a nearby neighborhood. One day Aunt was going there and I asked her to take me with her because I was curious about the process. We went to a little hut about fifteen minutes walk away from my home. To my surprise, it was Li's house and that was her family's occupation.

As I entered the dark little hut I saw a stone trough buried in the ground with a huge wooden staff that looked like a hammer hanging above it. To make the powder, the rice was put in the stone trough. The end of a long hammer handle was pushed up and down; the hammer rose up and fell into the trough and smashed the rice.

When we entered the room, Li's sweating father was wearing only pants. He had taken his turn and stood by to rest while Li's mother and Li pushed the handle. When Li realized who I was, she almost cried in embarrassment. She ran from the room and did not return until I left. I looked around and found her brothers and sisters playing in and out of the room. Their clothes were even more shabby than Li's. I could see their bony bodies through the large holes in their clothes. The scene was a shock to me. It looked like a completely different world. The following day Li would not speak to me, and I felt guilty, as if discovering her poverty were my fault.

My father certainly knew of the poverty around us, and he also seemed to be very conscious about our relative status and warned us not to be snobbish. He told my sister and me to keep a low profile about our family background at school. He didn't want us to feel superior simply because we had been born in a special family. He felt that one only earned respect through merit. His restrictive instructions made me feel awkward at school. Very often a teacher approached me to ask, "Is your daddy so and so?" My friends would then ask me why the teacher knew my father. I would become embarrassed, because I did not want everybody to know that my father was a high-ranking official, as this was so discouraged by my father.

Father also wanted us to understand that not all high-ranking officials were great and deserving of special respect. We were told not to judge people by their ranks, but by their merits, capabilities, hearts, and attitudes. Father did not like to be treated differently simply because of his rank, but he was very proud if people respected him for these other qualities. He always said that what made one noble was not rank, but character. The final judgment was to see how much one contributed to the country and how well one served the people.

The first time I really felt proud of my father at school was when an older boy said to me: "Boy, your father is really a good speaker. I listened to his speech last night at the school meeting hall. I wish I had a dad like yours." I knew Father had delivered a speech at my school the previous evening. The audience included all the teachers and staff as well as student representatives from the fourth and fifth grades. This boy was one of them.

My father had a reputation of being an excellent speaker. He often delivered speeches at schools, colleges, factories, hospitals, and other places. Many university professors came to know him by first listening to one of his speeches and then becoming friends with him. At his funeral, one professor told my sister "I still remember his speeches." Among the prominent Chinese Communists, former Foreign Minister Chen Yi was known as an excellent public speaker. When he gave speeches in Nanjing after the Communist takeover, the hall would always be crowded. A decade later, many people said that my father was the best local speaker since Chen. When I first heard that kind of comment from a schoolmate, I was thrilled. I could not wait to get home to tell my father. Young as I was, I already learned from my father what to be proud of and what not to be ashamed about.

VALUES COMING FROM PICTURE BOOKS

My father's department was responsible for many activities that greatly affected my life, though I did not realize it at the time. His department supervised four other departments in the city hall, and one of them was in charge of all the sports events and activities in the metropolitan city, including their promotion. One may wonder today why a government would have the responsibility of promoting sports. It is true that the Communist government did take too many responsibilities in hand at the time. One may cynically conclude that it is no wonder that the Communist system will fail; it tries to take care of everything and ends up not being able to take care of anything.

Under my father's supervision, many nonprofessional sports teams were organized in workplaces throughout the city. Big consolidated teams were established to represent different industries. For example, one team represented workers in manufacturing industries, and another those who worked in retail trade. Public school teachers had their own team, and so did the soldiers in the army bases. The municipal government provided space for games between those teams, allowing them to use the playground inside our residential compound. It was a well-equipped playground, with an eight-lane running track surrounding a soccer field covered by green grass. Almost every afternoon there were soccer games on the field.

Each afternoon after school I sat at the end line between the goal and the corner watching the games. One day as I watched, a player from the other side of the field got the ball and approached my side of the goal. I saw him raise his foot and kick it hard, aiming at the goal. The next moment I saw something flying toward the goal, and at the same time something flying toward me like an arrow. I dodged and something hit me on the back. It was so hard that I was pushed forward. When my feet hit the ground again, I still felt as if I were being pushed. I ran fifty feet before I could stop. What had happened? The player's sneaker had come loose and flown into the air toward the goal while the ball flew in my direction. The goal-keeper caught the sneaker in his hands and I was hit on the back by the ball. I both felt pain in my back and experienced loss of hearing. My ears echoed like a huge bell. I almost cried out, but pride made me hold up my head and walk home. As soon as I turned a corner and couldn't be seen from the playground, tears flowed like water from a spring. When I got home Aunt spotted something unusual and questioned me about it. I never revealed this episode to anyone. However, its impact on my life was profound. This simple hit on my back made me feel that sports were too violent for me and I never wanted to become an athlete.

Instead, I nurtured my love of reading. The day of television had not yet come, and one favorite pastime of kids my age was to read picture books. Each of us had only a few picture books as no family could afford many. So we liked to trade books or go to a special shop where books could be rented. For a penny you could rent a book and read it there in the shop. For two pennies you could check the book out overnight and return it the following day. This was a pretty good bargain and a lot of us liked to spend our late afternoon hours at a picture-book shop. The best part of this was that we could read books in series. Usually it took a series of ten to twenty picture books to complete a novel. I remember how I wished that I could save enough from my pocket money to buy one of my favorite series, but I never managed to.

These picture books were actually a very important part of our education, as they established and reinforced many values. reading the books we could easily distinguish the good from the l our young minds it became very clear that the Communist Party w. good and the Nationalist Party of Chiang Kai-shek was bad. Soldiers in the Chinese army were good and the Japanese or the American soldiers were bad. The Americans were brutal aggressors in both Korea and Vietnam. The chiefs of the enemies were Presidents Kennedy and Johnson and Defense Minister McNamara. As a kid, I was proud that I could spell their names in Chinese translation. We also learned that blacks had been slaves and were still oppressed. I vividly remember two stories. One was about a poor black child whose father was lynched by the KKK. Another, *The Children of Uncle Ho Chi Minh,* was about Vietnamese children fighting against American aggressors.

Another recurring theme of these picture books was modern Chinese history. We learned about the Red Army and its Long March, and we were encouraged to endure any hardships in our lives as the Red Army men had done in theirs. We were scared by the tortures that the Nationalist Party's special agents used in the prisons of captured Communists. Most often, these were the "underground workers," those undercover Communists who lived in the Nationalist-dominated territories, like my parents. Many of them were eventually executed. We saw these Communists as martyrs and heroes and those who betrayed them as worthless thugs. Of course, the Japanese aggressors were the most brutal animals of all. In fact, we never called the Japanese anything but "Japanese devils."

Reading picture books became a very important part of our education, because it was a part of our indoctrination in Communist values. For example, we were taught that it was a pleasure to help others. There was a soldier in the People's Liberation Army named Lei Feng. He did a lot of volunteer work on weekends and holidays, and before he died at twenty-three, he had helped hundreds of people who did not even know him. Most of his beneficiaries were elderly, young, or women. After his death, he was considered a model Communist and everyone was required to learn from his example.

At school, we were urged to do volunteer work as Lei Feng had done. As a result, I was often motivated to arrive at school early in the morning to clean the classroom before anyone came, because we were supposed to do good things without being noticed. This was just like Lei Feng, who always tried to hide his identity and did not want to get credit for what he had done. As a twelfth-grade student, my sister often organized her classmates to do volunteer work in community service. On

ild go to the railway station to help and serve pas-
vided drinks, carried luggage, explained route sched-
nges for those who could not read. Like Lei Feng, they
y, disabled, pregnant women, and young children. To
do things in the same spirit, my sister often bought me
iat had stories with this theme. I lent my books to my
d I believe they were also inspired.

Our entire generation was brought up with such values. In fact, the whole society was encouraged to accept them. Even today, I think some of these values are positive and necessary to a healthy society. Unfortunately, history followed a different course. During the following decade between 1966 and 1976, altruism was overemphasized to a ridiculous degree while the country experienced political instability and economic hardship. During his last ten years of his life, Mao, the man who had founded the new nation with its new ideological system, also destroyed it. During the next decade or so, in reaction to the absurdity of the earlier decade, the ideological values of the society were turned upside down. For example, volunteer work was no longer respected. Mao once said that we should support the American blacks in their fight against the capitalist government. Now, as the attitude toward Mao shifted from utter admiration and obeisance to mockery and hatred, new explanations about black problems came out. The urban poor in America was so poor because they were lazy.

Thousands of Chinese students came to study in the United States in the early 1980s. Disillusioned by our own social system under a Communist government, they came with all sorts of dreams and hopes, as well as myths and delusions about capitalism. We were brought up to believe that socialism was good and capitalism was bad. Now, we felt that we had been cheated, and thought that only the opposite was true. From my personal experience in the United States since 1987, I found that, among all the international students here, my fellow countrymen were the least critical of capitalism and Western society in general. It took some time for us to see reality in perspective. Through my own experience I see racism does exist in the United States.

Some other observations about American society make me concerned about the new values emerging in China today. For example, I find that volunteer work and the spirit of helping others are respected in the United States. That spirit, however, is disappearing in China today. The Communists did advocate these values in their earlier days, but they pushed them too far. As a result, when people began to abandon Communism, they also abandoned its positive values. Some universally acknowledged values seem to be ignored, unfortunately, in today's China.

History can be ironic in some unexpected way. I came to the United States at age thirty, and found that in many circumstances my understanding of America as a child was closer to the truth than that when I became an adult. In a graduate course in American civilization, I often heard my American classmates comment on the books we were assigned, saying how they were shockingly different from the high school textbooks they had read. What they meant was that through high school they had been taught mostly about the glorious part of American history and the advantage of its political and economic systems. Only in college and, especially in a graduate program in American civilization, did they begin to learn more about the other side of the matter. Now they read more about black history and the Native Americans. They also discussed the limits of capitalism. When I heard their comments about their earlier education, I was surprised. Now I found the picture books I read as a kid were closer to the truth, and much of what I had been told by the Communist authorities was true! The professor noted this contrast and commented: "Isn't it true that we were both good at criticizing the shortcomings of another society while trying to cover up our own problems at home?"

THE GATHERING WINDS OF THE STORM

By late 1965, I spent more time reading my picture books and saw my father less often. He changed jobs and moved to another city. He was nominated a deputy mayor of Suzhou, one of the most beautiful cities in China. Twenty-five hundred years old, it was known in the Western world as the Oriental Venice. His nomination looked like a promotion; however, it was actually another detour in his career because Suzhou was a much smaller city. A more natural promotion would have been to appoint him deputy mayor of Nanjing instead of Suzhou. Later I learned that this was not the first time he became a victim of inner-party power struggles. The news of his nomination surprised all of us in the family. My father had lived and worked in Nanjing for more than twenty-five years, and he was not ready, psychologically, to leave this city, which he considered his second hometown.

Father made the decision not to take the family with him, because he did not want to interrupt our lives. Within a year, my sister would be graduating from high school. Higher education in China had been free since the Communist takeover in 1949. However, college enrollment was so limited that there was no room for more than a quarter of the high school graduates. Therefore, the entrance exams were very difficult and selective, especially for admission to the top universities. My sister was an excellent student and would easily go to college, but my father's goal was for her to enter one of the best universities in China—either Beijing University or Qinghua University, also known as the Chinese Harvard and MIT. An abrupt relocation would certainly affect her scores in the exams, and Father did not want that to happen. Of course, my mother was another reason that Father did not move the family. She had her own career and could hardly tear herself away from her theater group. So, my father decided to move to Suzhou alone.

There were many tedious, little inconveniences after he moved to Suzhou. One of them was a kind of food stamp called *liang-piao*. Since the late 1950s, there was a rigid registration system to control the emigration of the population. Otherwise it was thought that too many people might flood a few major cities. Thus, each person registered as a resident of a certain place, such as a city or a county. People were not free to take jobs in another location unless the government asked them to. Without an ID card one could be restricted from doing many things, and, in fact, it was illegal to stay in another place longer than a week without applying for a temporary ID. It was a matter of surviving. For example, grain products were rationed in China: each urban resident could buy about thirty pounds of grains, rice, wheat, or corn, per month. A slip called *liang-piao* stating the amount of grain you were entitled to was necessary for each purchase. Even a bowl of rice in a restaurant required *liang-piao*. Because grains were the main food in China and there was a shortage of meat and vegetables, *liang-piao* was extremely important. Each month people picked up their *liang-piao* at the local grain-store after showing their ID cards. Different provinces had different kinds of *liang-piao*. In this way, the government could block any emigration.

When Father started his job as deputy mayor of Suzhou, he decided not to register as a resident of the city, and, instead, remained a resident of Nanjing. It was not only because he wanted to avoid paperwork and bureaucracy, but also because he feared that the registration system might someday hurt him and separate him from the rest of the family. Perhaps he had a sense of the forthcoming political instability and social upheaval. As a result, he could not get his *liang-piao* from Suzhou. Each month when we got our family's *liang-piao*, it included his share. So each month we had to send him his share by registered mail. I remember his saying, as a joke, that being the deputy mayor was illegal, since legally he was not even a resident of that city. It seemed that he began to have some concerns about the democratic nature of the nation, and wasn't that sure that it was "democratic," as he told me months before.

He was over fifty years old then, and this relocation and the separation from the family was not easy for him. He didn't take too much luggage with him, but among it was a multivolume book. It was the English translation of Chairman Mao's works. My father learned his English at junior high school, and one of his English teachers was an American missionary. My father's English was fairly good. In fact, he often taught English at schools to cover his identity as an underground Communist before the Communist takeover in 1949. Even after that, he found time to teach an evening course in English when he was the chief administrator of a technical school or a university. Despite the political changes and the fact that speaking a foreign language might not be a politically advisable thing to do, he always advocated learning English and other foreign languages. To keep up his English reading skills, he found the translation of Mao's works best suited his needs: no one could challenge him politically for studying Mao's works.

Besides, he really liked to read Mao's works. He felt there were many great ideas in Mao's writing that were both inspiring and deeply philosophical. Many others thought the same. For example, there was a prominent intellectual named Fu Lei, who translated most of Balzac's novels from French to Chinese. In his letters to his pianist son, Fu Lei wrote page-long comments appreciating Mao's philosophical ideas and wishing his son would benefit from these ideas as well. My father did the same with my sister, too, although not in letters but through talks.

When Mao's works were published in the early 1960s, they became best-sellers immediately. Although Mao was viewed as the founding father of the new China, most Chinese really knew little about this man. They had never seen him in person, on television, or in movies, because television was not available in China then and only large cities had a few movie theaters. Most Chinese had never even heard him speak, except for one sentence from the ceremony at the establishment of the People's Republic of China, which was played on the radio: "From now on, the Chinese people will stand up!" For a nation that had just broken the yoke of imperialist oppression and aggression, these words represented the beginning of a new epoch and were very inspiring indeed. The publication of Mao's works provided the first opportunity for ordinary Chinese to learn more about their leader and his thoughts.

This popular enthusiasm soon caught the attention of authorities in

Beijing, and an order came to promote the mass reading of Mao's works. In his position, my father was put in charge of this task at the local level, and he genuinely gave all his energy to carrying out the task. The movement had some positive effects at first. Many people were inspired by Mao's vision for the nation's future and obtained strength from Mao's words to deal with strife in their individual lives. However, as happened many other times, a positive thing soon became negative. The wave of reading Mao's works led to some unexpected and undesired results. Blind following of Mao's teachings took the place of independent thinking, and a personal idolization of Mao was growing fast. Now people followed Mao's words not because they were right but because they came from Mao's mouth. Once the blindfold was there, it was very difficult to restore sight again.

Not long after my father took the position in Suzhou, the Cultural Revolution began. For me, as a first-grade student, it started when our teacher brought in a picture of Chairman Mao. She told us that Chairman Mao was the Great Savior, and that, from that day on, we were going to keep his picture in our classroom. We had a loudspeaker above the blackboard in the middle of the front wall. Now the loudspeaker was put on the side of the wall, and in its place was Chairman Mao's picture. The school principal used to give orders through this loudspeaker, and it symbolically represented authority. Now it was very clear that Chairman Mao was in charge, and he could watch us at any moment.

Every day we were told how great the chairman was and how we should love him. In the middle of 1966, he wrote an open letter calling for a struggle against the "bourgeois headquarters" inside the Communist Party and encouraging everyone to write criticisms on posters. Our teacher told us that even we were not too young to join this struggle. Anyone could hang a poster in the classroom criticizing authorities, she said, including herself, the principal, or any higher-ranking officials.

On my way home after school I thought hard about what criticism I could come up with so that I could write a poster. It suddenly occurred to me that every morning when we started our class we would stand up and bow to the teacher, and the teacher then would respond by bowing to us. Since we now had the picture of Chairman Mao, it seemed to be a better idea to bow to his picture. Besides, when the teacher was bowing to us she was actually turning her ass to the great leader. Oh, it was such an insult to the chairman, and we must stop it! I was so persuaded by my own argument I felt as if I were about to stop a real crime.

When I got home I told my sister about my thoughts and she became excited, too. She thought I was very clever and that I had a good argument. So, with her help, I made a poster expressing my ideas and took it to school. Early the next morning before the classes began, I put it on the side wall in our classroom. All the students and the teacher read it. She even called in other teachers to see it. They all said nice things to me, praised my talent and courage, and agreed that I had a strong and correct political conscience. I was thrilled and felt like a real national hero. If an innocent eight-year-old boy like me could feel thrilled for what I had just done, it is not difficult to understand what millions of teenagers could be mobilized to do in the following months and years.

After my father took the position in Suzhou, each month he returned for a weekend with the family. Our favorite family pastime then was playing poker. We had a double-pack of beautifully designed playing cards, with each card featuring one of the "One Hundred and Eight Heroes" depicted in the classic novel *Water Margin*. I had heard almost all those stories from my grandpa, and each card refreshed my memory. These two packs of playing cards were fairly rare commodities. Father had purchased them at an airport while seeing off some foreign delegation, and we never found the same design again. We did not play with them often, and saved them for the weekends when my father was home. These cards were very dear to me and I could not believe my eyes when I woke up one night in the summer of 1966 to see that my mother and Aunt were burning the cards and other things in the kitchen. "Stop it!" I shouted and jumped to the stove, trying to snatch them back from the fire. Aunt stopped me and Mother began to explain why they were doing this.

The Cultural Revolution brought about a great many radical ideological changes. One of the articulated goals of the Cultural Revolution was to eliminate the "Four Olds": old cultures, old thoughts, old customs, and old habits. To answer the call from Chairman Mao, teenagers at high schools organized themselves as Red Guards. Their mission was to guard their great leader, Mao, against all his enemies. To identify such an enemy was their first task, and it was not that easy. No one would openly dispute with Mao. How could one find an enemy of Mao in those days? One thing the Red Guards did was break into people's houses trying to identify belongings that they thought bore the hallmarks of the Four Olds. Possession of these things was evidence of disagreeing with Mao, and therefore the person who owned them was his enemy. So, in a break-in, if such things were found, their owners would be publicly humiliated, mobbed, and beaten brutally.

Mother was very scared. With the help of Aunt, she burned and destroyed many things in our home which they thought might be considered to be the Four Olds. Playing cards might easily be considered something that only belong to the bourgeois and fall into the category of the Four Olds. To hide from their neighbors the fact that they were destroying possible evidence that might hurt them badly, they had put a heavy blanket on the kitchen window, so the neighbors would not be able to see the fire or the smoke. They thought I was sleeping and were not paying attention to me. Now, when they realized I had seen everything, they had to warn and scare me so I would never tell anyone about it. That night I was so upset I could hardly go back to sleep, although I was too young to understand that a political and social storm was coming.

RED GUARDS AT HOME

Like most youth at the time, my sister joined the Red Guards. In those days, almost every school had a couple of Red Guards organizations. These were grassroots youth organizations established by students in each school. Leaders were often those who were politically active, academically excellent, and athletically strong. The executive committee of the Red Guards in my sister's school had eight members, and my sister was one of the two girls on this committee.

The committee often held meetings at our home. Three members were from families of the air force officers; two came from blue-collar families. They were all considered to have "revolutionary" family backgrounds, and the Red Guard organizations were formed exclusively by such youth. If someone's father had been a capitalist before the Communist Revolution, he or she would be denied the right to join the Red Guards. At that time, to be able to organize or participate in a Red Guard organization was an honor that most youths desired.

When this eight-member committee held meetings in our living room, I liked to sit with them, listening to them talk. I was very glad to have them in our home because it made me feel that suddenly I had many older brothers and sisters. Although I did not quite understand all their conversations, I did learn that there was another Red Guard organization in their high school, and that there were some ideological differences between the two. It seemed that the one my sister belonged to was the more radical. They called themselves the Red Guards of Maoism while the other one was named the Red Guards of Mao's Thoughts.

The difference between the terms "Maoism" and "Mao's Thoughts" requires explanation. As a gesture of modesty, Mao only allowed his ideas to be referred to as "Mao's Thoughts," instead of "Maoism." The suffix "-ism" sounded more formal and Mao reserved that to honor Marx and Lenin. He insisted that the theoretical foundation of the Chinese Communist Party was Marxism and Leninism. However, along with the development of the radical movement within the Party, a personal cult of Mao was growing fast. Some radicals like Mao's wife argued that Mao's contribution to the Communist movement in history was second to none. Therefore, they suggested, it was only appropriate to use the term "Maoism," because this sounded as important as Marxism and Leninism. This difference may seem insignificant today, especially to an outsider, but at that time such a difference was as important as whether one calls a black person a black or a Negro in the United States today. To be politically correct meant not using the wrong word.

One major task of the Red Guards at the time was to remove all the Four Olds from people's daily lives. In addition, it was speculated that there were special agents of the United States, the Soviet Union, and Taiwan active in mainland China, who, together with the "bourgeois headquarters" inside the Communist Party, were trying to undermine and overthrow the Communist government. Therefore, the Red Guard organizations were to guard the "Red Headquarters" within the Communist Party led by Chairman Mao. A typical activity of the Red Guard organizations was to break into a targeted house at night searching for a trace of the Four Olds and other materials as evidence that the owner of the house was a bad person, and perhaps even a special agent. The Red Guards were particularly seeking guns, bullets, radio transmitters, or things like that.

When they searched people's houses at night, some Red Guards liked to beat people. This made me believe that violence was a human instinct that would surface if it were not subdued by morals and other considerations such as punishment. My sister never beat anyone in a break in. In fact, all her fellow committee members also disapproved of this behavior and felt personally uncomfortable about beating people. They even discussed this issue during the meetings at our house. They seemed to be still morally restricted from hurting another human being. But they felt it was very hard to curb this sort of behavior now. The targets were all labeled as enemies, and it was considered "revolutionary" to beat these people. What the committee members did was try to exclude those who they knew liked to beat people from the night actions by keeping the actions secret. But if those people heard about the plans they would always show up.

To help overcome the moral confusion and barriers and further mobilize the Red Guards, Mao appeared eight times on the top of the

Tiananmen Gate Wall between August 18 and late November 1966. There he waved his hands and cheered to millions of Red Guards in the huge square, giving them the moral authority to do what they were doing and whatever they dared to do.

The youth of this generation were brought up to adore Chairman Mao. They viewed the experience of seeing the chairman as the happiest moment in their lives. In those days, if someone said that Chairman Mao had once shaken hands with him, literally hundreds of people would jump to shake this person's hands to share the honor and the happiness.

To cultivate this kind of adoration, Mao gave an order that all those who wished to see him could travel to Beijing for free. So, the whole transportation system in China became free in 1966. Trains and trucks were packed with pilgrims. Furthermore, Mao said that the youth should have the opportunity to see the real world and local governments should give them the warmest welcome. Consequently, millions of young people could travel to any corner of the country for free. Wherever they went, free meals and shelters were provided. Most of the youth and teenagers took advantage of this unprecedented opportunity to travel. How I wished that I were five years older so that I could join this stream of travelers!

Accommodating thousands of travelers became a great problem for each city, and temporary shelters had to be provided. A quick solution was to open up all the schools, from elementary schools to colleges. Classes had already been canceled from grade seven upward, so it was relatively easy to turn all the unoccupied classrooms into temporary shelters. But that was still not enough, and classrooms in elementary schools had to be used for the same purpose. In my elementary school, it was decided to open half of our classrooms to provide shelters for traveling Red Guards. Classes were rescheduled into morning and afternoon shifts: half of the children would go to school in the morning and half in the afternoon, using the same classrooms. In this way, half of the classrooms could be used as shelters.

During this period of free traveling, my sister visited a dozen major cities, including the capital, Beijing. There she became one of the luckiest youths of her time: she saw Chairman Mao at Tiananmen. It was the third time Mao met with Red Guards. Organizing the event required tremendous effort. People were gathered together according to home location and institution. Early in the day, the organizers gradually ushered all the people into the huge square and let them stay there waiting for Mao to arrive. My sister, as a Red Guard from another city, was to sit in a remote corner of the square. For the purpose of keeping order, no one was allowed to move around the square without a special permit. My sister pretended that she had to go to a women's room and borrowed a special permit from one of the organizing workers. With the special permit, she gradually moved toward the center and front of the square.

A few moments before Mao arrived, one of the organizing workers spotted my sister on the aisle between the squares of people, and he questioned her identity. Because she could speak in pure local Beijing accent, the man thought she was a student from a top high school in Beijing. He ushered her to join those students who occupied the best positions on the square, right in front of the Tiananmen Gate Wall, as close as one could get to see Mao. No sooner had she joined those students than the ceremony began. From where she stood, my sister was closer to Mao than most of the people in the square. She was the only person in my family who ever saw Chairman Mao.

The square was so packed that many people got injured, and there were even rumors that some died. A remarkable phenomenon was that in such a crowd shoes might be pulled from one's feet. A great many people lost their shoes during the event. It was rumored that more than three thousand missing shoes were found on the square the following morning. The organizers opened a special lost and found office, and it took three days to dispatch those shoes. Looking back, the shoes were not the only thing lost on that occasion. The youth of a whole generation seemed to have lost their minds, too. Even older generations were soon carried away.

There was a famous quote from Mao at the time: "The most fundamental argument of Marxism is: It is right to rebel." Encouraged by Mao, the Red Guards began to rebel against all authority except Mao himself. It was a rare moment in history when the masses were mobilized to repudiate all bureaucracy and middle management and to respond to the highest authority alone. In Mao's vision, the real target of this movement was the "bourgeois headquarters" inside the Communist Party, namely, the entire bureaucracy including the president of China. However, it took awhile for the high school teenagers to reach that goal. The immediate targets were their schoolteachers.

A few teachers were easier targets than the others. They were often those who were old enough to have worked before the 1949 Communist takeover. They were forced to tell their personal history in public. For those who had worked for Chiang Kai-shek's government or those who had joined his Nationalist Party before 1949, there was not only public humiliation, but physical torture. Some Red Guards beat them with belts, and wooden sticks or steel rods. Joining the Red Guards were the rest of the teachers, who now claimed themselves as "revolutionary." Even school authorities joined the tide by giving away personnel records of the few teachers as evidence against them.

The political storm was soon carried over to my primary school. One day the whole school was summoned to a public meeting. The deputy principal announced that there was an enemy hidden among us and today we were going to expose him. The victim of the day was a math teacher who had served in Chiang Kai-shek's army before the Communist takeover. One after another, teachers and students came on the stage to attest to the wrong words that math teacher had said or wrong things he had done. He was immediately removed from his teaching position and was assigned to clean all the restrooms in the school.

Only a few weeks later, another public meeting was held and another enemy was announced. This time the victim was none other than the deputy principal himself. It was discovered that his father had been a landlord before the Communist takeover. By nature, he was a class enemy of the poor peasants who rented land from him. Now, the deputy principal was charged with trying to hide his criminal family history and waiting for revenge against the Communist Revolution that had redistributed his father's land among the poor peasants. Of course, as a school administrator, the deputy principal seemed to be a better target than the math teacher. Now a true enemy was identified, and everybody seemed to be quite satisfied. The deputy principal didn't have a pleasant personality, and even Aunt said he wasn't very nice. Now that he was exposed as an enemy, few really felt sorry for him. The day after the meeting, we all saw him come in and out of the restrooms, mops in hand, with the math teacher.

At my sister's high school, the two Red Guards organizations differed even more than previously, about almost every issue at hand, not just about some ideological terms they chose to use. For example, my sister's organization picked the deputy principal as their target while the other one chose the principal. Every day the students went to school, not for classes but to participate in all sorts of political activities. Public debates were often held, and representatives from the two Red Guards organizations had heated debates over various issues. A boy in my sister's organization was exceedingly good at those debates, and my sister was very impressed. He was also one of the eight members of the executive committee of the organization. Now, when the committee had meetings at our home, even Aunt and I could tell that he and my sister were closer to each other than the rest of the group.

However, love became taboo during the recent political and ideological storm. One was only allowed to love the country, the Communist Party, and the great leader, Chairman Mao. Even a married couple could not say they loved each other. Even though they were teenagers at the time, few Red Guards dared to admit, even in their own hearts, that they were in love. So, this relationship between my sister and her boyfriend remained dormant and then took the platonic form for ten years before they married. Like them, the entire generation of youth at the time experienced a psychologically distorted adolescent development.

"GOOD" REASONS AGAINST "BAD" PEOPLE

While love became taboo, sexual scandals were not. Officials who were involved in sexual scandals often became the first targets of Red Guard mobs. It was amazing how many scandals turned up during those days. Take our apartment building for example. Of the twelve families, ten had been married previously. Each man had been married to a country girl before coming to power in the 1949 Communist takeover. Once they became government officials they divorced their country wives. In traditional Chinese culture it was immoral to divorce a wife after becoming rich or powerful. Therefore, it was easy to mobilize resentment or hatred toward these officials. The Red Guards not only discovered these ignominious family histories, but, in many cases, brought the children from the first marriages back to the city to demand alimony for their mothers as well as child support. When people saw these long-ignored children with shabby clothes and uncultured manners, sympathy easily went out to them and anger was turned toward the fathers.

The irony was that, in many cases, these people had had good reasons to divorce many years ago. Before the Communist takeover, the traditional Chinese society was very patriarchal. Marriages were arranged by parents, especially fathers, and the youth did not have any choice. When the Communists advocated freedom in marriage, the youth who had been victims of forced marriage began to see new opportunities. They became followers of the Communist Party, and helped to found the Communist government. Under the new law, the old marriages were abolished and the youths happily remarried according to their own choice. No one thought that this former episode would come back to haunt them twenty years later.

Not all officials were at first assaulted by the Red Guards. Things had to make sense, and even mobs had to have reasons to justify their actions. Those bosses who were usually not very nice to the people working for them now became targets quickly. Indeed, it was true that certain government officials were less concerned about the people than themselves during the seventeen years between the Communist take-over in 1949 and 1966 when Mao launched this political movement called the "Cultural Revolution." The spirit of revolution during the early days of the Communist movement was eroded. What these offi-cials cared about was their own promotion with more power and a luxurious life. They put on airs in their daily contacts with ordinary people. Of course, people didn't like them. My parents didn't like these officials either.

My father often told me this story. When he was a young man he went into a public bathhouse one day and saw an antithetical couplet written in beautiful calligraphy on a pair of long scrolls hanging on the wall. It read: *It is hard to make this world fair and everybody equal, but once you are in the water in this house with nothing on, you will be truly free and equal with all.* We both liked the humor in it. He loved this couplet because he believed that all men are equal. While good clothes may make a good man better, better clothes never make a bad man good. The moral was that one should never try to look more important than one really is and never look down on any person because of their lower rank.

There was a barbershop in our residential compound. Before my father went to work in Suzhou I often went there with him. Usually there were many people waiting in line for haircuts. Most were residents in the compound and knew my father very well. Often they would offer to let us have our turn first because of my father's higher rank. They would say "You must be very busy" or "Your time is much more pre-cious" or "We can wait." My father would never accept these offers and would insist on waiting in line. Sometimes I saw people come into the shop and request to be served next. I never liked that, and as soon as the man left the shop I would ask my father who he was. My father would say, feeling a little uncomfortable, "I will tell you later."

Often it would turn out that the man was a high-ranking official, although his rank was not necessarily higher than my father's. I would feel very upset and wish that Father had not let the man get his haircut before us. But my father would always say that the man must have had a good reason. After all, my father would say, it was not worthwhile to care too much about trivial things. Peace and tranquility were far more important and harder to maintain. I knew he often embraced this kind of traditional Chinese philosophy. When he spoke like that, I always felt a compelling force in his voice that was much more powerful than it appeared on the surface.

My father had a gift for talking easily with people. He could have very natural and casual conversations with all sorts of people. For example, the barbers seemed to be much more comfortable having conversations with him than with many other officials. My father loved to talk to ordinary people, such as peddlers, shoe repairmen, gate keepers, and so forth. In fact, he owed his life to a gate keeper. That happened in the 1930s when he was an underground Communist working as a high school English teacher. One night when he came back to school after a secret meeting with another Communist, the gate keeper told him that someone had stopped by to look for him. The way he said "someone" was so deliberately emphasized that instantly my father understood that he meant the secret police had been there. After a brief and hearty thank you to the gate keeper, my father hurried to his room and gathered up whatever he could easily take with him. He did not go back to the front gate, but climbed over the side wall and with terror left the school behind in darkness.

I often heard my father say, "It was the people who had supported us in our earlier struggles against Chiang Kai-shek's government. Now we the Communists are in power, and we should never forget their support and abandon their interest." He would always quote Lenin to end his talk, "Forgetting the past means betrayal."

When Mao started the Cultural Revolution by criticizing these officials, most people, including my parents, could see some sense in his criticism. As officials, my parents earnestly looked at themselves to see if they had unintentionally behaved badly in their official roles. When they were asked to make self-criticism in public meetings, they did it in earnest. Despite her college degree, my mother felt her writing skills were limited. She had to come to my sister for help, and my sister also seemed to understand new ideas and ideological terms better and accept them more quickly. So, my sister often wrote drafts of self-criticism for my mother. To make it seem as if she had written it herself, my mother copied the drafts in her own handwriting and then destroyed the original manuscripts.

It is human nature to try to make sense out of things that do not seem to make sense at all, and many Chinese did this in the beginning of the Cultural Revolution. They had complete trust in the Communist Party and Chairman Mao, and once the idolization of Mao made him a demi-god, people's confidence in themselves lessened. When they couldn't understand something, their response often became: *Well, if I cannot see it, it's my fault. The great leader is much wiser, and what he says cannot be wrong.*

Most people felt this way when the Cultural Revolution began. Mao had two sets of messages for two different groups of people. The officials and Party members, who had followed him through their earlier lives, were asked to try to understand the new situation. He created a vision of continuous revolutions. To keep the spirit of the Revolution alive, he argued, sets of revolutions had to be launched continually. In his later years, he even specified that it had to be done every seven or eight years. In these ongoing revolutions, those who were once revolutionary might become reactionary forces. He warned them to keep open minds and always support the new revolutionary force. In the current case, it was the Red Guard organizations. Because Mao's words carried so much weight, those officials tried to understand the changes, even under the fists and belts of the Red Guards.

On the other hand, Mao encouraged the young Red Guards to dare to rebel against everything. Advocated by his radical followers, especially his wife, even violence was applauded and praised. They emphasized the animosity between classes, and dehumanized those who had been labeled as "class enemies." The effect was that often morals and common sense were eliminated. When a Red Guard was mobilized to beat an elderly teacher, he had to break with all the traditional morals. In his eyes now, the teacher was no longer one of the elderly whom he had been brought up from childhood to respect, but some great evil that threatened his own life and the general public interest. Today, perhaps it is very difficult to understand such a wild situation, but most people at the time were sincerely trying to make sense of it. It did have validity at first, because there seemed to be some "good" reasons to oppose "bad" people.

BEHIND THE BEDROOM DOOR

Like most others at the time, my parents were trying hard to make sense out of a situation that was increasingly out of control. Father still worked in Suzhou, but he often came back to Nanjing to spend a weekend with us. Although we had far fewer visitors now, two young men always came to our house when Father was home. I called them Uncle Wang and Uncle Jiang.

Uncle Wang was a manager of a cinema at the time. His relationship with my parents went back to the Communist takeover in 1949, when he was my father's security guard. The newly established government was more like a military system and all the higher-ranking officials had personal security guards. Uncle Wang was only a teenager then, and had joined the Communist army a year earlier during the civil war. Carrying a German-made pistol as my father's security guard, he followed my father everywhere, and stayed at our home at night. When my father established a modern technical professional school in 1953 with the assistance of the Soviet Union, Uncle Wang continued to work for him as an administrative secretary. Later, when my mother became the head of the local theater group, Uncle Wang worked for her as an executive administrator. Having worked with my parents for so many years, he had become our family friend.

Uncle Jiang also worked at the technical school. Like many of my father's colleagues there, he was very close to our family. Uncle Jiang had many brothers and sisters, and some of them lived in the United States. One reason Uncle Jiang felt close to my father was my father's knowledge and adoption of Western civilization. Many Communist officials had no exposure to Western culture and civilization at all before the Communist takeover. There was an anecdote about some Communist soldiers and officers after they captured the largest city, Shanghai, in 1949. Staying in a house with toilet facilities, a group of those armed men simply could not figure out the function of the toilet. It was so white and clean with some water at the bottom. Each time they pressed the handle fresh water came out and made a noise. Finally someone suggested that they might use the toilet to wash their faces. After each one used it they could push the handle and have fresh water for the next.

My father had a remarkable and distinguished manner. It set him apart from most of the other Communist officials and invited comments comparing him with Premier Zhou Enlai, who was widely recognized as a fine diplomat. When my father dressed up in a three-piece suit and tie he looked really sharp and impressive. At government-sponsored banquets for foreign visitors, most Chinese officials showed their hospitality in a way hardly appreciated by their foreign guests. They used their own chopsticks to serve food for their guests. Many foreigners must have been horrified and embarrassed when they saw chopsticks moving from a Chinese person's mouth into the serving dishes, picking up some food and dumping it into the foreigners' plates or bowls. In those circumstances, my father would always ask the waitress for an extra pair of chopsticks to serve with. I am sure the foreign guests appreciated it. Even in the mid-1980s I often heard people talk about my father's elegance in the 1960s. His distinguished public manner seemed to have made some people, such as Uncle Jiang, admire him.

Each time before Uncle Wang and Uncle Jiang came to visit, my mother would prepare two cups of tea and have two packs of good cigarettes waiting for them. In China, one's living room was open to any visitors because anyone could knock at the door and come to visit without an invitation. My parents wanted to have an uninterrupted conversation with Uncle Wang and Uncle Jiang, so, once they arrived, they would go into my parents' bedroom, so that an unexpected visitor wouldn't interrupt.

There were only two armchairs in my parents' bedroom. Each time my parents insisted that Uncle Wang and Uncle Jiang sit on the chairs and they sat either on the bed or on wooden chairs and stools. Out of politeness, Uncle Wang and Uncle Jiang refused to sit on the best chairs in the room, because their age and rank made such an arrangement awkward. But each time my parents' persistent sincerity would prevail. At first my parents tried to keep me out of the room so that I wouldn't hear their conversations, but after I promised never to tell anyone anything I heard, they allowed me to stay. After everybody sat down comfortably, one of my parents would ask: "What's the news?" These two men would then tell us all they heard about the political situation, at the local and provincial level and the rumors from Beijing.

In those days, word of mouth was almost the only reliable source of news. We heard about nearly everything politically important that was happening around the whole nation. We learned in detail how the Cultural Revolution was progressing. If someone in authority in Beijing, such as Mao's wife, Jiang Qing, met with a certain delegation of Red Guards and delivered a speech, no more than a week later my parents heard about it from Wang and Jiang. This was a very unusual way of getting political news. For seventeen years, important political events happening at the top level of the Communist Party would either be kept as a secret or the news was spread by official channels so that each level of officials let the lower level officials know a little about the events, but not all he knew. The highest authorities specified to whom and to what extent the news could be spread. Now, all this bureaucracy was broken, and rumors and news became the same thing.

Uncle Wang and Uncle Jiang would sometimes bring a printout of a speech recently made by some top leaders in Beijing. Usually it was a rough print, and sometimes it was a carbon copy. Uncle Wang and

Uncle Jiang often asked my sister to make multiple copies by rewriting it using carbon papers. In fact, this became the typical way to circulate important documents around China.

From these two men we also heard about local public meetings that had been held in the past week: who was targeted, what the charges were, who organized it, and how violent it was. We heard of disagreement and sometimes violence among the Red Guards. Based on the information from Uncle Wang and Uncle Jiang, my father tried to analyze the current political situation and predict future developments. His predictions almost always turned out to be correct. My mother teasingly gave him a nickname: Always Right, and both Uncle Wang and Uncle Jiang agreed with her. My sister and I would occasionally join in the predictions, although I was only eight years old. It seemed that my father was especially happy and amused when events proved that he was right and we were all wrong.

Despite the political storm in the outside world, inside this little bedroom we had fun by ourselves. Because all the adults in the room were smoking, every half an hour we opened the bedroom door for a few minutes to let the smoke out. Sometimes we played poker as we talked. Our cards were burned during the crackdown on the Four Olds a few months before, but Uncle Jiang brought new sets of playing cards every time he came. He seemed less scared than my mother, and claimed that he had some friends who were influential leaders of big, regional Red Guard organizations and no one would dare to hurt him.

At that time, neither Uncle Wang nor Uncle Jiang was a Communist Party member. They were not high-ranking officials as my father was. Actually, although my father made friends with almost everyone he met, most of those who were close friends were not high-ranking officials or even Communist Party members. Instead, my parents could have very natural and intimate conversations with ordinary folks like Uncle Wang and Uncle Jiang. During those conversations in my parents' bedroom, one topic was often discussed. My parents, especially my father, had not been promoted appropriately within the Communist system. Why? Both Uncle Wang and Uncle Jiang attributed it to my parents' relationships to their supervisors. They said my parents were truly loved by the people who worked for them, and my father was an exceptionally capable man. This might generate jealousy among other officials, including his supervisor. Additionally, my father was no one's protégé. It was difficult to be promoted unless someone at a higher level strongly supported or initiated the decision. Being no one's protégé certainly put my father at a disadvantage. Both Uncle Wang and Uncle Jiang said that it was partly my mother's fault, because she never made the social effort to make friends with the wives of my father's supervisors.

My mother took her job very seriously. She tried her best to do an excellent job in her own official position. Like my father, she spent most of her weekends with the people who worked for her, rather than with the people she or my father worked for. Many of the wives of father's colleagues did not take their jobs so seriously and would rather spend their weekends visiting the wives of their husbands' supervisors, playing mah-jongg, or shopping together. Uncle Wang and Uncle Jiang called that "wife diplomacy," and obviously my mother did not do that well.

Although the topic of these closed-door conversations was political and seemed beyond the comprehension of an eight-year-old boy, I gradually understood most of what they had discussed. It seemed they were saying that, on the one hand, there was some injustice in the current system. For example, promotion was not based on merit, but nepotism. Good, nice, capable officials like my father were not promoted properly, and sometimes even demoted. In that sense, they wanted to see some change and reform, and they could accept and agree to some of Mao's recent argument about carrying out a new ideological revolution. On the other hand, they seemed to be very confused, dissatisfied, and even shocked by the way Mao was handling the issue. Creating a political storm, economic chaos, and even criminal violence was certainly not a good solution to the problems they could recognize and identify. However, because of the idolization of Mao, it seemed almost sinful to question or doubt the wisdom of his argument and decisions. Apparently, they felt the contents of their conversations should not go beyond the room. So, they warned me again and again that I mustn't tell anyone anything I heard.

THE EARLY STORM
BARELY HITS OUR FAMILY

Grassroots organizations were mushrooming everywhere in China in early 1967. Earlier, Red Guards were organized in high schools, colleges, and universities. Now, organizations called "Revolutionary Rebels" appeared in almost every corner of the nation. Factories, hospitals, government departments, and nearly every workplace in all cities had at least one organization.

Across the courtyard from our grain store there was a small post office with one employee. One day on the door I read a poster announcing the establishment of a Revolutionary Rebel organization in the post office. I scratched my head and wondered: Only one man is working there; how many Revolutionary Rebels could this organization possibly have? That one postman must have been both the commander-in-chief and the only soldier in this organization!

As their names indicated, these Revolutionary Rebels were rebeling against their supervisors. At each workplace, the "rebels" held public meetings, denouncing their former bosses as "class enemies," a term borrowed from the class struggle theory of Marxism. Physical torture and abuse were common. Even within our residential compound, I often witnessed such assaults.

However, it was those in power who were less respected or who had made personal enemies of their employees who were usually attacked first. My parents certainly did not fall into that category. In my mother's theater group there was now a rebel organization. At first, they did not give her too much trouble except to ask her to sell propaganda papers in our neighborhood on Sundays. Even this was hard for my mother. If our neighbors saw her selling propaganda for the rebels, it would look very awkward.

My sister suggested that she and I sell the papers instead. Because of our age, it would not look as unusual as it would if my mother sat in the street peddling the papers. What my sister really meant, it turned out, was for me to sell the papers. She would keep an eye on me from somewhere nearby to see that no one robbed me of my papers or money. I was young enough to be talked into this, and felt very excited about it. The next morning my sister and I went to the shopping center across the street from our residential compound. We sat outside the front gate and put about half a dozen different papers in a pile on the ground and tried to sell them to people passing by. From time to time my sister would sneak away and let me do the job alone.

Various rebel organizations throughout the country printed these papers and claimed that they would be published regularly every week or two. But few of them survived more than three or four issues. A copy of each issue cost four pennies and usually I could sell between 50 and 100 copies every Sunday, although my mother would always carry more than 200 copies home each Saturday evening. On Monday morning, she brought the rest of the papers back to the rebels and they blamed her for not selling more. Sometimes she considered not returning the papers, simply saying she had sold them all, and giving them the correct amount of money. But she was afraid they might give her even more papers to sell. So she always brought some back and tolerated the blame and criticism.

I actually enjoyed my first job selling the newspapers, and I liked to read them, for they had many pictures and illustrations. They were all caricatures ridiculing various "enemies" of the Revolution. I was fascinated by those caricatures and even tried to imitate them. Pretty soon I became quite successful. Even my sister was amazed. She tried to imitate them too, but her illustrations were not nearly as good as mine. I was encouraged by this.

At school, in fine arts I was not the best student, as I was in many other courses. This was partly because I did not like the objects that our instructor often asked us to draw. Usually he would hang a picture on the blackboard and ask us to try to duplicate it. The picture was usually a portrait of a factory worker, a peasant, or a soldier. I felt it was very boring. The worst was when the instructor asked us to draw a picture of the Tiananmen Wall Gate. We were supposed to draw it from the front perspective, so that it would not look as if it were falling apart, even if we did a poor job. The teacher was also careful never to ask us to deal with the portrait of Chairman Mao hanging on the Wall. He would ask us to simply draw a frame there and leave it blank. He would be in trouble if we made a mess of Mao's portrait. Even so, I still had problems with my work, particularly with symmetry. I could never make the right side look exactly like the left, so the gates and lanterns and flags on one side would be either larger or smaller than those on the other. This annoyed me so much that I often cried over my work.

One day our instructor announced that he was going to organize a "Little Red Guards Artists Group." He would give extra lessons so that the children in the group would be able to use their pen as a weapon to fight the "Bourgeois Headquarters" and become more involved in the Cultural Revolution. Despite the lofty reasons, it was nothing more than an extra activity for school children. This was a good example of how people handled their daily lives by adapting to the new political storm. By using some of the most recently created ideological terms, people could find ways to justify what they wanted or were supposed to do, just as our fine arts instructor did.

Anyone could apply to join this Little Red Guards Artists Group, the teacher said, but only two or three would be selected from each class, because of the limited size of such an extracurricular group. He asked each applicant to draw something and he would then choose us based on the merits of our pictures. I was fascinated by caricature drawings, so

I prepared a caricature of Liu Shaoqi, the former president of the nation, now pointed out by Mao as the Number One Enemy, the chief commander of the "Bourgeois Headquarters" within the Communist Party, thus the Khrushchev of China. When I presented my drawing to the instructor, he could hardly believe that I had done such wonderful work. He asked me to draw another one as he watched and I did. He was very pleased and immediately accepted me as a member of his Little Red Guards Artists Group.

Another of my afterschool activities was to go with my sister to the municipal government office compound next door to our residential compound to read posters known as "Big-Character-Papers." There were basically two kinds. One targeted national figures, such as former President Liu Shaoqi and the general secretary of the Party, Deng Xiaoping, or other people such as governors of provinces. These were usually copies of the originals that had first appeared in Beijing or other provincial capitals. The other kind targeted local figures such as mayors, governors, and directors of various departments in our city or province. These would be written by local rebel organizations or anonymous individuals.

At that time, posters were the best sources of news. In addition to current events, which were not reported in newspapers, they carried gossip and rumors about public figures' private lives. For example, on posters one might read about an alleged relationship between a mayor and his maid. Pornography and any literature of that kind had been strictly banned in China since the Communist takeover in 1949. Now, in the form of "Big-Character-Papers," many lewd stories were produced. They immediately attracted a huge audience. Because of the nature of these stories, the language could become vulgar and I did not understand some of the words. Once I was reading posters with my sister and I came across a phrase similar to "fuck you." I certainly did not understand it, so I moved forward and approached the poster. I pointed at the dirty phrase with my little finger and asked my sister, "What does this mean?" The people all burst out laughing. My sister's face turned pink and she grabbed my wrist and took me away, leaving behind an amused crowd. On our way home I still did not understand what had happened. I kept on asking her what was wrong. She simply told me to be quiet and not to ask such silly questions. I did not understand the phrase until years later when I finally found it in a huge dictionary.

Among all the posters I read at that time there was only one criticizing my father. It was about an unexpectedly trivial matter. Because we always put an extra pair of chopsticks on our dining table to serve food, the author of the poster asserted that my father must have adapted this idea from Western table manners, and used it as an evidence to show how my father was Westernized and bourgeois.

A story like this certainly did not generate too much jealousy or hatred. Stories about other officials often involved alleged love affairs, or too much luxury, such as living in a fancy house or spending too much time on pets, fishing, or gardening at public expense. Compared with those officials, who were often brutally beaten and physically tortured, my father was spared during the first months of the Cultural Revolution.

SURVIVING THE STORM

For a couple of months my father did not come home on weekends as usual. I knew something must have happened to him, but wasn't sure what. A couple of times my mother sent my sister to Suzhou to see him. When she came back, they would lock themselves in the bedroom and talk for hours, but never mention my father to anyone else in the family. I hated this growing atmosphere of mystery within the family, but could do nothing about it.

It turned out that Father had been detained by the Revolutionary Rebels in Suzhou. When my sister went to see him, she witnessed one of the public meetings held against him. It was held at the city's stadium with thousands of people watching. My father, along with a handful of other high-ranking officials, was on the platform. All of them were charged as "power holders who would rather take the capitalist road than the socialist one." Each had two strong men standing behind him. From time to time, these two men would hold the arms of the man in front and force him to bend over till his mouth almost touched the ground. This form of torture was very common at that time in China and had a special name: "To take a flight," because the shape of the man in torture looked liked an airplane.

It was remarkable that even under such circumstances my father did not lose his humor and eloquence. During the meeting someone delivered a speech and charged him with saying that we should make friends with the American imperialists. He then openly challenged my father: "Didn't you say that?"

"No, never!" my father responded. The man was a little bit shocked and became very upset. He yelled at my father, "How dare you deny like that?"

My father struggled to move a step closer to the microphone and said, "I only said we should make friends with the American people. I said 'the Americans,' not 'the American imperialists.' There is a big difference here. Even today I would still say that we should make friends with all the peoples over the world, including the Americans."

The audience was moved. They seemed to agree with his argument. The man became very angry and shouted: "How could you deny that you said you wanted to make friends with the American imperialists? What if you did say that?"

"The truth is I never said that," my father calmly responded. "If I ever said things like that, then please feel free to smash my damned dog head." The whole audience broke into loud laughter, because one of the political slogans most frequently used in those days was: "Let's smash his damned dog head!" By applying that jargon to himself, my father made a fine joke, and no one missed it. My father turned the tables when given the chance.

Though he was an innocent victim of the current political storm, he still tried to convince himself that there might be some justice behind such chaos and violence. Mao charged that some officials had betrayed the revolutionary spirit and became bully bosses instead of servants of the people. My father earnestly accepted the argument and honestly searched in himself for evidence to prove Mao's words, just like a Christian might try to recall his sins before God.

One day after a public meeting, as my father was walking back to his apartment, a man of his age approached and stopped him by calling him "Mr. Deputy Mayor." My father was surprised, because few would use such an honorable title now. He stared at the man and could hardly recall when and where he had met him before. After a few seconds of silence the man said: "You don't remember me? We were classmates in high school almost forty years ago."

"Oh, yes! Now I remember," my father exclaimed. "Where have you been for so many years and what are you doing now?" The man admitted awkwardly that he had just attended the public meeting where my father was a target. He was a high school teacher and that day all public school teachers were organized to hold the meeting targeting officials in charge of public education. "Why didn't you come to see me before?" my father asked, excited at finding an old friend and wishing this reunion had happened earlier. The man looked at my father, hesitated for a moment, and then said: "Well, you are such a high-ranking official and I am only a school teacher. How could I bother you?"

My father felt his heart sink, and with a sense of guilt and regret he sincerely reached out his hand and shook the man's hand firmly, as if to say: This is all my fault, but I'm really glad that we finally got together. He invited the man to stop by for a cup of tea, and they had a long conversation. This incident made my father further believe that the Communist Party did have an issue to address: how to amend its relationship with the general public.

Not long after my father had been denounced at the public meetings in Suzhou, my mother became a target at home in Nanjing. One evening, as I was lying in bed, there was a knock on our door. Aunt answered and two actresses from Mother's theater group came in. They had been family friends for a long time. They were still on Mother's side and came that night to warn her that the following day the "rebels" would begin to target her.

Hardly had they finished their conversation, when there was another knock at the door. This time it sounded urgent and rude. My mother first let the actresses into her bedroom and closed the door, then she opened the apartment door and let in two other actresses who had also been family friends. They were now leaders of the Revolutionary Rebels organization in the theater group. They came to inform my mother that the next day she would lose her freedom to return home. She was to stay at work and be watched closely by the "revolutionary people."

Mother must have seemed too calm for them, for they asked if anyone else had spoken with her. She said "no," and then asked to be excused for a moment because, she said, she had to talk to Aunt before she went to bed and tell her what to buy at the market the next morning. The actresses could hardly stop my mother, because Aunt was actually our maid, and a maid was, by definition, more "proletarian and revolutionary" than an actress, according to Marxist class struggle theory. She had to be given the priority. My mother left the room and came into my bedroom and spoke very quietly into Aunt's ears and then left us quickly.

There was a small window high in the wall between my bedroom and my mother's. Quickly, Aunt put a small table under the window, stepped on it and quietly opened the window. She looked into my mother's bedroom, waved her hand, and the two actresses climbed into my room. Hardly had they touched the floor when I heard the other two actresses ask my mother why she kept her bedroom door closed, and they wanted to see if someone was hiding there. My mother opened the door and of course no one was there. The whole drama developed so fast that I could almost hear my own heartbeat. Thank God the two in the living room soon left and did not try to come into my bedroom. Probably, as my mother supposed, they would not because they knew it was also Aunt's bedroom, and it would be very inappropriate to search her room.

The next morning my mother went to work as usual, but she did not return home in the evening. She and several other managers were detained at work. At the time, the rebel organizations in all the theater groups were loosely associated because they all had been under the supervision of the Department of Culture of the municipal government. Now, all the leaders or managers of the theater groups were denounced as "powerholders who took the capitalist road." These people were ordered to do the lowest jobs, such as cleaning the restrooms, preparing food in the cafeterias, and cleaning garbage from the theater compound.

The detained group included some actresses and stars. Unlike my mother, who had joined the Communist Party before the 1949 Revolution and had been a social activist as an adult, the actresses or stars had never been involved in political struggles. Because of their popularity, the Party extended its membership to them and appointed them as directors or managers of their theater groups. Although they were Communist Party members and held managerial positions and seats in legislative bodies, they were not politically experienced and now were totally lost in this unprecedented political upheaval.

One of them was an actress who had been well known since the 1940s as a famous star in a local opera. She was forced to work in the cafeteria with my mother during the day and sleep in the next room at night. One day my mother discovered this woman was deeply depressed, and she was very concerned, because she thought that actress might commit suicide if she were left alone. My mother told the rebels her concerns and suggested that they keep an eye on her or let her stay overnight in my mother's room. Unfortunately, no one took her words seriously, and that very night the actress killed herself by drinking toxic skin-care oil and then cutting her wrist with a small knife. Afraid of being held responsible for more deaths, the rebels soon released the rest of the detained managers, including my mother.

Thousands of people killed themselves in similar ways during that period of the Cultural Revolution. Most of them were intellectuals and professionals, and some were government officials. In my extended family there was such a victim, my father's cousin. As a professor of mathematics and the head of her department, she became a target of the political storm. Unlike her cousins, she could not handle the situation, and decided to commit suicide. One day she sneaked into a tall building on campus, jumped from a balcony, and died immediately.

There were more deaths yet to come, however, and many victims were actually members of the rebel organizations. These organizations mushroomed in China for a while, and some of them took over the offices at various levels of government. Those who were left behind denied the legitimacy of such a takeover of power at local or provincial levels. The rebel organizations were thus split, and the conflicts between them grew rapidly into a civil conflict. In many other areas in the country, although not in Nanjing, gunfire was exchanged.

To control the chaos, Chairman Mao ordered the People's Liberation Army to take power at various levels, and formed Army Takeover Committees. Suzhou was the city where the conflict between rebel organizations became the most violent in our province. Foreseeing the forthcoming violence that would kill hundreds of innocent people in the city, my father wrote a letter to the Army Takeover Committee in Suzhou.

In his letter he argued that because he had lived most of his life in Nanjing, it would be far more convenient for others to investigate him through the department in Nanjing. Therefore, he should return to Nanjing and put himself in the hands of the revolutionary people at the Department of Culture, Education, Health Care, and Sports, where he had been the director for years. If he had ever done anything wrong to the people, he would apologize, take responsibility, and accept appropriate punishment; but, he added, he hoped history would prove his innocence. He apparently made a strong argument, for within a month the Army Takeover Committee approved his application. He returned safely to Nanjing in 1967.

A LEGENDARY MAN

Now, every morning my father went to the Department of Culture, Education, Health Care, and Sports, but instead of sitting in his director's office, he was assigned to mundane tasks such as cleaning the floor and restrooms, just as my mother was doing at her theater. Sometimes, the rebels would ask him to recall and write down his personal history before the Communist takeover in 1949. They knew he had been an underground Communist for seventeen years, but they did not want to admit he had a glorious history. They wanted to find out if he had done anything wrong, namely, betraying his comrades to the Japanese occupiers or Chiang Kai-shek's government, or working for these enemies as a double agent. Once they read his memoir, they interrogated him again and again, and checked with every witness they could find, yet they still could not find anything that showed my father wasn't the hero he seemed to be.

The more they read, the more they learned of the contributions he had made to the Communist Revolution. It was under his influence that both his brothers joined the Communist Party in the 1930s. What amazed the rebels was how "red" his entire family was. Three brothers and one sister, and their spouses, were all Communist Party members. It was really a family that contributed a lot to the Communist Revolution, not only during the final takeover in 1949, but also in the early years in the resistance against the Japanese invasion. In fact, the three brothers worked hand in hand in the resistance in late 1930s. I have rarely heard of all the brothers in one family serving the country this way. Many rebels found themselves attracted by the stories of the brothers. Years later, one of them told my mother she was thrilled when she read my father's writing.

The Japanese invasion of Shanghai on August 13, 1937, generated tens of thousands of refugees. They flooded into the American, British, and French concession areas in Shanghai. A temporary united philanthropic committee was established by various religious groups including Buddhist, Protestant, and Catholic, and it set up more than fifty refugee camps within the concession areas. A large number of social workers were desperately needed, and it was difficult to find so many people. The daily operation of these camps was run by a Buddhist leader named Zhao. He found himself lucky to have my father work for him, because, through my father, many responsible and educated people were soon recruited to work in the refugee camps.

They were all underground Communist Party members, including my father's two brothers and a cousin. She and my second uncle were the same age and later married. These underground Communists worked much harder than regular workers, because they did not work simply for payment but were highly motivated by lofty ideals. It was like a well-organized labor union secretly working hand in hand with management to help production and the productivity was incredible. Soon, the refugees were assembling toys and this helped the refugee camps financially.

The Communists also took the opportunity to advocate and organize the resistance against the Japanese. They set up educational programs, from literacy to complete primary education, in the refugee camps. My father and his brothers all became teachers, and they not only taught the refugees how to read but also advocated stronger patriotism. The first text they used to teach Chinese was written by my second uncle, and the title was "Our Great Motherland."

Many of the refugees were young people in their teens or early twenties. Most of them hated the Japanese invaders and wanted to fight them. However, these youths could not join the resistance, because the government led by Chiang Kai-shek had a lukewarm attitude toward resisting the Japanese invasion, and the resistance was not well organized. Chiang Kai-shek believed his army was not strong enough to fight the Japanese yet, and, above all, he was more worried about the Communists than the Japanese, for eventually they would be his rivals for the ultimate power in China. Under the circumstances, my father and his brothers saw a good opportunity to mobilize the youth to join the Communist forces in the resistance against the Japanese. The idea was supported by the Buddhist leader Zhao, because he was also tired of the lip service Chiang Kai-shek's government paid to resisting the Japanese and wanted to see more action.

Coincidentially, early in the summer of 1938, an urgent message came through an underground secret channel from a Communist army called the "New Fourth Army" based in Anhui Province. The army desperately needed to recruit youth to reinforce its forces immediately. The refugees in Shanghai seemed to be a good resource. However, it was very difficult to move hundreds of young people from Shanghai to the Communist army based in Anhui, because they had to pass by areas occupied by the Japanese and Chiang Kai-shek's army. Even the Western authorities in the concession areas in Shanghai wouldn't be happy to see such a large number of people join the Communist army. The task seemed almost impossible at first, but after consulting with the Buddhist leader Zhao, my father and his colleagues soon had a bold yet ingenious plan.

First, they convinced all the sponsoring religious groups of the refugee camps as well as the foreign authorities of the concession areas in Shanghai that it was in their best interest to move the youths to the countryside in the neighboring provinces such as Zhejiang and Anhui and run a self-reliance production program there in order to help the refugees become self-supporting peasants. It was also a financially attractive plan. The foreign authorities in Shanghai's concession areas were only too happy to approve the plan, because they wanted to get rid of the refugees who were such a burden to them now. My father negotiated with the foreign authorities so successfully that they even agreed to provide some relocation fees and second-hand clothes for the refugees participating in this emigration plan.

Meanwhile, because the areas neighboring Shanghai were still under the control of the Nationalist government led by Chiang Kai-shek, the action had to be approved by his government. At the time, Chiang had already moved his capital from Nanjing to Wuhan, an inland city hundreds of miles away from Shanghai. My father and his colleagues prepared a well-written proposal and sent it to the central government. Because its real purpose was not obvious, the proposal was soon approved by Chiang's government.

Due to careful organization, the true purpose of the movement remained hidden. To hide their destination, they chose a complex route. The first stated destination was a coastal city in Zhejiang Province named Wenzhou. There was a commercial water route between the concession areas and Wenzhou, but ships had to pass by a Japanese-occupied port. To pass safely without arousing Japanese suspicion, my father rented a British commercial ship named *Tycoon*. Once arrived at Wenzhou, they divided themselves into twelve groups, and walked toward the Communist army base in the neighboring province, Anhui. They deliberately chose the mountain areas as their route, because it was less likely to be detected by Chiang Kai-shek's troops in Zhejiang. Eventually, after a lengthy journey of about 200 miles, including the water and land route, my father led nearly 700 young people to the "self-reliance production program" in Anhui. The youth were immediately recruited into the Communist "New Fourth Army" and they greatly reinforced its capacity to resist the Japanese invasion.

In 1940 the Communist Party sent my father to Nanjing to reestablish Communist organizations in this Japanese-occupied capital city. This was the most amazing period in his life and difficult for the rebels in 1968 to believe. To live and work as an "underground Communist" in Nanjing was literally fighting in the heart of enemy territory. The last Communist organization in the city had been broken up in the early 1930s by Chiang Kai-shek's government, and all the captured Communists were executed at Yuhuatai, a little hill on the outskirts of the city. Following that, there was not any Communist activity in the city for almost a decade. The rebels wondered how my father could have possibly survived more than nine years between then and the 1949 Communist takeover without being discovered by either the powerful special agents of the Japanese and its puppet government or later the Nationalist government of Chiang Kai-shek. During those nine years and through diligent and cautious work, my father established an underground Communist Party organization that recruited more than 2,000 members before the Communist army took over the city in April 1949.

There were many legendary achievements during these years. Among the things that surprised the rebels when they were reading my father's writing, two were the most remarkable. After the Japanese surrendered in 1945, a civil war broke out between the Communist and Nationalist Parties. Partly as a legacy from Ambassador Hurley, the United States became a partisan in the civil war. When General Wedemeyer, head of the Military Advisors Group from the United States, came to Nanjing to discuss military strategies with Chiang Kai-shek, every new miliary movement resulting from these talks was closely monitored by the Communists, because at least five Chinese employees working for the American Military Advisors Group in Nanjing were underground Communist Party members under the leadership of my father. One of them was working as a technician drawing military maps!

In the final months of the civil war, the Communists had already taken over half of China, and Chiang Kai-shek was trying to use the Yangtze River as a natural defense to help him hold at least half of China. At such a critical moment, the underground Communists once again miraculously got the military maps of Chiang's armed forces along the Yangtze River. Those maps reached my father and he had the responsibility of delivering them to the Communist army on the northern bank of the river.

It seemed to be an impossible task, because Chiang's troops had blockaded all the ferries between the northern and southern sides of the river. Yet where there is a will there is a way. My father soon found a secret channel between the two banks. Because of the blockade on the river, certain commodities such as Western medicine became very rare on the northern bank. These were imported from the United States by Chiang Kai-shek's government. As a part of the sanctions against the Communists on the northern bank, there was a tight control on Western medicine. Speculative merchants soon found a very risky way to make money. They bribed high-ranking officials in Chiang's government and made illegal trips to the northern bank on official military ships.

Now, my father decided to try his luck. He purchased a suitcase full of Western medicine and hid the military maps in medicine boxes. To make it more realistic, my father and a woman colleague named Bai pretended to be a married couple who recently entered this risky business, for Bai was a more experienced underground Communist than my mother. They bribed a high-ranking official in Chiang's government and acted as his protégé, going to the city of Yangzhou, where other illegal merchants usually shipped their goods.

Right before they boarded the ship, however, a group of inspectors arrived unexpectedly. They opened the suitcase and removed the medicine to search for other forbidden goods, such as weapons, which were even more tightly controlled. They handled the boxes roughly and in the middle of the process some of the boxes broke. One secret map even became loose and slid out of the box. As soon as it happened, my father pushed the map back into the box before the inspectors could notice! Fortunately, the inspectors didn't find anything suspicious, and let Bai and my father go. They eventually reached the northern bank and delivered the maps in person to the headquarters of the Communist army!

At home, my mother had prepared for the worst. At the time, she and her fifteen-month daughter were living in a little hut on the bank of the Yangtze River. They were in hiding from the police, because only a month before a Communist colleague was arrested after being betrayed by another under his supervision who had been arrested earlier. For safety's sake, my mother searched her little hut carefully and burned all the progressive books that might attract a policeman's notice. The Party organization even arranged other temporary housing, and moved my mother and sister to an apartment with other underground Communists.

A month later, on April 23, 1949, the People's Liberation Army launched the final attack, crossed the Yangtze River, and took over the capital city, Nanjing. On the following morning, my father and his "pseudo wife" entered the city with the marching army. Before my father began his journey north, both he and my mother knew that they might never see each other if he were stopped by Chiang's troops and they discovered the real purpose of his journey. Now when my mother, with her fifteen-month daughter, saw my father again in his new army uniform, tears poured down her cheeks.

CHAPTER 3

THE REBELS DIDN'T GET
WHAT THEY WANTED

Despite his incredible record of achievements and contributions to the Communist Revolution, by 1968 my father had become an alleged enemy of the Revolution. He was thought to have caused tremendous damage to the revolutionary cause in the past, although there was no evidence against him. His only "fault" was being an administrator, and now Mao claimed administrators were enemies of the people.

One afternoon in the spring of 1968, while reading in my bedroom after school, I heard some loud noises downstairs. I realized that a mob was attacking someone on the street. Now mobs occurred in our residential compound so often that I usually didn't bother to look. Suddenly, I heard my father's name. I felt a chill down my spine, because I knew that it was my father who was being attacked.

I rushed on to our balcony, cautiously approached the edge, and peeked out. As a ten-year-old, I was afraid to expose myself to the mob for fear they could hurt me. Yet I was anxious to see what was happening to my father. His hands were tied behind his back and he walked ahead of the crowd. He had a two-foot-high pointed paper hat on his head and a board on his chest hanging down from his neck. Words on both the hat and the board said, "Down with him, a betrayer, spy, and capitalist fellow traveler," typical charges of the time. The mob was shouting slogans, and alternately hitting a drum and a gong. I saw them pass by our house and head back to the office compound of the municipal government. Because I kept my eyes on my father, I didn't even see who was in the mob. Once they were out of view, I started to cry. I did not understand the feelings I had, but they certainly were painful and I was miserable.

That evening my father came home a little late at dinner time. He looked exhausted and sat down on a chair as soon as he came in. Although it was still very cold in early spring, I could see sweat on his forehead. My mother rushed to the bathroom and came back with a warm, wet wash cloth, and put it in Father's hand. My grandma came over slowly on her bound feet and handed him a pack of cigarettes and a match box. Grandpa stood by, making some noises of coughing to announce his presence. My sister started weeping.

The dinner table had been set, and Father glanced at the table and tried to cheer us up a little bit by giving us a smile and saying: "Let's have dinner now." After he sat down Aunt handed him a cup of tea, saying: "You must be very thirsty now." Father took the cup from her hand gratefully and said: "Thank you very much." The house was unusually quiet. No one seemed to have an appetite, and the dishes on the table were almost untouched. Father finally broke the silence by saying that this was a part of the Cultural Revolution and that we should all try to understand it. He forgave the mob: in his mind these people were only doing what they were told to do. He tried to convince my mother to view this new experience in their political career as a test of strength.

Almost all the government officials at the time were puzzled and trying to understand the situation. They seemed to be trapped by the political upheaval launched by the Party and its chairman, a leader they had trusted and loved so much. There must have been millions of questions in their minds.

Early one morning three or four months later, there was a knock on our door and a dozen people came in. I recognized them as my father's colleagues at the Department of Culture, Education, Health Care, and Sports. I used to greet them as "uncles and aunts." This was considered good manners in China, and my parents had trained me to do so when I was a little boy. Yet that morning my greetings seemed to make them uneasy and embarrassed. Some of them gave me an awkward smile, and some tried to look away, as if they did not see or hear me at all.

The Rebels Didn't Get What They Wanted { 65 }

A man with a thin, gaunt face stood in the center of our living room and announced that the rebel organization at the Department of Culture, Education, Health Care, and Sports had come to search our house. He said this was a necessary revolutionary action, because my father had failed to confess to the people all the crimes he had committed during his past evil life. So, they came to search for evidence that he was lying.

It was surprising to learn that they were all revolutionary rebels, especially those who had been so friendly. When the rebel organization was established, only the director and deputy directors of the department were excluded. All the others, from chauffeurs and secretaries to the managers of different sectors, had joined in the organization. Now they were all "revolutionaries." Almost all of my father's colleagues who used to come and work with him on Sundays turned on us; we had become their "enemies." This was certainly confusing and hard to understand for a ten-year-old child.

Picking up my school-bag, I had headed for the door to go to school as usual, but was soon stopped by one of the "aunts." She told me that I would not have class that morning and that my teacher had already been notified. While talking to me she removed my school-bag from my shoulder and began to search it inside and out. I resented what she was doing, because I hated to have other people touch my things. Yet I did not dare say a word, but carefully watched her remove my books and other things from the bag and place them on our dining-room table.

The others began to search each room, and the search was incredibly thorough. There was a wardrobe in my parents' bedroom, and the mirror on its door was attached by four screws at the corners. The rebels suspected that something might be hidden behind it so they removed all the screws to make sure that nothing was there. They completed their search by lunchtime and apparently found nothing they really wanted. Yet, before leaving, they collected various things and put them into a huge bag. They made a list of every item, and said they would "borrow" these from us. They asked my parents to sign the list.

The rebels came to look for evidence that my father had some sort of connection with the "Bourgeois Headquarters" inside the Communist Party and therefore had been inappropriately promoted. To their disappointment, what they found only proved that my father had not been properly promoted since the Communist Party took power in China in 1949. For example, the rebels found a certificate of my father's appointment signed by Premier Zhou. After the Communist takeover, Nanjing was under the direct leadership of the central Communist government in Beijing. It was given such priority because it had been the capital of Chiang Kai-shek's government. Administratively, it was treated like a province rather than a city; all the officials in the municipal government were appointed by the premier. My father was appointed deputy chief-of-staff of Nanjing, and this was the highest position to which he had ever been appointed.

In addition to the certificate, the rebels also took away some old photos. The most cherished ones were those taken of my father and Premier Zhou in 1960, when the latter was inspecting the technical school that my father had directed for six years. Despite being demoted from a higher position in the government hierarchy, my father had worked hard and turned the school into a model for training high-tech professionals, and its influence was nationwide. The rebels came to search for evidence against my father, yet only found evidence of his achievements.

The rebels also suspected that my parents had betrayed their comrades when they were underground Communists living under Chiang Kai-shek's government or during the Japanese occupation. Again, what they found indicated just the opposite. For example, they found a photo of a prominent Red Army general, Fang Zhiming, who had been captured and then executed by Chiang Kai-shek during the "Long March" in the 1930s. The picture was taken immediately before the execution. On each side stood a comrade. The three of them had on shabby overcoats, worn out by torture, and they had handcuffs and heavy shackles on their hands and feet. They looked both calm and firm, and seemed ready to die for the ideology they believed in. My family acquired the picture in an unusual way. During the civil war between Chiang Kai-shek's Nationalist Party and the Communist Party in the late 1940s, my father's youngest brother was a commander in a Communist army. The photo was among the things captured after they had occupied a Nationalist army's headquarters. More than a decade earlier, it was this unit that had defeated General Fang Zhiming's army, captured him alive, and later executed him. My uncle was touched by the photo and he sent a copy to my father. If my parents ever betrayed their underground comrades, how could they possibly possess and cherish such a photo?

During the search, the only real surprise or discovery, for both the rebels and my family, was that Aunt, our house maid and baby-sitter, had more money in her bank account than either my parents or my grandparents. That made the rebels very disappointed, too. They had hoped to find evidence of my parents' wealth. Then they could accuse my parents of betraying the proletarian revolutionary cause and becoming a bourgeois within the Communist Party. Now, although they took a huge traveling bag of "borrowed" materials, none of the rebels left our house victorious. Of course, we all knew that wasn't the end. There were surely more troubles ahead for our family.

A FAMILY TORN APART

In September 1968, a few weeks after our house had been searched, my father was detained at work. Someone was sent to our house to fetch his personal belongings. When I came home after school I was told that father would not be coming home that evening and probably would not return home for quite a long time. I was very disappointed, although not totally surprised. By that time many officials living in the municipal residential compound had been detained. I knew this would happen to my family sooner or later.

Several days passed, and I missed my father very much. One afternoon Aunt noticed I was feeling blue. She took me to Father's workplace, and asked the guards to let me see him. We were told that we needed to get a permit from the executive committee of the rebel organization. None of the members was present at the time, but one of them lived not far away. We went to his home and found him.

He was a man in his late thirties and had just started to grow fat. After Aunt told him why we came to see him, he said: "He is not your son. Why did you bother?" "The kid is innocent," Aunt said. "I don't care what his father did. The boy is missing his dad. Look at his eyes. Don't you have a child, and can't you tell?" The man looked a little embarrassed. He awkwardly mumbled: "I'm not married yet. Aren't you single, too?" This time it was Aunt's face that turned red. Without further conversation, the man accompanied us to see my father.

When I entered his room it was dusk and I saw him in the twilight. My father was surprised to see me. Yet he did nothing but smile at me and offer me a glass of water, because the traditional culture forbade emotional action and intimate behavior in public. We were not supposed to embrace or kiss each other in such a situation. However, from his slightly shaking hands I could tell his feelings. I wasn't allowed to stay long. A few days later, my mother was detained at work also. This was certainly too much for me, a ten-year-old boy. Yet it was only the beginning of a long nightmare.

Early in October, an enormous change came about. Chairman Mao gave the instruction that all the former government officials, including almost all of the employees working for various levels of governments, should work in the countryside like peasants and reform themselves through farm labor. The rationale was that these people had worked for many years in offices and they must have lost touch with reality. They needed to return to field work to keep their minds suitably proletarian. The vast countryside was a good school for them all.

Hundreds of labor camps called "officials' schools" were built throughout the nation over night. Almost all the employees in the municipal government in Nanjing were sent to a labor camp called "October 4th Officials' School," because Chairman Mao's comment was made on that date. Those who had earlier formed rebel organizations were not spared, and they were sent to the labor camp as well. My father was moved to that labor camp immediately. My mother, with her theater group, was first sent to another place to do farm work, and months later joined Father in his camp. A year later, the camp was relocated to the other side of the city, and Father and Mother were separated in two locations miles away from each other.

The camp was quite far away from the city and it was not easy to get to. No one could return home daily. In fact, people in the camp were only allowed to return to the city the second and fourth weekend of each month. Yet neither of my parents was allowed to come home at all. They were detained there, always guarded.

In December 1968, my sister left home too. After stirring up a whole generation of youth at the beginning of the Cultural Revolution, Chairman Mao now redirected the millions of Red Guards into the vast Chinese countryside and let the huge land absorb their unused energy. To glorify this movement, it was described as an exciting, wonderful learning experience for young people and they fell over each other to participate. One incentive Mao gave was that they had a better opportunity in the countryside. With their education, he said, they were needed more in the countryside than in the cities.

Most of my sister's schoolmates settled in a county in the northern part of our province. However, if someone could find another place in the countryside where she or he had some relatives, she or he could settle there. This was thought to make the settlement smoother.

My sister, my grandparents, and Aunt had a serious discussion. At first, my sister seemed to prefer to go with her friends and classmates. My grandparents and Aunt favored her joining some relatives. An extended family member always seemed to be more reliable than her teenage friends and classmates. Besides, all the youths were in the same situation, and were more likely to ask for help than to give it. Finally, they decided that my sister should join some relatives in the country-side. At first they thought of the home village of my father's parents, but we had no contact with anyone there. Then it occurred to them that there was someone related to us living in Anhui Province.

It was "Elder Sister Xiuzhen," whose grandmother was my mother's aunt. Xiuzhen's mother-in-law was living with her two daughters in the southern part of Anhui where my father's grandfather was born. Since we had frequent contact with Xiuzhen's family, her mother-in-law's house seemed an ideal place for my sister to settle. My sister went to see my mother at her camp and told her about the alternatives. My mother also felt that it was a good idea for my sister to live with Xiuzhen's mother-in-law. Although my mother was detained at the time, her maternal concern made her brave enough to confront the rebels, asking for a day's leave to go home and handle the issue. Because she had been a beloved leader, many rebels were sympathetic and they issued a special permit. Mother came home and met with Xiuzhen and her husband. They both agreed to let my sister live with their mother and promised that she would be well taken care of. Although Xiuzhen was only a second cousin and none of us had ever seen her mother-in-law, my mother felt much better now that her daughter was going to live with someone she felt she could trust.

The government provided about 200 yuan ($100) relocation fee for each young person going to the countryside. The amount was more than five times a worker's average monthly wage, and it sounded like a lot of money. Half of the money, however, went to the village where the person was going to settle to cover the initial settlement cost. The re-maining part was given to the youth in cash, but it was not even enough for initial preparation for the moving. For a couple of days, my sister and Aunt went shopping all over the city, comparing the prices for each item they wanted in every store. They spent all of my sister's relocation fee before they were even halfway through the shopping list. That was when I began to understand why people worried about money.

When the young people were leaving for the countryside, there was usually a big farewell meeting. Huge crowds gathered at the railway or long-distance bus stations to see the young people off. Some band of drums and gongs played loud music. All the youths wore red paper flowers, which were a symbol of congratulations for having done some-thing glorious. However, my sister had to leave the city alone and quietly, because she did not join her classmates and, instead, went to Anhui on her own. When the day of departure came, only Aunt and I saw her off at the railway station. We hired a cycle rickshaw. The cycle rickshaw was so small, there was no room for my grandparents. They were too old for such an uncomfortable journey, anyway. Neither of my parents could come because they were detained at their labor camps.

As soon as we got on the cycle rickshaw Aunt began to cry. My sister tried to cheer her up, but failed. When we arrived at the station and Aunt reached into her pocket for the money to pay the cycle rickshaw driver, she cried even harder. For a moment, the driver didn't seem sure what to do. Then he decided to help us carry the luggage into the station, which was not really his job.

The station looked shabby and dirty. The trains leaving from this station went to small inland cities and towns. There was another station that connected the city to other major cities in China. The passengers here were mostly peasants or peddlers. This image only convinced us that my sister was going to some place that was backward and full of hardship. After giving her a last hug and having said our final words of farewell, we watched her through the windows on the train, until it moved away. Although we had said "See you" to each other many times, we really did not know when we would be able to see each other again.

On the way home I felt a loneliness I had never experienced before. I realized that from then on I was going to live alone with my grandparents and Aunt. Although they were very close to me and loved me, they were not my immediate family. My family had been broken to pieces. Each of my parents was detained at a different place; my sister was traveling hundreds of miles away to farm in a strange land. To me, only ten years old, our apartment suddenly looked bleak and lonely. What I didn't know then was that there were millions of other families in China who were being torn apart, and millions of lonely kids like me.

VISITING MY PARENTS
IN THEIR LABOR CAMPS

While my parents were detained they no longer received government salaries. Now, each month we received only a small stipend. Each of us, that is, my parents, my grandparents, Aunt, and me, received a survival allowance of fifteen yuan a month. Another eighteen yuan was given to Aunt as her salary. My sister had already relocated to southern Anhui and was working as a peasant, so she was not eligible for any stipend.

The monthly stipend of fifteen yuan each gave us very little to live on. It was about half of the average salary of a worker. During those years when my grandparents, Aunt, and I lived together, we could only afford to buy a quarter pound of meat for the whole household every other day. I became one of the poorest of my classmates. In primary school, if your family income per capita was fifteen yuan a month or less, you could apply for a tuition waiver. I remember how embarrassed I was when, for the first time in my life, I had to tell my teacher that I could not afford to pay my tuition.

My parents were detained in different places, so Aunt and I visited each on alternate Sundays. We arose early in the morning, usually around five o'clock, because it was a several hour journey each way. My father's camp was on the northern bank of the Yangtze River. At that time the long bridge over the river was still under construction, so we crossed by ferry. Although it was sad to visit a detained parent, each journey actually felt like an adventure, especially as we crossed the river on the boat, for neither Aunt nor I could swim.

Each time we arrived at the labor camp, we went through the same procedure. Aunt always brought something with her, such as an old shirt or sweater for one of my parents. She would give it to the rebel who was on duty that day as a "watcher." It would be carefully examined to make sure nothing was hidden in it, and after that given to my parent. Then Aunt would request that I be allowed to see my parent. Usually I was granted this privilege.

Fifty to a hundred people lived together in a huge barn, and two people slept on a single bunkbed. The floor was cemented and looked quite damp. Birds flew through the beams and often made quite a lot of noise. When I sat down with my parent, I was required to encourage him or her to confess past crimes. I was supposed to quote from Chairman Mao, saying that those who made confessions would be punished less severely or not at all, while severe and certain punishment awaited those who did not confess. I always felt awkward playing that role, because I was not used to speaking to my parents in such a condescending manner. Besides, I hated to add any pressure to their already heavily burdened hearts.

I was terrified by the story of my sister's girlfriend. Her father was a general and the Commander-in-Chief of the Naval Academy at Nanjing. His heart was affected earlier in the Cultural Revolution when he was attacked. When his wife and children pressed him to confess to crimes he had not committed, he felt that even his family could not understand him and he became deeply depressed and committed suicide. I certainly did not want such a tragedy to happen to my family.

To balance the quotations from Chairman Mao and the pressure on my parents to make confessions, I always liked to quote another sentence by Chairman Mao: "Believe in the people and believe in the Party. Every problem will be solved eventually." The connotation of this quotation was pretty explicit. I was encouraging my parents to believe that eventually they would be absolved of all unjustified charges and history would prove their innocence.

After these rituals were finished, we had a normal conversation. The "watcher" would usually find something to read, keeping an eye on us and listening to our conversation at the same time. My role as a two-faced young man sometimes excited me. I compared my role of visiting the camps with that of my parents when they were working as underground Communists. In my fantasy I often imagined I might be arrested because of my secret communication with my parents.

During these visits I began to develop an ability to make instant judgments about people. I learned to distinguish lukewarm friendliness from hidden hostility and to gauge a person's sincerity. I could tell which "watchers" were friendly, so I could feel more comfortable talking freely in their presence. This experience made me more inquiring and analytical, and it certainly made me grow up quickly.

I enjoyed those visits to the camp. In addition to seeing my parents, I looked forward to them because the camp cafeterias were probably subsidized, so the food was better than what we ate at home. In addition, my parents always bought the best dishes when I visited. They had the same stipend we did every month. That meant they must have been very frugal during the week to let me enjoy a good meal.

I was very thin and pale at the time. Each time my parents saw me they would ask Aunt to try her best to find me some more nutritious food. While watching me enjoy my lunch at their camp, each would smile at Aunt and express their hearty thanks to her for staying with the family at such a hard time and plead with her to take good care of me. Each time Aunt would answer, with tears in her eyes, "Don't worry. I will take care of him as if he were my own son."

MY SISTER IN THE COUNTRYSIDE

My sister was now farming in the south of Anhui Province. My father's family originated from that area of Anhui. It was on the border with another province called Jiangxi, where the Communists had established their first military guerrilla base in the late 1920s. The area was mountainous, and that had helped the Communists in their guerrilla war against Chiang Kai-shek's government. It was extremely inconvenient to travel there. From Nanjing, my sister went by train and bus, and then had to walk seven miles to the tiny village where my cousin Xiuzhen's mother-in-law lived.

Language posed a major difficulty for my sister. She lived with Xiuzhen's mother-in-law and her two daughters. She could speak Mandarin with them, but few of the other villagers over twenty years old understood Mandarin, which was the standard or official Chinese. Only teenagers who went to school after the Communist takeover learned it, because the new government made it compulsory to speak Mandarin in school. In fact, that was an important improvement made under Communism. It had a strong impact on nationalism, and helped communications among people throughout the country.

Spoken Chinese is so varied in accent and dialect that a person from one location often finds it difficult to understand someone from another. I had similar experiences later in my life and know what a hardship it must have been for my sister. The first time I had a language problem was after my marriage. I found I was totally unable to communicate with my wife's family. She comes from a small village in our province, about 200 miles away, but I could not understand her family, especially her mother. My wife had to interpret for us. My father-in-law could understand me a little when I spoke Mandarin without a Nanjing accent, but he could barely speak Mandarin himself, so the communication was one sided. Even my wife's brother and his wife could not speak much Mandarin, although they had learned it in school.

When my sister was in Anhui, few people were able to interpret for her. She felt fortunate that Xiuzhen's mother-in-law spoke fairly good Mandarin. In fact, she spoke Mandarin even better than her two daughters. That helps explain why she became a local leader. She joined the Communist Party after the Communist takeover. There were very few people in the village at the time who could serve as a link between the isolated villages and the outside world. When my sister was there Xiuzhen's mother-in-law was no longer serving as a village leader, but her ability to speak Mandarin had helped her progress socially.

My sister was quick to pick up the local dialect. Within a year, when she came back to visit us during the Chinese New Year holiday season, she could have a conversation with Xiuzhen's husband in the local dialect. I sat there listening to them talk for about half an hour and could not understand one single word.

Language was certainly not the only difficulty my sister encountered. The economic hardship seemed devastating. Although the area was not the poorest in the nation, the living standard in that isolated village was much lower than I could imagine. My sister farmed with local peasants and barely survived. Except for the winter months she worked ten to twelve hours a day. During the sowing and harvesting seasons she had to work at least sixteen hours a day! Like all the peasants, she worked under a system called the "people's commune." At the beginning of each year a meeting was held in the village to evaluate all the workers and assign a rate for their strength. Most men, for example, were given a rate of nine or ten points and women only seven or eight. Those who were rated at ten points earned one full credit for each day's work. A woman rated seven only earned seven-tenths of a credit each day. The earning difference was based on physical strengths. However, women were often assigned to do the same work as men. Almost all the housework was also done by the women. During the sowing or harvest seasons, a wife often had only two hours of sleep each night. In addition to sixteen hours of farm work, she had to cook and prepare meals in the early morning and wash the clothes after midnight.

Even though my sister's life wasn't as bad as that of a country wife, some of her tasks sounded extremely difficult. For example, she transplanted the cultivated rice sprouts to a farm field. That required standing in a water-covered field, burying her feet in the mud, bending over, carrying the sprouts in one hand and planting a few of them into the mud with the other. After sixteen hours a day of such harsh labor, her hands became swollen lumps, and she could hardly straighten her back. The skin on her feet turned white and peeled off, and her legs became numb because she stood in water so long. Even the native-born peasants could barely cope with the hardship. It was incredible that my sister endured and survived.

Despite her heavy workload, each day she only earned a Chinese dime (approximately five cents). Under this system, her annual income was only thirty-seven Chinese yuan (twenty dollars), just enough for her share of the rationed grains and hay for cooking. Under those circumstances even eggs became a luxury. One egg cost about a day's work!

My sister gave Xiuzhen's mother-in-law and her two daughters almost all the money she earned. But when dinner was served her bowl was often a little less full than the other two girls'. Sometimes Xiuzhen's mother-in-law would cook an egg for each of her daughters but not for my sister. She would bury the egg in the rice in her daughter's rice bowl so that my sister would not see it. She might even ask her daughter to go outside of the house to eat so that my sister would not notice the special treatment. This made my sister feel just like Cinderella.

Although she didn't feel a true member of Xiuzhen's family, she found acceptance in some other places. When she had her lunch with other peasants in the field they offered to share their steamed bread and other food. They knew her situation at home and felt sympathetic. It is typical for a Chinese peasant, who is perhaps less well off than anyone else in the world, to have sympathy for others and offer help. The peasants were almost illiterate, but they were generous and kind. My sister has never forgotten those lovely people.

Another place she found comfort during her years in the village was a big public barn where people gathered in winter. For a couple of months, the weather was too cold for field work. The villagers had to stay home even though they preferred to have some work and income. Bored in their houses, they would gather at the public barn. Before my sister and other youngsters emigrated there, the barn was only a place for talk. Now the young people brought music as well. They sang songs, played musical instruments, and organized performances. This sort of activity was encouraged by the authorities in Beijing, especially Mao's wife. She loved to play the role of a patronizer of arts, although she was very picky in terms of style. She insisted that only art that met her taste was "revolutionary," and she banned everything else. As a result, only a handful of Beijing operas and a dozen songs were performed. She advocated that these songs be sung and the operas be produced throughout the country. Young people, like my sister, took this opportunity to have some fun in their otherwise hard and boring lives. As an unexpected result, their presence brought new life to the little mountain village.

The former Red Guards mobilized by Chairman Mao to immigrate to the countryside also brought a more civilized life. At the time, most of the country areas were very backward. Many did not even have electricity, and habits and customs were far from modern. For example, in many areas local residents did not use public restrooms. When men and women were on the street and felt the call of nature, they just urinated in public. People from the city were often shocked when they saw this. Under their influence, villagers soon abandoned this behavior.

Health care was another big issue. In many counties of 100,000 residents, there was only one hospital. Without modern transportation, a sick person often died on the way to the hospital. City youth knew of this situation before they left home, and they often brought nonprescription medicine with them to the countryside. In addition, many of them tried to acquire some rudimentary medical knowledge, especially acupuncture.

My sister bought a self-teaching acupuncture book and several needles. She practiced with her needles on her own body. She also persuaded me to let her experiment on me. She first tried to identify those points on my body related to some common symptoms, such as sleeplessness, stomachache, or loss of appetite, according to the body maps in her book. Then she would try to put her needles into my body at those points. She asked me whether I felt a special swelling feeling in the area where she put in her needles. This was supposed to happen if she put her needles in successfully. Before she left for Anhui, she learned some basic acupuncture. If I had a cold or a stomachache, she would put a needle into my hand where my thumb and the first finger join together. It would relieve my pain immediately. Once she arrived in the countryside, she began to use her knowledge. During the two years there, she helped cure more than one hundred people, both in her village and in the surrounding areas. It pleased her that, in this way, she was able somewhat to return the hospitality she had received from the uneducated, kind local residents.

LIFE FOR "ART'S" SAKE

My life at home was easy compared with the hardships my sister had in the countryside. Many of us learned to play Chinese musical instruments. Because of Mao's wife's advocacy, almost every school in the city formed a music group whose official mission was to "spread Chairman Mao's thoughts." In reality, it was no more than extracurricular musical training. I became involved in these activities during my last few years at primary school.

Although my family was torn apart, I, as an eleven-year-old boy, seemed to pay more attention to peer pressure than to my family tragedy. One day, one of my classmates' parents bought him a Chinese violin—a musical instrument with two strings. We call it *er hu* or *hu qin* in Chinese. *Qin* means a musical instrument, and *hu* refers to an ancient tribe who were ethnically different from the majority of the Chinese, the "Hans." Hundreds of years ago this musical instrument was adopted into the Chinese culture and was called *hu qin*. It was also called *er hu* because of its two strings ("two" is pronounced as "er" in Chinese). The boy invited us to his house to see him play it. In fact, we only saw him play *with* it. However, we were all fascinated by the instrument. Within a few weeks, five others in my class convinced their parents to buy the instruments for them.

I also asked Aunt to buy me one, but was told it was too expensive. It cost five yuan, while my monthly stipend was only fifteen yuan. Aunt suggested that if I cut spending on something else, she might be able to buy me one. She also had an idea as to what to cut. Ice cream was a luxury, even during the summer. To cool off in the humid heat, people usually bought cold drinks or juice. The least expensive cold product was an ice bar, which cost about four pennies. Aunt and I had agreed that during the summer I could spend four pennies a day to buy an ice bar. If I wanted something fancier one day, I couldn't have anything at all the next day or two. In this way, I learned to budget by the time I was eleven. Aunt suggested that if I didn't buy any cold treats for a whole summer, she might be able to find enough money to buy me the musical instrument I wanted. So I agreed and eventually got my *hu qin* for four and a half yuan.

With my *hu qin* I joined the music group at school. Every afternoon after regular classes we convened in the music classroom. The music teacher gave us a little extra musical training using an upright piano. Just like our fine arts teacher, the music teacher used this opportunity to give us more education. As teachers, their first wish was to let their students learn more no matter what political winds blew. It was these ordinary people who saved us from wasting our time and growing up to become ignorant adults. Our generation lost a great deal during the political frenzy of the Cultural Revolution, but because of these devoted teachers, we learned much of what we needed.

The piano in our school was very old and the music teacher often needed to tune it. If we ran in the room, the quivering floor would mean the piano had to be tuned again. The music teacher was often annoyed by this. After spending almost every late afternoon with her for a month, I began to develop a very sensitive ear for tuning. Whenever a string instrument was ever so slightly out of tune, I could detect it. So each time before we gave a performance, I would see to it that we all had our instruments accurately tuned. Probably because of that, I was soon promoted to be the leader of the instrumental division of our music group. This made me quite happy and excited. It seemed that, despite my disgraced family name, I was doing well at school. For a child of my age, the influence of school was much greater than that of the family. The dominant value system came from school. As long as I was doing well at school, life didn't seem so miserable.

The rest of the music group were singers and dancers. One was a girl two grades younger than I. She had a pretty, smiling face, and I was very fond of her. Although she was not in the instrumental division, she showed a great interest in the instruments. During the break she liked to pick up a *hu qin* and try to play it. Most often she would only manage to loosen the strings and then she would come to me for help tuning it. Of course, it was a great pleasure to do this for her. Other than that, we rarely spoke. Before I graduated from primary school, she was recruited by a professional dance group in the Chinese Army and left school to join it. I didn't know how strong my feelings for her were until an unexpected incident occurred.

Our school was closed during the summer. For security reasons, each day some of the students were assigned to patrol the campus. One day while I was on patrol I found the student ID card of that pretty little girl with a photo on the card. I could feel my heart beating faster as I held her card in my hand and stared at her photo. I felt I found a treasure and wanted to keep it, although both at school and at home we were told to return things that didn't belong to us. A moment later I became discouraged because I realized that, even if I decided not to return the card, I did not have a private place to keep it. In China, we did not have school lockers, and at home, we did not have any privacy, either. It would be dishonorable for a boy to be found keeping a girl's photo. China was an extremely puritanical society at the time, similar to Victorian England. Any affair between a man and a woman who were not married would become a great scandal. Even a rumor could ruin one's life forever. I might be treated as a criminal both at school and in public, and even at home. So, after much thought, I decided to leave the photo card where it was. After staring at it for a long time and giving it a rushed kiss, I put it back. I was hoping to be able to find it again, but when I revisited the classroom a week later, to my surprise, the room was empty. All the desks and stools had been moved elsewhere. My heart sank, and I knew I had lost that photo forever.

I enjoyed being a part of the music group for another reason. One of the few things we were allowed to perform was a play in the form of Beijing Opera. It was entitled *The Story of a Red Lantern*. By then, Mao's wife had banned almost everything, from Western classical symphonies to Chinese folk songs, except a few plays in Beijing Opera that she herself had helped to revise. *The Story of a Red Lantern* was one of these. It is the story of a railroad worker and his family in the resistance movement against the Japanese occupation of northern China. He was an underground Communist who was betrayed by a former colleague and arrested by the Japanese. They tortured him, but failed to get the secret information they wanted. Eventually, they executed both him and his old mother.

Each time we gave a performance we selected a short piece from this play, since we did not have too much else to choose from. Others might get bored, but I had a personal reason to love this play. In fact, I could almost recite the entire script, because I could easily associate the hero in the play with my father. Just like that railroad worker, my father was once a train conductor in the northern China as a cover for his real identity as a Communist. Like the hero in the play, my father was part of the organized resistance movement, endangering his own life for the country he loved so much. To me, my father was always a hero. Yet he was wrongly charged now. The society did not see him as a hero, as I did. This conflict could make a child very confused. Now, fortunately, the play came to my rescue. Such a well-known image of a heroic underground Communist helped strengthen my faith in my father and reconcile the clash between personal belief and public conviction. As the result of art, life became less confusing and miserable.

NANNY GETS A NEW JOB

I was not the only person who had to solve the problem of clashing values. Aunt had the same dilemma. As my nanny and my parents' housekeeper, she needed to believe in my parents and to justify her continuing friendly attitude toward our family when my parents were labeled as "public enemies." Several times the rebels tried to persuade her to provide evidence against my parents. She either gave them none or gave them a few trivial pieces. It was not difficult for her to defend her decision to stay with us, because it was her job and no one could offer her a better one. However, she had to be careful, because she was not supposed to have a close emotional tie with us. In other words, many would criticize her as less "revolutionary" if she remained friendly toward us. She was not a well-educated person, but she knew what she was doing. She didn't change her attitude toward us very much at home, but, outside, she became a new person, a local activist. Her strategy was to get involved in many "revolutionary" activities, so that she would be viewed as very "revolutionary" and therefore she could "afford" to be a little less "revolutionary" at home, associating with an infamous family. She was seeking a balance. She became an activist in the "Neighborhood Committee" in our residential compound. In Chinese cities, each neighborhood has a neighborhood committee. Only the head of such a committee was on the government payroll. The rest of the members and the people involved in its activities were volunteers. Each neighborhood committee needed a couple of full-time volunteers and many more part-time ones. Most volunteers were housewives or retirees, and they were usually illiterate. People with some level of education were desperately needed. Aunt had a fourth-grade education, and according to what was believed to be orthodox Marxism, her class status as a housemaid made her a member of the most "revolutionary" class in the neighborhood. In addition, she now had more time to herself because my parents were not at home. So she became more and more involved in the activities organized by the neighborhood committee.

The neighborhood committee wasn't a government agency, but it often functioned as one and had many powers. It had inherited a tradition of thousands of years of governing experience in China. Each ruler, from a feudal emperor to a modern political party, needs some kind of grassroots organization to help stabilize the reign. Under the Communist rule before the Cultural Revolution in 1966, the responsibility of such a committee was to keep the neighborhood clean, quiet, and safe. To make it clean, the committee needed to raise funds to hire regular cleaners and to organize voluntary thorough seasonal clean-ups. To keep the place peaceful and quiet, the committee had to help reconcile family quarrels and fights. For security, the committee cooperated closely with the local police office. It helped patrol the streets, reported on suspicious strangers, and tried to identify wanted criminals.

At the expense of individual privacy, these grassroots committees helped build an incredibly effective anti-crime system. My cousin, "Elder Sister Xiuzhen," had a wonderful experience with the effectiveness of the system. After she graduated from high school she began to work as a bank teller in the early 1960s. Her office was right beneath her apartment. She had a brand new bicycle, which was considered quite a luxury, especially when it was not needed as transportation to go to work. Because her apartment was very small, she locked her bicycle outside her unit. One day while she was working at her bank desk she received a phone call from the local police station. The policeman asked: "What is the registration number of your bike?" She answered and asked: "Why?" The policeman verified the number against his and then said: "Please stop by the police station after work. Your bike is here. It was stolen from your apartment about half an hour ago. With the help of the neighborhood committee, the thief was stopped near your house. Your bike is here, undamaged." Xiuzhen was astonished that the police could find her bike before she even noticed it had been stolen.

Now, the tasks of neighborhood committees changed. The idolization of Chairman Mao spread throughout the whole country, and participating in the movement became a dominant activity for each neighborhood committee. Formal rituals of idolization were developed and adopted everywhere. Every morning, people had to gather and stand in

Nanny Gets a New Job   { 81 }

front of a picture of Chairman Mao, recite some of his quotations, and wish him a long, long life. This ritual was performed in every workplace first thing in the morning. For those who didn't go to work, the neighborhood committees organized the rituals. Part of the ritual was to sing songs praising Mao and the Communist Party and to dance to the music of these songs. In our residential compound, people from the same block gathered to partake in the ritual every morning. Aunt was the organizer for our block. My grandparents were also required to go, although they were over seventy years old. They had little talent for singing or dancing, but they had to join the others at the exercise. The sounds that came out from the group weren't too pleasing to the ear!

In the afternoons, the neighborhood committee often held meetings, and Aunt would always attend. Usually the committee chair would read the newspaper to the audience, who was mostly illiterate. Because Aunt was one of the few who could read, when the chair needed a rest she often asked Aunt to read an article. Aunt would take over the paper and read it aloud. She loved the job, and felt proud of herself. Even I felt proud to have her as my nanny. Most nannies in our residential compound could not read, and many had to come to her for help when they received letters from their families. They needed her to read and write responses for them. Who would have thought that the day would come when she would not be my nanny any more?

I was quite surprised when she told us that she had found a job in a mirror factory recently built by a group of nearby neighborhood committees and that she would stop working for us the next day. Because of her contributions to our neighborhood committee, she was rewarded with this job, which offered some health care and a retirement plan, benefits she did not have as a housemaid. As a single, childless woman she felt life would be much more secure with this change. She also said that she would still live in our house and do as much housekeeping as she could in the evenings and weekends in exchange for free room and board.

By this live-in arrangement she saved even more money. A few months after she started her new job she purchased a wristwatch, which was a great luxury at that time. Only two factories in China produced watches and each watch sold for 120 Chinese dollars, which was about four times an average factory worker's monthly salary. A factory in our city became the third one to make watches. Unlike the high-quality watches made by the other two factories, their product sold for thirty Chinese dollars each. The government regulated the price so that it was affordable for more people. Aunt bought one, and she took meticulous care of it. Every day when she came back from work she would put it in a little paper box she made and store it in a drawer in our bedroom. She warned me again and again to never touch it.

Although she still lived with me, she was no longer my nanny. I could not help feeling somewhat abandoned, because she was the adult I knew best since childhood. With my parents detained at labor camps and my only sister farming hundreds of miles away in an isolated mountain village in another province, I felt very, very lonely and unsupported.

BRAINWASHING AT SCHOOL

I was in fifth grade then, and most of my time was spent in school rather than at home. I cared less about what happened to my family than what we were told about our country at school. We were told that China might go to war with the Soviet Union. A few shots had already been exchanged on tiny Treasure Island on the border between the two countries. We were told that the Soviet Union was a more dangerous enemy than the United States, because it was more likely to invade us. We learned that throughout history Russia had taken vast amounts of land from China. The newspaper called the Soviet authorities the traitors of Lenin and Stalin, and they were believed to be as aggressive as the czars. The only difference was that it would be a modern war this time and nuclear weapons would very likely be used.

We were taught how to deal with nuclear attacks, and after class we dug trenches on the campus. Our textbook directed us to dig trenches at least six feet deep. However, because of the high water table in our city we could hardly dig three feet before hitting water. None of our trenches would be of any use, and we were very disappointed and frustrated. We put a lot of manpower into making them. All classes above the second grade joined in the effort. Most of us were exhausted by the hard labor, but our spirits were high. Many of us got blisters on our delicate hands, which were not used to such work. Yet we were highly motivated, and each of us felt very proud. If someone got five blisters and I got ten, I was delighted because it showed that I had worked harder.

Our morale was strengthened by the training in composition class, where we were forced to think in a way that we were told was correct. We were asked to write about our thoughts during hard labor on the trenches, yet there was only one story we were supposed to tell. Everyone was to write in more or less the following formula. First, we were to describe the hardships we encountered, and then admit that we were just about to give up. At that moment, we were supposed to say, some quotes from Chairman Mao occurred to us and we were inspired anew. We would then recall how heroes had overcome the difficulties they had faced. Our heroes could be a range of people living in different times. They could be Red Army Men during the Long March, or "revolutionary martyrs," that is, those who had been executed by Chiang Kai-shek's government or the Japanese occupiers. Or they could be someone closer to our own times, such as Lei Feng, the young army truck driver who had helped hundreds of strangers who did not even know his name to write him a note of thanks. After reporting all these thoughts, we were to conclude our compositions by saying that we were greatly inspired and found the strength to continue and finish our laborious tasks. Everyone had to follow this basic pattern. The victims not only lost their creativity, but also began to tell lies, both skillfully and naturally.

The problem with this kind of education was not so much in the spirit it tried to teach as in the way it enforced conformity and encouraged hypocrisy. As a matter of fact, many of the quotes from Mao were inspiring. They either emphasized endurance of hardship, or strengthened people with exhortations to some lofty ideals. Altruism and patriotism were often praised. Some of the spirit was quite similar to what John F. Kennedy inspired when he said: "Ask not what your country can do for you but what you can do for your country." In fact, years later—in 1980, when I was a college student majoring in English, I read that this was a well-known quote of Kennedy. I could hardly believe my eyes. How could Kennedy sound just like a Communist leader? Today, I realize that the difference is not so much the idea, but how it is spread in society. In a healthier society, an idea inspires people by its moral power. When administrative authorities were used to enforce an ideal or ideology, it often led to serious problems. One of the great contributions of the American Revolution to modern democracy was to firmly establish the principle of separating religion from state. Unfortunately, the Chinese Communist government had transgressed this principle. They wanted people to believe in communism as if believing in a religion, and they also used the power of the state to coerce people into this belief. Therefore, they had to suffer the consequence.

Despite our high morale and strenuous efforts, the trenches we dug turned out to be of little use, just as unfruitful as many other things people did that the authorities had ordered them to do. However, a new order came: again, it was in the name of preparing for the impending war against Russian invasion. This time, a large population of residents in major cities were ordered to be temporarily evacuated to the countryside.

As fifth-grade students, we were very excited when we were told that we were going to leave the city for a week to walk around the city, a distance of about sixty miles. We had to bring many things with us, ranging from tooth brush and toothpaste to a change of clothes and a quilt. Each one was taught how to pack up everything into a square bundle and carry it on his back just like a soldier in the army. Competitions were held among classes and individuals to see which person and which class could do the best and quickest packing job. Once we learned to tie up the packages and carry them on our backs, the teachers asked us to jump up and down. At first I didn't understand why, but soon I knew. Before long, those who did not do a good job of packing were embarrassed as their bundles loosened and fell apart.

After a couple of days of basic military training, we set out in very high spirits. Our class was labeled Number One, and we walked ahead of the other four classes. Our teacher walked in front, carrying a huge red flag. Following him, someone was supposed to hold a portrait of Chairman Mao and walk ahead of the parade. The teacher assigned this job to me because I was the tallest in the class. I was thrilled to be trusted with such a glorious job, and that night I was inspired to write the first poem in my life in the diary. The first two lines were:

> With a red flag blowing in the wind,
> Our Great Teacher is leading us to win.

Here, "Great Teacher" referred to Chairman Mao. In the idolization movement, Mao was given four great titles: "Great Leader," "Great Teacher," "Great Commander," and "Great Steersman." Big signs with these words could be seen on walls and boards everywhere in China. The effect of such propaganda on people was really strong, and I was also greatly affected. I did not even realize that I had been influenced until the following incident.

During our long walk, we went through many military exercises, including air-raid drills. We were told that if we heard an alarm we should immediately get off the road and hide in the bushes. This was to avoid being spotted by incoming bombers. When I heard the alarm, I rushed off the road like everyone else. I was just about to lie down on the ground when I suddenly realized that I had the portrait of Chairman Mao in my hands. What should I do with it? Without any hesitation I did something for which I was highly praised later. I put the portrait on the ground, knelt down on my knees, bent over, and covered the portrait with my body. All I wanted to do was to protect Mao's portrait from the simulated air-raid. After the raid was over, our teacher noticed my awkward position on the ground and understood my intention immediately. He summoned the whole class and praised me for my wise choice. He said my deed showed that I loved Chairman Mao more than everything, including myself. I don't know whether that was true, but the brainwashing at school did seem to work.

HOME, SWEET HOME

The long walk around the city was my first opportunity to observe the lives of peasants. Their clothes looked very shabby and their houses were all in shaky condition. Their skin was darker because of so much exposure to the sun. The dishes on their dinner tables looked even more awful than what I had at home. As an inexperienced observer, I could not describe the great differences between city life and country life in any more detail. I noticed that after living in the countryside for a few days, everything at home seemed so colorful—the different color paints on the floor, the wall, the windows, and the doors. When I arrived home I felt certain that our house had been repainted while I was away, although it hadn't!

Although our house had not been repainted, there was some good news waiting for me. In 1970, shortly after I came back from the long walk, my mother was released from detention. Then, months later my father was freed as well. The turmoil of the Cultural Revolution seemed to be over, although the charges against my parents were not yet removed. We were only told that it was no longer necessary to detain them. Now, they were treated like most other people in the labor camps and could come home for a weekend every other week.

When my parents were at home, the atmosphere in the house seemed to lighten. Father often said, "Oh, it's so wonderful to be home again!" He would hum a tune that became familiar to me. One day when I asked him what it was, he began to sing it in a language I did not know. It was the song called "Home, Sweet Home," and he seemed to remember the first line only. He explained that he was singing it in English and encouraged me to try to imitate him. Then he explained the meaning of the words "Home, Sweet Home" to me in Chinese.

From my early childhood my father enjoyed teaching me. He taught me to read before I went to school. With a world map, he taught me the names of countries, and explained which were socialist and which were capitalist. He also explained that other people spoke different languages. He could speak English, read a little Russian and Japanese, and now he wanted me to learn English, because, he said, so many peoples in the world spoke that language.

It sounded interesting to me, and we started immediately, with the alphabet. We sat down at a desk in my parents' bedroom. My father searched the drawer and found a blank notebook that had a school logo on the front cover. My mother had bought it for her classes at college fifteen years ago but had never used it. Now it became mine for learning English. My father wrote down the twenty-six English letters, in both capital and small letters. He went over each letter repeatedly until I could follow and read them. He then asked me to learn them by heart in the right order. He said it was very important to remember the order because that would help me later on to use a dictionary. He then began to teach me a few words. Each word began with a different letter, starting from "a." So the first three English words I learned were "America," "banana," and "China." To my father, it was quite natural that I learned the word "America" before "China," although many others might think differently. To an orthodox Chinese, it could be a political crime to learn the word "America" before "China."

When my father read the word "America" aloud, both in English and Chinese, and asked me to repeat it, my mother became uneasy and nervous. She thought it was not wise to mention the word "America," because the United States was officially China's greatest enemy. She was afraid that the neighbors might hear us and report us to the authorities. We might be under suspicion of espionage or something like that. My father wasn't that afraid, however. He still insisted that we could make friends with the American people. Since we were learning English, how could we not learn the word "America," he asked. So, we continued our lessons, and my mother just went out of the room to make sure that the apartment door and windows were properly closed.

My parents always called to each other with a "*ha-luo*" at home, but I did not understand why. Now after I learned the English word "hello," it made sense to me. My parents had apparently adopted the word and pronounced it to sound just like a Chinese word, but without a clear meaning. Since few knew the meaning of the sound, it gave them a special sense of intimacy and love that was not shared by anyone else. Now I found a secret romance between my parents and thought it was very interesting. It *is* interesting, because it shows how a Communist couple kept a taste for romantic love even after the Communist Revolution.

In September 1970, shortly after my father began to teach me a little English at home, my school began an English course. This was my last semester at primary school. I was surprised, because the English course usually started in the first year of junior high school. We were told it was a part of the curriculum reform, and my school was selected as a demonstration model. To my father, an experienced politician, this event indicated a change of the national political wind. The radical frenzy of the Cultural Revolution was over, and the country was going to be back to normal again. Behind doors at home, my parents resumed their political conversations, which they had to remind me again not to mention at all in public, just as they did years before. Now they seemed to have a little more hope for the future, both for the country and for themselves.

They were right, and we soon heard a piece of good news from my sister in Anhui. She was recruited into a college, and became one of the few in the nation who was so lucky. Since the beginning of the Cultural Revolution in 1966, all of the universities and colleges in China stopped recruiting students. Many of these institutes were closed and dismantled. Now, after closing campuses for five years, Mao let a few universities recruit students again in 1970. This happened in three places: Beijing, Shanghai, and Anhui Province. Six universities in Anhui recruited students that year, and quotas were assigned to local administrations. Because of her hard work and extra services, such as giving the peasants acupuncture treatments, my sister earned high respect in her village, and when that village was given the opportunity to send one youth to college, the peasants picked her.

Of course, traces of the earlier radical movement could still be found everywhere. Take our English textbook, for example. We were not starting with ABC. The first English sentence we learned was: "Long live Chairman Mao!" Then we started to learn the letters, and the first letter we learned was "l," because the first sentence started with the word "long."

This change in order also brought my attention to the word order in an English sentence. I soon found some differences between English and Chinese. For example, in English we say "Good morning!" while in Chinese we say "Morning good." Instead of "Long live Chairman Mao!" we say "Chairman Mao long live!" After a little while I felt I had figured out some rules and told everybody in my class that foreigners speak backward instead of forward. They all seemed to be impressed. With my father's help at home, my English soon became the best in the school.

Across the street, only a block away from our school, there was a professional school called Nanjing Foreign Languages School. It was a special type of school oriented toward training future diplomats and foreign language specialists. Only a handful of major cities in China had this type of school. In fact, when my father was in charge of the city's education department, he had held a position somewhat equivalent to chairman of the board of trustees of the school.

The Cultural Revolution interrupted the enrollment of this school for a few years. Now it began recruiting again, and fifth-grade students were wanted as well to make up for the loss in the student body. A recruiting team came to our school, and a few students from each class were selected to be interviewed. Because of my good English, I thought I would certainly be invited for an interview, but I was wrong. The school had a policy that it would only recruit students from "revolutionary" families. As my parents were still suspected of being "public enemies," I would not qualify as a candidate.

At the same time, I learned that one of my childhood playmates, Mingming, had been interviewed and was accepted. This made me even more upset. Mingming's father had been the treasurer of the municipal government and they lived next door to us in a single-family house with a huge courtyard around it. Because his house had much more space I often played there instead of at home. During the Cultural Revolution, both our fathers became targets of the movement, and they were both sent to the same labor camp. Only a year later, however, things had changed quite dramatically. To control the chaos, Mao now wanted Premier Zhou to take measures to reestablish authorities and governments at local levels. One-third of those who were placed in power were former administrators. The other two-thirds came from the army and the rebel organizations. Mingming's father was thus returned to power.

As a result, his family was provided with a car and a chauffeur, and every evening his family received theater tickets and invitations. Mingming's family also had a housemaid, whom Mingming also called "Aunt." She and "my" Aunt were best friends. When Mingming's parents and sisters and brothers had all seen a performance and his father still had more tickets, this woman would invite Aunt and me, and the four of us would go to the theater together. On those occasions I would nostalgically recall the days when my father was still in power. I was twelve years old then, and old enough to realize the advantages of having a father in power.

RICE PUDDING ALMOST LEADS TO SUICIDE

Although both my parents could now come home almost every other weekend, they were still required to do physical labor in their camps. Because my mother had heart disease for more than twelve years, she was very weak and unable to do heavy work. She was often asked to do light jobs, such as sitting in a field, acting as a human scare crow.

It was quite a different story for my father. He was a strong man, and he was always required to do very heavy work. As a matter of fact, whenever a tough job came up, he was the first person to be called upon to do it. He was even nicknamed the Number One Laborer in the camp.

He was not only capable of carrying heavy objects, but he also had many other skills that former officials usually did not have. For example, once they were asked to move half a dozen huge vats containing human excrement from latrines to the farm field to fertilize the crops. As in other places in the countryside, the latrines in the labor camp were in the open. There were huge vats containing human excrement buried in the ground. In front of these vase-shaped vats, a group of former officials fell silent. No one seemed to know how to lift them and move them, yet they knew what the political consequence would be if they could not finish the job.

My father looked around and went away for a moment. He came back with some solid branches to be used as sticks. He cut them to fit the size of the opening of the vats. Because the vats were vase-shaped he could slant one stick into a vat and then level it so that it could not pop out. He then put another stick in the vat to make a cross. At the node of the cross he tied a cord and made a ring so that he could put a shoulder pole through it. Now, two people could carry the vat with the pole on their shoulders.

After my father was released he often told us stories like this about the years of his detainment. On a weekend evening when both my parents were at home, he told my mother and me that he had something to confess. The seriousness on his face was so obvious that I immediately sensed that he was going to say something quite important and unusual. After we all sat down he said that about a year before he once had a very bad idea in his mind.

"What's that?" my mother asked anxiously.

"I was thinking of committing suicide." My father's voice was quavering a little.

A chill ran down my spine. I looked up at him, and then at my mother. Both of their faces were too sombre to reveal anything. My heart began to beat faster as I imagined my life and my family without my father. How could I live without him? Even the thought of it was intolerable. I stared at him with surprised fear.

"Why? What had happened?" My mother asked. My father then told us the following story.

In April 1969, the Ninth National Congress of the Chinese Communist Party was held in Beijing, and Marshal Lin Biao became the acknowledged successor of Chairman Mao as the vice-chairman of the Communist Party, to replace the previously ousted, former president of China, Mr. Liu Shaoqi. Lin's status as the successor was even written into the new charter of the Communist Party.

Since the beginning of the Cultural Revolution in 1966, the legal system in the nation had not functioned, and the constitution had been abandoned. Now, the new charter of the Party became a document that not only guided Party members but, in fact, regulated what every citizen should or should not do. The whole nation was requested to study the new charter. First of all, everybody was expected to hail Lin as the successor to Chairman Mao.

One day there was a study session of the new Party charter at the labor camp. During the discussion my father made a reckless comment. He said that it seemed that the new charter would continue in effect for at least five years, because it was specified in the charter that the next revision would take place in five years. Before the discussion was over, someone had already reported to the authorities of the labor camp that my father was implicitly opposing the content of the new charter: it had just been revised and now he was talking about revising it again!

A public meeting was held immediately, forcing him to admit guilt and confess his real motivation. One person after another criticized him as an incorrigible capitalist road traveler who refused to accept the new leadership of the Communist Party headed by Chairman Mao and Vice-Chairman Lin. What made my father sick was that now everyone was joining together to blame him, including those former government officials who could not move the vats of human excrement without his help. In fact, it was one of them who had reported him to the labor camp authorities in the first place!

The meeting went on for over three hours. At the end, my father was exhausted. When he went to the cafeteria for dinner, he found one of his favorite foods on the menu on the wall: a special sweet rice pudding that was usually only served in the Chinese New Year season. Exhausted and frustrated by what had just happened in the afternoon, he decided to buy two servings, instead of one.

Someone immediately reported this to the authorities, and it was used as evidence that he ignored what had been said about him in the afternoon and stubbornly insisted on his "counterrevolutionary" position. Right after the dinner, another public meeting was held to denounce him further.

Surrounded by the unified voices of so many different people, he felt a loneliness that he had never experienced before. He felt doomed, and his life seemed to be a waste. He felt so powerless that he could not make any positive change. The nation was in big trouble, and so was he.

He had also had severe trouble with hemorrhoids at the time and had to go to a hospital. The authorities in the labor camp had to send someone to escort him to the hospital because he was still in custody. Once aboard the ferry crossing the Yangtze River on his way back to the city for the hospital visit, he suddenly wished to jump into the river.

"It flashed through my mind for only a second. I soon realized that everything would not end there," my father said. "I had my family, and they would have even more trouble after my death. I couldn't do this to them. In addition, there were hundreds of underground Communist Party members who had worked with me before 1949 and they needed my testimony to prove their innocence. If I killed myself, many of them would probably never have a chance to prove their innocence. For their sake, I had to live on."

My mother put her hand on the back of his hand and said: "It was so nice that you thought about us. You always cared about others more than yourself!" Mother's voice was quavering, and I could tell she had much more to say than she could speak. Father finished his story by reassuring us that we should always be optimistic and should never, never follow his example in contemplating suicide! When he finished his story, I felt I had suddenly grown up; within minutes I became an adult, although I had not had my thirteenth birthday!

Young as I was, I had already experienced many things. I had the rare chance to observe elite life; I had also suffered extreme economic hardships. I had been surrounded by many friendly faces; I had also seen them become cold and indifferent. I had learned much that only an adult would know and care about; I had also lost the opportunity to enjoy being a child, that is, to be carefree and have dreams. Now I had even learned what circumstances could lead a strong-willed man like my father into thinking of finishing his own life!

CHAPTER 4

A FORMER MEMBER OF
THE COMMUNIST PARTY

As I grew up, I gradually learned more about my extended family. The most remarkable member was my uncle in Shanghai. My father had two brothers: one lived in Beijing, and one lived in Shanghai. My father was the eldest, and the one in Beijing was the youngest. I called the one in Shanghai Second Uncle, and the one in Beijing Third Uncle. For many years, all I knew about the second uncle was that he was a former member of the Communist Party. At a time when it was a great honor to be a member of the Communist organization, the word "former" raised a question in my mind. Why wasn't he a current member of the party? I learned the little I did know about him as a result of an incident at school.

Every year, each of us was supposed to fill in a form at school listing all of our relatives and their background information, such as their occupations and positions. This was a common practice in China after the Communist takeover. School children as well as employees were required to do so. The information was collected, updated, and kept on file in each person's dossier. The purpose was to give the government more control over all the individuals. There was a column in the form labeled "political attitude," where one was supposed to tell if a relative was a member of the Communist Party. The number of Party members was very limited; the Communist Party had never wanted to extend its membership to the general population. So, in most cases, most of the relatives one listed on the form were not Party members. To fill in that column, one usually put down the word "regular," because Party members were considered "outstanding." Of course, if one had many relatives who were members of the Communist Party, that person's social network appeared "revolutionary" and positive. I could claim many of my relatives to be Party members, including my second uncle's wife. However, I was told to write "a former member of the Party" for him. As a child, I never knew more. Recently I learned a lot more about his life.

Like my father, my uncle made remarkable contributions to the Communist Revolution in 1949. He was two years younger than my father, and under my father's influence, he had joined the Communist Party in the mid-1930s when he was only a teenager. In 1937, they worked together in the refugee camps in Shanghai as a part of the resistance movement against the Japanese invasion. Later, my father was sent to Nanjing to open a new frontier for the Communist movement while my uncle took over the leadership of the Communist organization within the refugee camps in Shanghai. By 1949, my uncle was in charge of an underground Communist network of over a thousand people in the suburban areas of Shanghai and a couple of nearby cities.

At the time, the Communists controlled northern China, but the South was still in the hands of Chiang Kai-shek. Chiang was trying to use the Yangtze River as a natural blockade to resist the Communist takeover. Both Nanjing and Shanghai were on the southern bank of the Yangtze River. They were the last two strong thresholds of Chiang's power. Chiang's troops, equipped with U.S. arms, were holding the last military defense along the river. Morale was very low and the people in the South were awaiting the imminent Communist takeover. The underground Communists in the South had successfully collected some important military information. For example, at the risk of his life, my father had broken the blockade on the river and delivered the maps about the military force in Nanjing and other areas to a Communist headquarters on the northern bank. At the same time, my uncle, who worked in a different branch of the Communist organization in Shanghai, risked his life to deliver a map about the military force in Shanghai to another Communist headquarters in the North. Both brothers had miraculously accomplished their missions and were warmly welcomed at the headquarters as heroes. Few knew, however, that the two most important maps that helped end the Chinese civil war were delivered to the winning side by two brothers.

After the Communist victory in 1949, my uncle assumed many responsibilities within the power hierarchy. He was put in charge of the Communist Youth League organization in Shanghai and nearby areas for a few years. In 1953 when the Communist government started to transform private enterprises into a public and private partnership, he was appointed the deputy director of the bureau in charge of all the light industry section in Shanghai. His task was to transform about 5,000 businesses, which manufactured commodities such as rain boots, locks, glasses, plates, and clocks. It was believed that this structural change would tremendously increase the production rate. The rationale was that the workers would become more productive, because they were working for the public instead of private owners and that the workers would now be the "masters" instead of "slaves."

In a short period there were some positive signs and the economy was strong. Technological progress seemed miraculous, and my uncle contributed to it. Until then, China was very industrially undeveloped; it did not manufacture many common consumer goods. For example, it did not produce wristwatches. In 1954, the director of the economic planning bureau of the central government in Beijing visited Shanghai. He asked the local government in Shanghai to produce the first Chinese watches because Shanghai was China's largest and the most industrialized city. A task force was created, and my uncle was responsible for its leadership.

Although China had never made watches, some rich Chinese had bought imported watches from several countries. When these watches didn't work, they needed to be repaired, and the repairmen were Chinese. My uncle began by organizing the clock and watch repairmen in Shanghai. Each clock-and-watch repair shop in Shanghai was visited; and he gathered about forty people to work on this project. These included repairmen, some technical workers in the clock factory in Shanghai, a young mechanical engineer, and a diamond craftsman. The government sponsored the project, and it took them only three months of experiments to manufacture the first eighteen watches ever made in China!

This story is a good example of how some technical advancements could be achieved in Communist countries more successfully than in a capitalist society. Bigger and more prominent examples were the first satellite by the Soviet Union and China's first atom bomb. For a limited number of selected projects, a powerful government such as a Communist one had the ability to mobilize and organize in a faster and more successful way. However, whether such initiative is capable of achieving a sustained rate of growth for the entire economy is another question. I do not want to argue that a socialist or a communist system could work well in general, but in the early 1950s the socialist bloc did achieve something that showed strength and potential. I think it is worthwhile to reexamine this period of history more carefully.

Perhaps because of this kind of success, some of the leaders became arrogant and despotic. They seemed to think that they could do whatever they wanted. They began to set goals that were not achievable and give orders that produced deletrious or disastrous results. They could not tolerate different opinions, and they abused their power by punishing those who dared to disobey. My uncle soon found himself working for two such leaders in the municipal government in Shanghai. One of them was the mayor, Ke.

From time to time, my uncle found these two leaders impossible to work with. One of them frequently intervened. For example, once he asked why a specific worker in one of the 5,000 businesses under my uncle's supervision had not yet been accepted as a member of the Communist Party. The mayor, on the other hand, always set goals too ambitious to achieve. Despite the fact that each of these 5,000 businesses was required to negotiate its own agreement acceptable to both the state and the private owner, especially with respect to the equity capital to be assumed, the mayor wanted my uncle to provide him with a comprehensive plan with detailed schedules of how and when to accomplish the transformation for all of the 5,000 businesses, and he wanted the plan in five days!

Observing the unreasonable leadership, my uncle felt he could hardly remain silent. He gave very careful thought to this, and decided that the best way was to raise the issue in an official meeting of Party members. This would keep the issue confidential among a few Party members. Up till then, he had been told that a responsible member of the Communist Party should raise any issues or concerns at a Party meeting, but nowhere else. The idea was that one should criticize in a constructive way and keep the criticism inside the Party.

At the end of 1956, there was a Party conference at which representatives in Shanghai were to cast votes to elect the local Party leadership. He felt it was his duty as an honest and loyal member of the Party to raise his concerns during this meeting. He spoke three times urging a leadership change. He felt the leaders in the municipal government had digressed from the democratic style that the Communist Party advocated.

He even made a bold speech criticizing the mayor for his despotism. He said he had once witnessed the mayor talking to the deputy mayor like a bully. He then quoted Lenin's living will when Lenin warned of the danger of Stalin's despotism. Finally, he said: "Mayor Ke was one of the few in our Party who had met with Lenin, and we all respect him very much. I am willing to cast my vote for him, but I really and sincerely hope that he will make some changes in his leadership style."

His words had the impact of a huge stone falling into quiet water, creating a very loud splash and huge waves that immediately attracted attention. Even the journalists from Beijing heard rumors of his speech and chased him down outside the conference room. He immediately sensed the tension in the atmosphere, and found other participants looking at him differently than before. He began to realize that he had probably said too much, and decided to say no more, especially not to the journalists. However, it was too late. The mayor had heard his words and would never forgive him. Ke waited for an opportunity for revenge.

That opportunity soon came. Earlier in 1956, Chairman Mao had invited open criticism about the policy made by the Communist Party after it came to power, and wanted people to help improve it. Many people, especially the intellectuals, truly believed Mao's sincerity and began to speak out. Yet as soon as these outspoken people expressed their thoughts, Mao and some officials found the criticism too much to tolerate. In 1957, Mao launched a political movement persecuting these people. It was called a movement against the rightists. Hundreds of thousands of people fell victim. Because of this ridiculous persecution and an actual conspiracy over a period of two years, my uncle became one of the last victims in Shanghai, and was eventually expelled from the Communist Party in 1959.

"A MAN CAN DIE ONCE, AND ONLY ONCE!"

In the late fall of 1957 when my uncle was still a member of the Party, Chairman Mao came to Shanghai and delivered a speech to a select audience of about 200 Party leaders and government officials. Like most others in the audience, my uncle sat straight in his seat attentively listening to this long-time legendary leader. He had the most pious feelings one could have. Mao was a great speaker, and my uncle was very impressed. The speech was full of humor, and Mao cited history as easily as counting his fingers. Yet, as my uncle reflected on the event over thirty-five years later, few in the audience truly understood the real and implicit meanings of Mao's speech.

There was no organized discussion as there usually was after a leader delivered a speech. The mayor, however, soon announced that there was a lot of catch-up work to do in terms of carrying out the campaign against the rightists in Shanghai. Earlier in the year, many people had been labeled rightists in Shanghai, as well as everywhere in China. There really wasn't anything to catch up with! It was apparent that the mayor now wanted to have more people labeled rightists and persecuted. The mayor thought that was what Chairman Mao really meant by his speech, and he proved to be correct. Later in life he was promoted, almost to being Mao's successor, but he died prematurely of a heart attack in the mid-1960s.

By secret instruction of the mayor, the first attack against my uncle began at the end of 1957. At a Party meeting, he was asked to explain why he had criticized the mayor during the Party conference in the previous year. He was ordered to make a self-criticism and an apology. Not everyone participating in this meeting had attended the previous conference; when the story was retold it became dramatic and distorted. My uncle was described as having challenged the mayor's leadership and that of the Party as well. After hearing so many false charges, my uncle felt he had to defend himself. He denied all the charges and cited his more than twenty-year loyalty to the Party. He asked the participants to stop interpreting his words with evil intentions and asked: "Why can't you trust me, my comrades? Why do you suspect there is always something evil in what I said?"

His words irritated his colleagues, and they asked him to self-criticize his attitude first. The next day he admitted he had a poor attitude and promised to prepare a thorough self-criticism. During the next three days he examined his inner heart like a religious person, searching for any evidence of sin. He exaggerated every mistake he had ever made at work and viewed it as a defect of his loyalty to the Party. He delivered his self-criticizing speech at the next Party meeting, using most negative terms. Yet what he received in return was a further denunciation. Some said that he hadn't prepared well and didn't criticize himself enough. Others said that he had prepared only too well, and did everything possible to disguise himself as having bourgeois ideas while actually he was upholding capitalist individualism. In the Communist lexicon at the time there was a big difference between "bourgeois ideas" and "capitalist individualism." While the former was often used to describe a fellow Communist who held unorthodox ideology, the latter was enough to disqualify someone from being a Communist. My uncle felt his heart sink when he heard such a negative phrase used to describe him. Instinctively, he knew that something even worse would happen. When the meeting was over, another one was scheduled to continue this denunciation.

At the next meeting, new charges appeared. Someone reported hearing my uncle advocate "independent thinking," and the word "independent" was now interpreted as rebelling against the Party's leadership. Another asked: "Why did the private business owners have so many positive words to say about you?" My uncle really didn't know how to respond. The previous year, he was asked to transform 5,000 private businesses into public and private partnerships. Because he was fair in considering both the public and the private interest at the same time, he retained a good working relationship with the private sector; that helped him make the transition more smoothly than many industries not under his jurisdiction. Yet his success now worked against him; it became evidence used by his accusers to portray him as being closer to the capitalists than to the Party. No one seemed to remember that the Party had been just as close and friendly to private business owners up until the previous year.

Now with their de facto ownership of all businesses, the Communist Party started to revise its policy, and began to treat former business owners as enemies rather than friends. They had been useful in the coalition against the previous government, but once the Communist Party came to power and stabilized the economy, these people became less important. Just like destroying a bridge after crossing the river, the Party abruptly cut its connections with the former business owners. The men who helped build the bridge, such as my uncle, were also victimized.

A concurrent international event made my uncle's case go from bad to worse. Three years after Stalin's death, his successor, Khrushchev, made a confidential speech during the Party congress denouncing him. The ideological fight between the Communist authorities in Beijing and in Moscow became public. Leaders in Beijing charged the new leadership in Moscow with being revisionists, who were betraying the revolutionary course and representing only the interest of Western capitalism. My uncle's criticism of the mayor was not seen as an isolated incident. It was alleged to be associated with Khrushchev's confidential speech against Stalin and my uncle was accused of collaborating with international revisionists and capitalists. Then, another misfortune befell him. His wife was diagnosed with a malignant tumor in her urinary tract. When my uncle first heard the diagnosis, he decided not to tell her about his political trouble. She needed to have surgery to remove the tumor, and he had to give her all the support he could. The hours of waiting for her outside the operating room were the longest in his life. He thought of all the possibilities. Her life-threatening disease might soon kill her and leave him alone to deal with his political demise. Or his political life might soon end and have a detrimental impact on his wife's physical recovery. Even worse, the mutual detrimental effects might strike so severely that neither of them could survive either physically or mentally.

In the next couple of days, he managed to come to the hospital after work, saying nothing of his day, during which he had suffered such serious charges and denunciation. However, as his case worsened, he had trouble being cheerful. So, on the third day after her surgery, he lied to her and said he was too busy to visit her every day. She gave him a smile, with such understanding and trust that it only hurt him more deeply. Before, he didn't want to tell her the truth; now he didn't know how. When he held her hand to say good-bye, he felt he might never be able to see her again. It was a very frightening thought.

They had to wait a month for the biopsy report. When it finally came, fortunately, it was a great relief. She didn't have cancer. Only then did he tell her what had happened to him during the past month. He was still very naive and thought that he might have a chance to survive the political crisis if he could make an acceptable self-criticism. He asked her to help him reexamine his thoughts and deeds to see why he was not doing what the Party required him to do. She moved home and together they reviewed their lives during the past decades, beginning with the first days of their romance when they shared a common ideology and the enjoyment of their comradeship. He asked her to point out his faults, and she answered with sincerity that she couldn't find any.

With a little more confidence, he proceeded cautiously. The person in charge of his case suggested he have conversations with his old friends, especially those who had worked with him as underground Communists. A little less naive, he carefully thought about the suggestion, and decided not to contact anyone, in the fear that others might become involved and victimized. Several weeks passed and that person spoke to him again. This time he explicitly asked my uncle who had supported his anti-Party and anti-socialist activities. Apparently this person was seeking a chain of dissidents. My uncle held his breath and rejoiced in his heart that he had not done as suggested. If he had contacted anyone, he would have jeopardized them and many others as well. There was a built-in incentive in the system now; the more people you persecuted the more you were rewarded.

In the following months, while waiting for the final conviction, my uncle felt very lonely. He described it as being a prisoner waiting for his execution, with no hope at all. He couldn't sleep and lost his appetite. He dared not write to anyone, and there were few he could talk to. He could not even sit quietly at home because he had lost his peace of mind. For hours he wandered in parks, and did not notice what he was doing. Sometimes he buried himself in libraries, reading novels and trying to forget himself.

October 1, 1959, was the tenth anniversary of the People's Republic of China. On the same date five years before he had been happy and excited, celebrating with the rest of the nation. Now he was a lonely outcast. At seventeen, he joined the Communist movement and put his life in danger for fifteen years working for a Communist victory. Yet, in less than ten years, he went from a victor to a victim. "Why was the spring of my life so short?" he asked himself. There was no answer.

He was sent to work in a machinery factory as an apprentice. After the night shift he was trying to get some sleep when an urgent phone ring interrupted his bad dreams. He was told to go to the human resource department of the municipal government to read the conclusion of his case. He had been waiting for this moment for a long time. Yet when it came he felt he was too weak to face it. Before, he had the courage to fight the Japanese and Chiang Kai-shek's government, because he was a member of a strong organization and felt supported by thousands of comrades. Now, he had no protection. He was a lonely victim facing a cold world. He felt chilly and was shivering. Everywhere he went he met indifferent eyes, mean voices, spiteful laughs, and cold shoulders. The only one he could turn to was his wife, who, at the time, was recovering from a second operation. Because of suspicious bleeding from her left nipple, her physician worried about breast cancer. To prevent malignant development, she was advised to have her breast removed. While she was in the hospital, her husband called. She told him to come and meet her outside the front gate of the hospital. She quickly took off the hospital pajamas, dressed in her own clothes, and sneaked out of the building. Before her husband arrived, she was there waiting for him.

As they walked around the hospital, she helped analyze the situation, and asked him to be prepared for the worst. "It's not the end of your life, you know," she assured him. "Even if you are convicted as a 'rightist' and expelled from the Party, you can still be a revolutionary. As long as you have a clear conscience, it doesn't matter if you are guilty in the eyes of others." Her words gave him the courage to show up for his appointment. As she predicted, he was convicted as a "rightist" and was expelled from the Party. Before he went to the factory for the night shift, she called. "Please be very careful and do not let an accident happen. You have to remember that a man can die once, and only once!"

Yes, the old spirit in him died, and my uncle was reborn. A loyal member was expelled from the Communist Party, and his only crime was his loyalty. How could the Party have avoided such a tragedy? He could never have imagined this when he joined the Party as a teenager. What was wrong with this organization? In the years since, he is still haunted by this question.

THE EMPEROR'S NEW CLOTHES

While my uncle was in trouble, my father could not give his younger brother any help, for my father had been victimized by the same man before. Even before my uncle made his mistake of criticizing Mayor Ke, my father had warned his younger brother about the danger of working with this despotic man. However, the younger brother turned a deaf ear to an elder brother's warning and concerns. My father knew this despot far better, because he also had worked for this man. Mr. Ke was the mayor of Nanjing before he became the mayor of Shanghai. As the deputy chief-of-staff in Nanjing's municipal government, my father had two encounters with this man in 1952.

At the time, the Korean War was on. The United States occasionally sent its bombers and reconnaissance planes over Shanghai. It scared some Chinese leaders, and Mayor Ke of Nanjing was one of them. The mayor was very concerned and feared that the bombers might come further inland and hit Nanjing, especially the municipal compound. He asked my father to organize an emergency task force to dig five holes through the wall at the back of the government compound, so, in case of an air raid, the municipal government workers could climb through the holes and find better places to hide.

It was not an ordinary wall he was talking about. It was part of the city wall. In ancient China, each city had a huge square wall surrounding it, just like the Great Wall in Beijing. The municipal government office compound in Nanjing was located right inside the city wall. After discussing the plan with the chief civil engineer of the municipal government and several other engineers, my father realized that the mayor's plan was unrealistic. First of all, it wasn't safe, because if the wall were damaged, it could collapse at any time. Second, the ancient wall had cultural value and should be protected, despite the need of air defense. Instead, my father decided to tear down a twenty-meter stretch of wall and build a new gate; on top of the gate they would reconnect the old wall. With this alternate and safer plan, the wall would remain mostly intact and protected. It also provided a second access to a natural park right outside the wall for the city residents. Until then, only one gate in the wall provided access to the park, and it was two miles from the municipal compound, far from any significant residential districts. With the approval of the deputy mayor, my father built the new gate and named it the "Liberation Gate," as a memorial to the Communist take-over in 1949. Among many of his colleagues, however, it was known by my father's name, Qiluan, because he was chiefly responsible for it.

The air raid never happened, but the new wall gate served its peace-time function. The natural park became a part of the city and millions of residents and visitors have enjoyed it ever since. From the perspective of city planning, the gate created a new node in the city that led to a series of developments in that area. The eastern side of the city grew, and the old residential district in the south became connected with the industrial district in the north. In short, it had a strong impact on the future layout of the city.

However, the mayor wasn't happy to hear that his original plan was considered inadequate and hadn't been implemented. Above all, he didn't like to be seen as ignoring the value of the old wall. Instead of admitting his own mistake, he falsely accused my father of opening a new gate in the old wall and destroying a historical site, and called him an unworthy descendant of our ancestors. All the power was in the mayor's hand, and my father could hardly defend himself, even if he had a thousand mouths!

Soon, the mayor blamed my father for another matter for which he was not responsible. Orders came from Beijing to start a campaign against corruption and bureaucracy. One Saturday morning Mayor Ke delivered a mobilizing speech to all municipal employees. By afternoon, he learned that the union for municipal employees had scheduled a ballroom dance that night. He decided to use this as evidence of corrup-tion in the municipal government, associating ballroom dancing with a capitalist lifestyle, although ballroom dancing had always been allowed by the Party leaders because it was a common practice in the Soviet Union.

Mayor Ke liked to play a more radical role in the Party and he claimed to be more "revolutionary" than his colleagues. The trouble was that such people never stop. They ultimately claim to be the *only* "revolutionaries" and charge those who do not agree as "counterrevolutionaries" or enemies of communism. In many cases, however, they are just hypocrites, and never believed in what they advocated. Or they only banned others from doing what they themselves wanted to do. For example, Mayor Ke himself was once a fan of ballroom dancing, although few people knew or even suspected that, because he left an impression that he was its greatest opponent. During the past decades of Communist rule, China has seen too many hypocrites of this kind. I always wondered at these dual personalities, and wished I could have understood them better.

The mayor held my father responsible for scheduling the dancing party because the municipal employee union was under my father's supervision, even though my poor father knew nothing about it, and did not even know how to dance. The mayor especially condemned the timing of the dance. In his view, my father deliberately set up the event to offset the importance of the mayor's speech! To make it more serious, the mayor charged that my father did this in defiance of the new campaign designed by the highest authorities in Beijing.

Mayor Ke ordered three different agencies to take initiatives to investigate the case immediately. He even planned to publish the case in the local daily newspaper the following Monday, picking my father as the first target of the new campaign. However, after long talks with each investigator, my father convinced all of them that he was innocent. They agreed to report the truth to the mayor.

The mayor was still livid and he summoned my father to see him. When my father arrived at the mayor's office, the mayor gave him a cold shoulder and ignored his existence. Finally, when he turned to my father, he pointed his finger at his face, screaming: "You just read tomorrow's newspaper. I assure you, you will be very famous!"

As soon as he returned home, my father began to write a memo of self-criticism. My mother asked him: "Why do you criticize yourself when you have done nothing wrong?" "You don't know," he said. "The mayor was really upset. Even if he was convinced by investigators that I have done nothing wrong, he would still feel that he had lost face." Father knew Mayor Ke would never admit making a mistake or misjudging a good comrade, and my father had to let him save face. "If the case were publicized in the newspaper, the chance of any correction would be very slim indeed, because then the Party would lose face." My father's caution prevented him from being expelled from the Communist Party. But the mayor put a statement in my father's dossier limiting his future promotion. This became a barrier in my father's career, and it haunted him until his death.

After Mr. Ke became the mayor of Shanghai, my father warned his brother of the danger of working with this man. However, the younger brother had a strong trust in the Party organization. He didn't argue with my father, but he didn't pay much attention to my father's opinion, because he had been promoted more often within the Party hierarchy and was holding a more important office at the time. The Communists had been in power for only a few years, and he believed there was nothing to worry about under this new system. Even though it was because of my father's influence that his brother joined the Communist movement, the younger brother now felt he knew more about communism than his elder brother.

Yes, communism had such appeal that it seemed easy to understand! Anyone could believe that he understood communism while actually confusing the ideal with reality. My uncle's son once thought he understood communism, when he was only nine years old. My uncle and his wife took their son to visit a deputy minister in the central government at a local hotel. It happened that another guest was Marshal Ye Jianying, who was later to become the president of China in 1980s. Because the deputy minister had a close friendship with both the marshal and my uncle, he invited them for dinner. It was a great honor for my uncle to have dinner with such a prominent figure. My uncle asked someone in the hotel to take care of his son. When the adults sat down to eat, the hotel employee, quite panic stricken, reported that the nine-year-old boy was missing. After a long, thorough search they finally found him hiding under a bed. When his angry and embarrassed father demanded an explanation for such weird behavior, the precocious nine-year-old responded: "What a shame that you call yourselves Communists! You don't even want to share your food with me."

At first, everyone was shocked, then they burst into laughter. The nine-year-old understood textbook communism. What he didn't know was that if there had not been an especially close relationship among these three men he might have destroyed his father's career. Just like the boy who had found the true nature of the emperor's new clothes, my cousin bluntly told the truth as he saw it.

100 YEARS AFTER THE PARIS COMMUNE

Of course, my cousin soon learned more about communism than was described in his textbook. After his father was expelled from the Party, he experienced a lot of discrimination at school. For example, he was denied membership in the Communist Youth League, which was supposed to recruit every outstanding student at high school. Having a membership was seen as a great honor and being rejected by the League for political reasons was looked upon as a stigma, by both other students and their parents. In a society with such rigid moral codes, a person with such a blot had to carry a heavy burden of shame. Those who have read *The Scarlet Letter* by Hawthorne will understand this predicament.

Unfortunately, it took years for the society to be aware of its injustice and try to correct its mistakes, especially when the school system educated children with the same set of old values. Fifteen years after my uncle's fall and five years after my own parents had become victims of the same sort of injustice, I was taught, and continued to hold, Communist beliefs and was just as enthusiastic as any of my classmates when we joined the Communist indoctrination activities at school. My parents never instructed me any differently! They dared not. If they did, I might betray them and expose them to the authorities. Or, if I did express any dangerous heresies, I would get myself into trouble. No parent wanted to see that. Even they had a hard time sorting out what was happening, adjusting themselves, and reconciling reality with the ideological beliefs they had adopted earlier in their lives. It took years and very dramatic political events for the nation to abandon communism as its dominant ideology.

In January 1971, I graduated from primary school. In China, schools for secondary education are called middle schools; some of them have both junior and senior sections, some only junior sections. The one I went to was called the No. 13 Middle School and it had both junior and senior sections. Where children went to school depended on where they lived. I was lucky to go to this school because it was one of the best in the city. In fact, it was the only middle school with both junior and senior sections that had been built in Nanjing since the Communist takeover in 1949. From the outside, the main building looked magnificent with a huge traditional Chinese-style roof just like that on the Tiananmen Gate Wall or on the Forbidden City. Inside, it had modern facilities like science labs, and each classroom had movable double blackboards with a layer of thick glass on the surface so that it was really smooth to write on and easy to erase. Many universities in the United States still do not have such nice blackboards in their classrooms.

Life in middle school was very restricted, just as in primary schools. Each student had an assigned seat and shared one desk with another student. The desks were arranged into four lines, with the students in each line forming a small group. Despite this rigidity, there was some fairness in seating assignment. Short students sat in the front and tall ones in the back. Those who were near-sighted were usually allowed to sit in the front. To protect the students' eyes, every two weeks the line on the right moved to the left and each of the other lines moved to the right, because there were diagnosed cases where students developed walleyes after sitting in one side of the classroom for too long.

The Cultural Revolution brought many radical changes to school life. Much of my time at school was not spent in class, but on extra-curricular activities. For example, because I had learned to play *er hu*, a Chinese violin, I was recruited into the musical group, and many after-noons and some mornings I was with this group. As in the primary school, this was called the "Team to Spread Mao's Thoughts." We began our rehearsals in mid-February and our opening performance was on March 18, 1971, the centennial of the Paris Commune of 1871, the first Communist mass movement in the world.

The theme of our performance was the centennial of the composition of "The Internationale." The words had been written by Eugène Pottier in 1871; its music was composed by Pierre Degeyter after the Paris Commune movement was crushed by the French government. Our performance consisted of a poetry reading by two girls while the orchestra played background music, including "The Internationale," at the back of the stage. Our poem was written by our talented Chinese language teacher. I was moved by our performance. I felt a beauty in both the poem and the verses of "The Internationale." One line in "The Internationale" moved me the most: "We were nothing—thus let us be everything!" It just echoed my young teenage feelings, and gave words to my young dreams. The world looked much more promising than it really was.

In addition to the centennial celebration of the Paris Commune, there was a nationwide campaign to require everyone to sing "The Internationale." Few realized that this was part of Chairman Mao's new political maneuver. In one of his speeches Mao asked the whole nation to read Marx's and Lenin's works carefully, not just his own. Of course, I began to read *The Communist Manifesto*. Even though both my parents were still forced to do hard physical work in their labor camps, and even though the book was somewhat beyond the comprehension of a thirteen-year-old, I felt proud of myself. Every night I read the book for about an hour, and noted this in my diary.

Few people understood why Mao advocated this reading. Most people, including many of the teachers at my school, interpreted it as the modesty of a great man. Things were seldom that simple and his request was politically complex. Approximately a year before, one of the few members of the standing committee of the politburo, Chen Boda, was removed from power at a politburo meeting at a mountain resort in the Lu Mountains. For a few months, this news was kept from the general public. In my family circle, however, we figured out what had happened. We detected it from an article in a leading newspaper that for years had served as a mouthpiece for the highest authority in China. This article warned about the danger of some ambitious man usurping power because he had successfully pretended to be humble. We recalled that Chen liked to call himself a "humble man" on public occasions, and it was true that we hadn't seen him in public for quite some time. It must be Chen to whom the newspaper article was referring, and he must have been removed from the center of power.

Chen had been Mao's personal secretary and he wrote drafts for many of Mao's speeches and articles. During the Cultural Revolution he climbed the power ladder rapidly by associating himself closely with Marshal Lin Biao, Mao's wife, and other radicals. We rejoiced to see his downfall, but we didn't know that this was only a prologue to the downfall of Marshal Lin.

To flatter Mao, Lin once advocated a nationwide campaign to read Mao's works, especially three of his articles, which Lin claimed to be the core of Mao's thoughts. The themes of the three articles were "to serve the people," "altruism," and "where there is a will, there is a way." Now, by emphasizing a careful study of the European Communist classics, Mao was implicitly indicating that Lin's advocacy was wrong and that Lin would not be an appropriate successor to him. However, because Marshal Lin was the Number Two strong man in the nation, few people could imagine his downfall.

With the political winds changing so fast and secretly at the top level, ordinary people could easily be fooled or victimized in their political life. My first class teacher at the junior high school was such a person. She was born and brought up in Indonesia. The coup d'état there in the early 1960s was followed by a persecution of ethnic Chinese residents that resulted in the deaths of many thousands and also sent a huge number scurrying back to China. For some reason, our school had many of these returning Chinese as both teachers and students.

Usually, one could tell these people from the rest of us by noticing their accents and their clothes. Our teacher, Ms. Xie, stood out especially because of her dress. She always wore colorful clothes and made herself look pretty. She changed her clothes very often. She changed her shirt every day or twice a day, whereas most Chinese wore the same shirt for three to five days, and perhaps even a week.

All this made her look quite bourgeois. But in politics, she did not let anyone get ahead of her. She was as radical or "revolutionary" as any teacher could be, in her effort to become a member of the Communist Party. In order to be accepted as a Party member, one had to have many achievements or merits, which required one to work harder than one's colleagues. Of course, the most important thing was to follow the ideological Party line very closely. For someone with her background, it was even more difficult to be accepted into the Party, but Ms. Xie hardly seemed discouraged.

When I entered the school, the current political campaign was called "Deepening the Great Revolutionary Criticism." It was a continuation of targeting the so-called Riders on the Capitalist Road such as the former president Liu Shaoqi and his colleague Deng Xiaoping. As usual, local representatives were also targets. At our school, the former school principal was the local target. This man was blamed for any problem at our school before the Cultural Revolution. The format of the campaign was a little different this time. Instead of mobs and rallies and posters in public places, in this instance a team show was required.

Of course, our teacher Ms. Xie would not let this chance pass. She enthusiastically involved herself and our class and worked very hard to obtain an outstanding record. Competitions of Great Criticism were held between classes. Each class had five or six students on the stage reciting critical essays written in a literary or rhythmic style. To win, we needed some well-written articles of criticism. The teacher selected a few students, including me, to write the first draft. Then she polished our articles.

Parts of our essays criticized the former school principal. He also happened to be a friend of our family. He often visited my home when my father supervised the city schools. He also had been in the Communist underground under my father's leadership in Nanjing before the Communist takeover in 1949. I did not believe he was a "public enemy" and I hesitated to write anything against him. I asked my father for advice, and he suggested that I avoid direct attacks, if at all possible, especially avoiding name calling or finger pointing. Therefore, I offered to write the part dealing with national figures such as Liu Shaoqi and Deng Xiaoping, and let others do the former school principal. Then I tried to avoid participating in the team show on stage. I suggested to Ms. Xie that I should not be in the show, because of scheduling conflicts with my music group. Since the music group was a school-level organization, our class interest had to come second. I made my point well, and was off the hook.

Our class's team show did win the competition; however, Ms. Xie did not have time to harvest the advantage before the political wind changed direction dramatically. The power struggle made political targets such as Liu Shaoqi and Deng Xiaoping obsolete. The targets of the new political campaign were Marshal Lin and his radical friends, who, after the exposure of their alleged conspiracy against Mao, tried to escape the country and died in an airplane accident on September 13, 1971. Life went a full circle. Because Lin came to power during the Cultural Revolution by attacking Liu and Deng and others as "capitalist roaders," those who had followed closely in attacking Liu and Deng and other "capitalist roaders" now became vulnerable. Many rebel leaders were targeted, accused of being Lin's associates or local representatives. Fortunately, Ms. Xie was not one of them, and wasn't hurt much by this shift. However, a good month of hard work in organizing the team show against the "capitalist roaders" did not earn her a single bit of credit, and she was still not accepted as a member of the Communist Party.

The tragedy of Ms. Xie was really twofold and instructive. On one hand, she had probably already been discriminated against in her effort to become a Party member, simply because of her background as a returning overseas Chinese. Yet, on the other hand, it was amazing to see that a person with such a background was so eager to conform to the norms, and to try so hard to become a Communist Party member. One hundred years had passed since the Paris Commune movement in France. The Communist system established in China turned out to be very different from the original ideal. Yet, inside the system, most people were still firmly following the doctrine. The downfall of Marshal Lin made many people rethink their plans; that year seemed to be a turning point for communism in China.

MY MOTHER LOSES HER FREEDOM AGAIN

To our family's surprise, a few months before the accidental death of Marshal Lin, my mother was detained again in May 1971. This happened so quickly that it was difficult to adjust to. I was old enough to ask why, and I learned that, this time, she was detained for a totally different reason. It began in 1966 at the beginning of the Cultural Revolution, when Chairman Mao encouraged the Red Guards, and later, the Revolutionary Rebels, to take action against the so-called capitalist powerholders. As a result of that political storm, almost every person who had been in any managerial position became a potential target of the political persecution. Both my parents became its victims. Many officials tried to avoid harm by positioning themselves with the Revolutionary Rebels at their workplace. By distancing themselves from the "bourgeois headquarters" within the Communist Party, they tried to convince the rebels at their workplace that they had been fooled by the "bourgeois headquarters" and were victims, instead of supporters of public enemies such as Liu Shaoqi and Deng Xiaoping. Some administrators joined the rebel organizations. Some went even further, and created their own rebel organizations.

One day a manager of a drama group approached my mother with an exciting idea. Instead of being political targets of the rebels, managers should now form a rebel organization of their own, targeting the bureaucrats at the Department of Culture and other higher-ranking officials at the municipal and provincial government. They thought they could cut their links with the old system and join the rebels following Chairman Mao's leadership in this "Second Revolution" of the Communist movement. My mother was easily talked into this idea and became a member of this organization called the Rebels of Grassroots Managers at the Department of Culture. In reality, other than holding a few regular weekly meetings, these people did not do or change much. The rebels at the theater groups continued to view them as targeted capitalist powerholders rather than fellow rebels.

Five years later this came back to haunt them, because the leaders of the rebel organizations became the targets of the new political campaign. Like many rebel leaders, they were now accused of being members of an alleged secret "counterrevolutionary" organization called "May 16th." It was on that date in 1966 that Chairman Mao started the political campaign that was later known as the Great Proletarian Cultural Revolution. Now it was rumored that there was a secret organization named after that date whose members behaved just like other revolutionary rebels in public, but who were actually opposing the leadership of Mao and Communism by misinterpreting Mao's revolutionary policy.

The first victims were a group of leaders of Red Guards in Beijing, and they were jailed for their earlier actions, which had actually been approved by Mao himself. Soon the targets of the persecution included many rebel organization leaders throughout the whole country, and finally many innocent people who had nothing to do with either Red Guards or rebel organizations at all. It was estimated that more than two million people were victims of the persecution throughout the whole nation. In my province, the persecution against this alleged underground anti-Communist organization went on for more than a year. These people were detained, interrogated, humiliated, and even tortured. Many could not tolerate the torture and committed suicide. Some were sentenced to prison or executed. There was a snowball effect. The targeted victims were forced to give lists of other people who they knew were also members. If one person gave a list of a hundred people, a hundred more fell victim to this cruel persecution.

One day someone "confessed" that the Rebels of Grassroots Managers at the Department of Culture were affiliated with this nationwide "anti-revolutionary" organization. As a result, all the people involved, including my mother, were charged as public enemies and immediately lost their freedom. The irony was that years ago these managers had not succeeded in escaping the charges of being capitalist powerholders by siding with the rebels. Now their fruitless effort haunted them. My father was upset because he thought my mother had made a very stupid mistake.

Psychologically, this was a particularly hard blow for my parents and the whole family, because the nature of the charges was not the same as the earlier ones. Previously, the whole managerial class rather than individuals were involved. There was a kind of invisible peer support and broad sympathy in society. Most people being charged had the confidence that they had been wronged, and since almost everybody in a managerial position was wronged, the chance of getting things straightened out sooner or later was fairly good.

This time it was quite different. After a few years of suffering, many of those people were cleared. Most of them were free to go home. The new wave of persecution targeted the persecutors in the earlier wave. In the public eye, many of those rebels, who had persecuted others before, deserved punishment for the wrong they had done. My mother certainly did not belong to this group. She felt ashamed to be considered a part of this group, but also less confident that things could be straightened out, because she didn't believe this group was so innocent. If the group as a whole was guilty, the chance of her being singled out as innocent was slim.

To be detained now was much more disgraceful than it had been during the earlier wave. Even within my extended family, things changed. For example, Xiuzhen visited far less often. At her bank, she was put in charge of more business, and she seemed to be moving smoothly in her career path. Of course, she did not want to jeopardize her bright future by associating with an aunt whose name was tarnished.

Aunt still lived with us, although she now worked in a factory. She was reluctant to take me to visit my mother, because she heard a lot of gossip within the residential compound and felt ashamed about it. Even my father, who had recently been released from his detention in the labor camp and came home on weekends, felt he should not visit her. If he visited her, he argued, he would be "playing into their hands." He sensed a trap waiting for him, fearing he would be charged and punished severely as the "black hands," a Chinese political jargon meaning the master mind behind the scene. Similarly, the Beijing regime was punishing the so-called black hands of the Tiananmen Incident of 1989 more severely than the mass of student protesters.

Only when this wave of persecution went too far and victimized half a million people in my province alone, did the public begin to have sympathy. Actually, the whole post–1949 history of Communism was a recurring cycle of persecutions. In each wave of persecution, only a small portion of the population was hurt, and the crime was done in the name of the public interest. Only after decades of persecutions that victimized at least one member of every family did people begin to realize how they had been fooled by this system. It was then that the system began to fall apart.

SIX FAMILIES IN ONE HOUSE

The situation was particularly bad when my mother was detained this time. We really needed her at home to help us move. Since my father was no longer working with the municipal government, our family was asked to move out of the residential compound. Many other families were also asked to leave the compound and make room for those who were currently working at the municipal government.

An army officer and executive member of the Revolutionary Committee was already scheduled to move into our apartment. In the new government his place was equivalent to my father's old position. Therefore, he thought it was his turn to live in our apartment. However, after we moved out and he came to see the place for himself, he was very disappointed: it was far poorer than he had anticipated and he refused to move in.

In the years between the Communist takeover in 1949 and the Cultural Revolution in 1966, army officers often had quite elegant houses, and, usually, higher salaries than their counterparts in civilian positions. It was a nice balance between power and wealth. Army officers had control over fewer people, but they lived more luxuriously than the government officials who controlled many more lives.

The Cultural Revolution had removed most of the civilian officials from power and replaced them with army officers and rebel organization leaders. These army officers were happy to have more power, of course, but they were not ready to accept the meager living conditions. The officer who had looked at our apartment demanded better housing.

The irony was that the Cultural Revolution was supposed to be a second revolution to keep up the momentum of the Communist movement, which had appealed to people by guaranteeing fair and egalitarian allocation of social wealth. Yet, now that power had changed hands, the elite class had even more privileges. They had both power and wealth.

When we moved from our old apartment Aunt decided not to come with us. As a factory worker, she belonged to the workers' class, which Chairman Mao claimed to be the leading class of our society, and therefore she had far more bargaining power in her negotiation with the municipality. She was allowed to stay inside the compound and the municipality found her a studio apartment right across the street.

Our new place, assigned by the Revolutionary Committee of the municipality, was a single-family house now shared by six families. Before the Communist takeover in 1949, it had been the residence of the Catholic Archbishop of Nanjing. It was a Western-style building with two floors, an attic, and a two-story garage with a bedroom on the second floor for the chauffeur. Now, one family was placed in the attic and another in the garage. Two families shared each of the two floors of the main building. It was a nice old building; but now it had to house six families! The style of the building really amazed me. The windows moved up and down, instead of the usual type that pushed outward. There was a chimney on the roof and a fireplace downstairs in the original sitting room. It was the first time I had seen a fireplace except in pictures in an English textbook. As I stood beside it, I felt as if I were inside a picture.

My family lived on the second floor, and we occupied two large bedrooms and a tiny room that had been a toilet room. The six families shared one men's room and one women's room downstairs in the courtyard. My family also had a small room adjacent to the women's room as our kitchen, which had been the bathroom of the house. Because it was so inconvenient to use the toilets downstairs during the night, we used a couple of chamber pots. They were shaped like drums, and it was a dirty job to clean them. Traditionally, this was not a man's job, but the pots were too heavy for my grandma to carry downstairs, so I had to do it. After they were cleaned I took them back upstairs again.

Our new home was far less convenient to transportation and shopping. Although it was not far from the city center, it was not on any bus or trolley route. The closest store was almost as far away as downtown. I did not like walking twenty minutes to reach a store and another twenty minutes to return.

There were other inconveniences to deal with. For example, there was not a single water tap on the second floor. Our kitchen was downstairs and too small to dine in. So, my grandma had to cook downstairs and then I had to carry the food upstairs. After the meal, I took all the dishes downstairs again for washing.

Worst of all, we had no place to take a bath. In our old home we had a bathroom with a toilet and a bathtub, but no shower. Most houses in China did not have showers because there were no facilities to provide hot water. Even the mayor's house did not have a hot water boiler. Previously, we heated water in big pots on the stove and poured it into the bathtub. Now we did not even have a bathtub.

In fact, most families in the city did not have bathtubs. They were a luxury that was accorded the people living in the municipal government residential compound. Other people either went to a public bathhouse or took a bath at home using a wooden basin. After we moved into our new home we used a wooden basin. I seldom went to a public bathhouse except in the winter, when it was freezing in the house because there was no heat at all.

In China, only a few northern cities had heating systems inside buildings. In cities like Shanghai and Nanjing only a few fancy hotels had heating systems. In the winter, the temperature could be as low as ten degrees below zero centigrade. People slept in bedrooms where everything froze. In our new home this problem was even more serious because all the kitchens were separated from the main building and the heat generated by cooking could not warm the bedrooms.

I remember that the first winter in our new home was unusually cold. That year my sister's boyfriend came to stay with us during his vacation from army camp. He arrived one day before my sister. As most boyfriends would do in such a situation, he tried hard to do things that he thought would please his girlfriend's family. The following morning he got up very early and mopped our wooden floor. Minutes later the wet floor became so slippery that no one could walk on it. Everybody had to sit down and wait for the warm noon sun to melt the icy floor!

Despite all the inconveniences at our new home, there was one thing I loved about it. The neighbors were very open and friendly; life there was quite communal. Each family's life was almost an open book. None of the six families could close its doors to the others, because there weren't any doors. Since each family had its kitchen in the little buildings separated from the main building, everybody knew what the other families were cooking. Families would talk to each other while cooking or washing in their kitchens. The little courtyard in front of all the kitchens became a public area where many people spent most of their time at home except when they were sleeping. This made our lifestyle more like that of the blue-collar, low-wage workers residing in the other end of the city. I really loved my new neighbors, especially Mr. Zhang. This was the man who once, for politeness's sake, didn't pass wind while meeting with a group of businessmen and injured himself. The six families lived together almost like an extended family.

A TRIP TO VISIT MY REDETAINED MOTHER

Because Aunt did not move with us to our new home, I had to travel alone to see my mother at her labor camp. The first of these trips was quite an adventure for a thirteen-year-old. Careful preparations were made for my trip. Grandma cooked some of mother's favorite dishes. It was early autumn and I packed a sweater for her. Because my mother had serious rheumatism, I took her a few herbal wristbands that were particularly helpful in relieving her pain. I also took her a pair of cloth shoes that were more comfortable than sneakers for her rheumatism.

The chief mission of the trip, however, was to try to cheer her up and keep her from having a nervous breakdown or attempting suicide. As I mentioned before, this second detention was a much harder blow. To be a target earlier in the Cultural Revolution was more generic; everybody was in the same situation. Now it was quite different. The situation was improving and there was widespread hope that with the power of the radicals waning, everything would soon go back to normal. At this point, to be associated with radicals and become a political prisoner again was a double insult.

I set out at 6:00 a.m. First I took a local bus and transferred to another one to get to the terminal for long-distance buses. By the time I arrived there it was almost 7:00 a.m. I wanted to take a bus to the Crane

Gate, the closest bus station to my mother's camp. To my surprise, I saw a big sign at the entrance of the bus terminal saying the two scheduled buses on that line had been canceled that morning.

Checking with the information desk I found that I had two alternatives. I could either wait for the afternoon bus, at about 3:00 p.m., or take another bus to the Yaohua Gate where my father's camp was located. I could get off in the middle of the route at the Unicorn Gate and then walk about five miles to my mother's camp. I hated to wait for the afternoon bus and I was afraid that I wouldn't be able to catch the last bus coming back to town. So I decided to take the other bus and get off at the Unicorn Gate.

At the Unicorn Gate station I asked a man how to get to the Crane Gate by foot. He looked at me as if I were insane, and asked me why I did not take the bus. When I explained my dilemma, he said it would be a long, long walk. Following his directions I started toward the Crane Gate. The road was straight, and looked endless. It was lined with poplar trees. All I could see ahead was the road with two lines of trees leading to the horizon. I walked and walked. More than forty minutes passed and I saw no changes; still the endless road with two lines of trees leading to the horizon. I was exhausted, and the bag on my back felt very heavy.

Hungry and thirsty, I sat down for a rest. My stomach was churning and I could hear loud noises coming from it. I could smell the dishes my grandma made for my mother that were in my bag. "No," I said to myself, "I should not touch that. That is for my mother." But the smell was really tempting. So I took out the container of food and put it under my nose, just to smell it. I was determined not to touch it and I didn't!

After another hour and a half of exhausting walking I finally arrived at the camp. There were rows of one-story buildings in front of me. At one end of the first building I saw a sign indicating the headquarters. I entered the room and saw a tall fat man about fifty years old. I told him I had come to see my mother. He asked me, "What's your mother's name?" I told him, and he said: "Oh, you came to bring her something, right?" I said yes.

This man then carefully searched my bag and examined every item in it. Finally he said, "OK, I'm going to pass all these to your mother. You may go now." I was very disheartened. After such a long walk I wasn't expecting this kind of cold refusal. I begged him to allow me to see my mother, just for five minutes. He was tough and wouldn't give me even a minute.

I left the headquarters room, but I did not want to give up. Instead of going back I went further along the rows of buildings. Someone looked at me with curiosity. I pretended to be looking for the men's room and asked him where it was. He gave me directions. On my way back from the men's room I roamed among the buildings. All of a sudden, through an open window I saw my mother sitting on the edge of her bed. I cried out: "Mom, I came to see you. I walked for two hours. But they wouldn't allow me to see you. I brought something for you and they took it from me."

My mother was surprised to see me. She looked much thinner and darker than before. She stared at me and her movements were far slower than they had been. She mumbled a few words asking about my father and grandma. I said they were fine. Then, looking around and finding no one watching us, I spoke to her in a low voice: "Dad wanted me to tell you to take good care of yourself and not think too much." We were trying to persuade her not to think about suicide.

Just at that moment I felt someone approaching from behind. I raised my voice and quoted my favorite saying from Mao: "Believe in the people and believe in the Party. Every problem will be solved eventually." Then I said a quick goodbye to my mother, and turned around. The tall fat man was right behind me. He yelled at me angrily: "Why didn't you leave as I told you to?" "I just went to the men's room," I said. Then I passed him and walked toward the bus station without once turning my head. I was very scared and expected he might have me detained at the camp. Nothing happened, and I got to the Crane Gate bus station. It was about 2:30 and I was just in time for the first bus back to town.

Arriving home I told my father every detail of my trip. He was very glad that I fulfilled the mission so well. He praised my cleverness and compared it with what he had done as an underground Communist. To me, that was a very big compliment, just what I wanted to hear from him. I felt I was a real grown-up now and was very proud of myself.

Three days later, however, I was summoned into the deputy principal's office at school. She was a thin woman in her forties. Because of my performance in the school's music group she easily recognized me among the thousands of students. Usually she was nice to me and she always gave me a smile when we saw each other on campus. But that day her face was very perturbed as I entered her office. I soon found out why. Sitting next to her in an easy chair was no one else but that tall fat man from my mother's labor camp. I knew immediately that I was in trouble. She asked me to take a seat and said: "This gentleman came to tell us something about what you did over the weekend and I don't think you need me to introduce him to you." Silently, I sat down.

The tall fat man tried to be pleasant this time. He gave me a forced smile that exposed his yellowish teeth. He spoke to me in a soft voice that sounded very unnatural compared with his large body. "Who told you to do what you did last Sunday?" I knew he wanted to hear my father's name and pin him as being behind my behavior. "What did I do?" I asked. "Don't play dumb with me," he said. "I told you not to see your mother. Why didn't you listen to me?" I said, "Well, I was on my way from the men's room and I saw my mother by accident." "What did you say to your mother?" "Nothing but take care of yourself." "What does that mean?" "Well, take care means take care. What do you think?" The man became upset now. He warned me not to do anything against the Revolution. After whispering to the thin woman, he left the room and I was alone with the woman.

This time she gave me a little smile, almost unnoticeable. She then asked me an unexpected question: "Do you believe that your mother is a member of the May 16th organization?" I was taken aback and after a little pause, I said, "I don't think so." "Why?" "Well . . . ," my mind began to scan all the evidence to support my answer. All of a sudden I thought of the person who had been the manager of a local drama group. It was she who came to my mother with the idea of organizing the managers of local theater groups into a rebel organization at the beginning of the Cultural Revolution. If their organization were a collective member of the so-called May 16th organization, an alleged anti-revolutionary organization, as they were charged now, it must have been this woman who recruited my mother. Yet, as far as I knew, she was still free. Perhaps it was because her husband was a high-ranking army officer and was still in power. But the simple fact that she was free seemed to give me the best reason for believing in my mother's innocence. How could my mother be guilty if this woman were innocent? I put this question to the deputy principal, and without a word she dismissed me from her office.

What really surprised me in this episode was that, from my description, my father was able to figure out who this tall fat man was: one of our previous neighbors in the residential compound! Before the Cultural Revolution, he was a deputy department director in the municipal government, only a few ranks lower than my father. It seemed to me that he should have been more sympathetic toward my family. But that was not the case. From then on I came to realize that it was very difficult to judge people accurately, and any kind of generalization could be misleading.

Unfortunately, even in China today, such generalizations have often been made. For example, looking back at the history of the Cultural

Revolution, people tend to think of the Red Guards as totally evil and all the government officials as victims. The authorities in Beijing have even stated that those who were Red Guard or Rebel leaders should not be promoted to any important government positions, while anyone who was targeted by the Red Guards or Rebels can easily claim it as a political credit. Yet the truth is that none of these generalizations really help in determining a person's integrity or character. This fat tall man tried to entice me to betray my father as the instigator behind the scene so that he could persecute him as well as my mother, just like the person who was in charge of my uncle's case and had tried to entice my uncle to betray his old friends. Both men had crooked and cruel hearts, although they belonged to the same group of administrators and long-time Communist Party members as my father and uncle. How could we make a generalization that since they had been mobbed by Red Guards during the early months of the Cultural Revolution they should deserve more respect and promotion than some innocent teenage Red Guards? New injustice is occurring because wrong assumptions are still being made.

IT WAS TOO LATE

My grandparents were not happy about our recent move. My grandma often complained she had suffered more in her life because of her association with my father than she had benefited from it. I think she was right.

When my grandparents lived with us in the municipal residential compound, they did not enjoy as many privileges as they might have had as a result of my father's position because my father was very careful not to abuse his power. For example, although he had a car and a chauffeur, both at public expense, my father seldom gave my grandparents a ride. My mother could ride when she was going to work, but not to go shopping, and even then, only when it was an emergency or she was late. Otherwise my father always asked her to use public transportation. When Father went to theaters, which was a part of his job, and took the family with him, we could all get a ride in his car. If we went to different theaters, we had to take buses.

For me, therefore, each ride in my father's car, an old black four-door Ford, was an excitement, and almost every day I would ask if I could get a ride. I was greatly disappointed when the car was suddenly replaced by a small new jeep. The municipal government told my father that the car had been identified as the one used by Zhou Enlai in 1946 when he headed the Communist delegation participating in the nego-tiation with Chiang Kai-shek's government in Nanjing to end the Chinese civil war. (General Marshall from the United States served as the mediator and he failed.) Because the car was seen as a historical antique, the municipal government now wanted to display it in the museum founded on the location where Zhou's delegation had stayed. Twenty years later, when my mother became the curator of that museum, the car was still there.

If a few rides in my father's car were the rewards of living with my parents, my grandparents must have paid dearly for them when my parents had lived with them before the Communist takeover. Because then my parents were underground Communists, they could have been arrested and executed at any moment, and that had been a daily worry for my grandparents. Besides, they could have been arrested, too.

Once, one of the Communist colleagues had a high fever. Because he was single and lived with others who were not Communists, my father was afraid that in his raving he might reveal his status as an under-ground Communist. So my parents took him home and cared for him. His temperature was so high that he raved. Once he even mentioned the word "Communism" and it scared my grandparents because they were afraid the neighbors on the other side of the bedroom wall might hear it. If the neighbors reported it to the police, the whole family could be arrested and executed.

When my grandma told me these stories, I could tell that she was truly disheartened. She never devoted her life to any ideology or idealis-tic cause like communism. All she did was to respect her daughter's choice to marry a handsome young man who turned out to be a Com-munist. Before the Communist takeover, she had suffered because of this marriage, and she could understand that. But she could not under-stand why she should suffer again now, twenty years after the Commu-nist takeover.

Both my grandparents were from middle-class families. In my grand-ma's youth, girls did not go to school. Among each of my grandma's six sisters only the youngest had any schooling. Unlike my grandma, that sister did not have her feet bound, because this terrible custom had been abolished by the Revolution of 1911. By the time she was of school age, a few schools in large cities had begun to accept girls. Although her father was strongly against the idea at first, eventually he gave in to his youngest daughter's will. My grandma was fourteen years older than her youngest sister, and throughout her life she wished that she were fourteen years younger. As a victim of society, she was forced to have her feet bound at age three and as a child she didn't know how to read.

However, she was very smart and later learned to read quite a few words by herself. The most amazing thing to me was that she learned arithmetic without formal training. In fact, she never used a pen or pencil to do her calculations. Instead, she did them all in her head. Very often she was faster than I was with a pencil and paper.

At home, we all recognized that my grandma was far more intelligent than her husband and her children. Her marriage to Grandpa was arranged by their parents. My grandpa inherited some money from his family to open up a small shop selling cigarettes and match boxes. But it was actually my grandma who ran the business behind the scene. With her good management, their business was quite successful. By the time my mother was a grownup their shop had expanded to sell dozens of different commodities.

When my mother met my father, neither of her parents knew that he was an underground Communist. Even my mother only learned this later. Before they were married, my mother joined my father in the Communist movement, and two years after the marriage she became a member of the Communist Party. They did not inform my grandparents about their involvement in the Communist movement. At the time, my father seemed to be an ideal son-in-law. He was handsome and had a decent, well-paid job as a high school English teacher and he was highly respected. He did not drink and never used opium or other drugs. Unlike many other men at that time, he did not visit brothels. What else could my grandparents dream of for a son-in-law?

When my parents married, my grandparents didn't realize the danger they were in. Later, they came to suspect that my parents were underground Communists. By now they had no other choice but to try to keep this secret. Their house often became a meeting place for my parents and their colleagues. They set up a mah-jongg table and sat around pretending to be playing mah-jongg. If the secret policemen suddenly broke into the house, they would not be able to find anything suspicious.

So, my grandparents became involved with the Communist movement unintentionally, but as my grandma told me these old stories she seemed to be very proud of her role in them. I think I could understand her feelings. When the Communists took over China and my father became an important government official, it was great and surprising news to my grandparents' siblings and their families. They all congratulated my grandparents on having raised such a wonderful daughter and choosing such a great son-in-law. Of course, no one anticipated that my parents could be out of power again twenty years later.

After we moved into our new home in 1971 my grandparents were physically isolated from the outside world. With her bound feet, it was almost impossible for my grandma to walk to shops or stores by herself. My grandpa was aging and his health deteriorated quickly. He wanted to go downtown, but he could not handle the traffic by himself. He would stop at the intersection and be too afraid to cross the street, even if it were the pedestrians' turn.

He needed to go to the barber once a month, and the closest one was downtown. He had to ask me to go with him whenever he needed a haircut. After a few visits he became too weak to walk that far. He asked me to find out whether any barber would be willing to come to our home to give him a haircut. I talked to the barbers at that shop. Every time they said, "Oh, yes, but our schedule is full this week." After a few weeks I realized that they did not take me seriously and did not mean what they said. I was furious and asked them: "Don't you serve the people as Chairman Mao asks everyone to do?" "Yes," they said, "we serve workers, peasants, and soldiers. What is your grandfather? Is he a worker or a soldier?" I felt my throat choke. In those days, the word "people" had long been interpreted by radicals as to refer to workers, peasants, and soldiers only. My grandfather was none of those. How could I tell them that he had been a small business owner before the Communist Revolution in 1949? That would certainly exclude him from any definition of "people."

At home I had to persuade my grandpa that he just had to wait another week. But soon I knew it was too late. One day I found he could not get out of bed. My grandma had to bring him everything. She had to help him wash his face and brush his teeth. She had to bring him his food, although he could only eat very little now. He had to use a chamber pot in the bed and often he did not even know that he needed it. But he never forgot that he needed a haircut. Once he pointed to his head and smiled: "See how long it is now. Where is the barber?" I had to hold back my tears and told him the barber would come soon.

One afternoon I was home a little earlier than usual. My grandma was preparing dinner in the kitchen. I went into my grandparents' bedroom and saw my grandpa lying in his bed motionless. I approached him and thought he was sleeping. But when I turned my back to him I heard a sound. It seemed that he was trying to cough, but could not do it easily. My instinct told me something was wrong and I hurried downstairs to get my grandma. When grandma came and held grandpa's head in her arms, he made the last movement in his life. We heard a noise from his throat, and then everything was quiet. After a moment we both knew that he was gone.

That was the first time I had seen a dead man. I was very frightened. But my grandma seemed much calmer. She slowly put my grandpa's head back on the pillow. His eyes were still half open. After three tries she managed to close them. Then she straightened out his body and moved it to the middle of the bed. After that she walked away and sat down on an armchair. Only then did she begin to cry. Her crying became louder and louder. Between the cries she mumbled a few distraught words. I was even more scared then and did not know what to do.

It was almost dinner time and most of the neighbors were at home. A few minutes later people from downstairs came up to find out what happened. As it was not a weekend and my father was not at home, a neighbor helped to telephone him, and he came home later that evening. My mother could not be reached on the phone, nor could she come home because she was still detained in the labor camp. One neighbor downstairs had been in the same labor camp and he offered to try to negotiate with the camp authorities to let my mother come home once, or at least to attend the funeral.

The funeral was held at the public funeral home. It was a rainy day and the road leading toward the funeral home was very muddy. It was difficult for my grandma to walk on her bound feet through all the mud. Fortunately, Aunt arrived at our house early that day, and she helped my grandma walk to the funeral home down the muddy road. I could tell that her arms were supporting almost all of Grandma's weight. All of the relatives on my mother's side who were living in Nanjing came to the funeral. It was the first gathering of the extended family since the Cultural Revolution. Unfortunately, my mother had not been allowed to attend her father's funeral.

above left
The author's maternal
grandfather, early 1950s

above right
The author's third
uncle with his family,
early 1950s

The author's
father (*left*) with
Russian and
Chinese faculty
members at the
technical school,
1956

The author's father
(*right*) meeting with an
East German visitor in
December 1959

The author, at age one, 1959

Foreign Minister Chen Yi (*far left*), Premier Zhou Enlai (*middle*),
the author's father (*right*), in 1960

The author on International Children's Day, June 1, 1960, with his sister (*left*) and nanny (*right*)

The author's second uncle with his family, early to mid-1960s

The author's sister, 1969, her first year in the countryside

The author's sister's future husband, 1968

The author in primary
school, late 1960s

The author in the early to mid-1970s, during high school years

The author's father's sister (*front left*) and her family.
Her son-in-law (*center rear*) was a movie actor who played Lei Feng,
the "model Communist soldier." Chinese New Year, 1973.

Survivors of the Cultural Revolution:
the author's second uncle and father, mid-1970s

A family reunion in the mid-1980s: the author's mother (*left rear*),
second uncle's wife, second uncle, father, and third uncle (*left to right*)

The author's father at a holiday party in the mid-1980s

The author with "Uncle Zhao," a prominent Buddhist leader, 1987

The author's maternal grandmother, with his niece (*right*) and second cousin, late 1980s

The author's sister, father, niece, wife, and mother (*left to right*) in 1989
after he came to the United States

Mourners at the author's father's funeral, 1990

The author's
mother at home
after his father's
funeral, 1990

The author's
mother and sister
in front of his
father's statue,
early 1990s

The author
with his wife,
Meirong, and elder
son, Alexander,
1993, in the
United States

The author
in front of his
father's statue,
1996.
The calligraphy
on the base is by
"Uncle Zhao."

CHAPTER 5

"WHAT DO YOU WANT TO BE?"

Because Aunt did not move in with us, housework became a heavy burden. Domestic work was still usually done by women, but in my family there were not many women around. My mother was detained at her labor camp. My sister was in Anhui Province, hundreds of miles away. My grandmother was too old to do much. My grandpa wasn't a help at all when he was alive, for he had never learned to do any housework. My father was still in the labor camp and could only come home on weekends. So, the food shopping became my chore and my grandma did all the cooking. I had to buy fresh food every day because we did not have a refrigerator. In fact, the word *refrigerator* was not even in the Chinese vocabulary. Washing machines were also unheard of and all the clothes were washed by hand. Every other weekend when my father came home from the camp he and I did two weeks of laundry.

I enjoyed washing clothes with my father because it gave me an opportunity to be close to him and spend time with him. I finally received the paternal love and attention that many other boys had much earlier. It was during those evenings that my father began to tell me about his life and our family history. His stories fascinated me because they contrasted so much with my life. Many times I wished that I could have lived in his time, instead of mine, because his seemed much more colorful.

For example, I knew he had worked as an English teacher for many years before the Communist takeover, but now I learned that he had also been a journalist. Of course, his stories of working as a wartime journalist, reporting from the front, fascinated me. On August 13, 1937, the Japanese attacked Shanghai for the second time, five years after its earlier attempt had been defeated by the heroic 19th Route Army led by General Cai Tingkai. The day after the gunfire started, my father saw an advertisement in a local newspaper, *Evening News*, recruiting trainees to be front-line reporters. It offered a very decent salary. As my father was looking for a better job to support himself as an undercover Communist, he applied immediately. Two out of the forty trainees completed the training, but only my father got the job. The other one decided not to take it because it was too dangerous.

Indeed, it was a dangerous job. Every midnight my father rode on an old Red Cross vehicle to the front. Sometimes it was an ambulance, other times it was a truck. It carried him right to the battlefield where fighting had taken place earlier in the day. The roads were terrible, full of mortar holes. Quite often there was sporadic gunfire too, sometimes not far overhead. By one or two o'clock in the morning, my father would arrive at the front and meet with soldiers and officers in their trenches or shelters. By 4:00 a.m. he would be back at home writing his report, and at 6:00 a.m. he would deliver it at the headquarters of the *Evening News*. He then would go back to his studio to get some sleep. He liked this maverick work much more than a regular office job. It sounded like more fun to me, too.

There is one story that he didn't tell me, but that I learned later from my second uncle. It really fascinated me and helped me know more about the three brothers. It turned out that when my father was a journalist in Shanghai, his two brothers were also in Shanghai as squad leaders in the army reserves. Although the reserve force was officially under Chiang Kai-shek's leadership, the battalion my uncles belonged to was actually controlled by the undercover Communists. Both my uncles were undercover Communists. Chiang's special agency soon detected something unusual about this battalion and sent a new commander to take over. It was not easy to discover which individuals in the battalion were undercover Party members, and that may have led to the following incident.

The battle against the Japanese turned out to be very difficult and

Chiang was considering a strategic retreat. However, on the night of October 20, the battalion suddenly received an order to move to the front. By 1:00 a.m., the company my uncles belonged to arrived at a small village named Huacao, very close to the front. Without further orders, the company stopped moving and rested in the village. My second uncle felt too nervous to sleep, so he wandered outside the village. There he encountered his platoon leader, who also sensed something wrong. It didn't make sense to send one ill-trained reserve unit to the front when the entire battle seemed to be lost and a military retreat was imminent. The platoon leader summoned another squad leader and the three men had a serious discussion among the bamboo outside the village. My uncle was not sure whether the other two were also undercover Communists, but they all felt that there might be a political conspiracy, and that the battalion was simply being sent to the front to be destroyed by the Japanese.

Their discussions went on in the bamboo grove until around 4:00 a.m. when the Japanese bombers suddenly arrived, dropping many bombs right over the small village. Hardly had the bombing stopped when the three men ran back to the village to see what happened to their troops. Passing by a small pond, they encountered my other uncle, who had gotten up early and come out of the village to wash his face by the pond. The two brothers stared at each other, and both instantly and instinctively realized that they were lucky survivors of the Japanese air raid. When they got back to the village they learned that over half of the company had been hurt or killed, many of them under the collapsed walls of an old theater where they had spent the night.

From dawn to dusk, the survivors didn't eat or drink anything while trying to uncover the dead bodies from the rubble, pay their last respects, and bury the bodies. By evening a retreat order finally came from the battalion headquarters. The exhausted men carried their wounded companions and set out under a mourning moon. The long shadows behind them suddenly reminded my second uncle of a scene from a Russian novel named *The Rout* by Aleksandr Fadeev. It was also about a troop defeated in battle, and the nineteen survivors walked silently in the moonlight. Even today, my uncle clearly remembers that passage from the novel.

The survivors trudged along the road through the night until they saw two army trucks come by. They waved their hands desperately, and the trucks stopped. A man jumped down from the first truck. To the great surprise of my uncles, it was my father. He had just come back from his nightly visit to the front. The three brothers embraced each other, and none of them could hold back his tears. My father was the first to recover from this temporary and unexpected joy. They soon moved all the wounded onto the trucks. Once back on the truck, my father waved his hand and tried to cheer up the rest of the group. "Don't worry. We'll get them to the hospitals right away. You have all done a great job. We as civilians salute you!" He was a good journalist and always knew just what to say.

After I heard this story I couldn't help thinking of the three brothers as wartime heroes. My father changed his jobs more than twenty times after that, but he said the jobs he liked the most were teacher and journalist. He called them freelance jobs because he could work on a schedule more flexible than 9-to-5 office work would have allowed. Also, he said that these jobs allowed one to have a longer career and did not force one to retire at an early age. After hearing so many of his stories I really felt sorry for myself because life for my generation seemed so monotonous.

One night, while we were doing laundry together, my father asked me what I wanted to be when I grew up. I was both surprised and puzzled, and did not know how to answer. According to the formal education my generation received, this was not even a legitimate question. Since kindergarten we had been told to do whatever the Communist Party wanted us to do and to be what the Party wanted us to be. It never occurred to me that, as an individual, I had the right or even the chance to choose.

After observing what had happened over the past few years, I really did not think one could become whatever one wanted. For example, although I did not know exactly what my sister wanted to be, I was quite sure that she never intended to be a peasant. Even though she was now at college and majoring in the Chinese language, I did not see how she could plan her future. Basically, I did not see how anyone of my generation could have any career choice because everyone's fate was totally dependent on the political wind. I felt extremely powerless.

I remember that I had wished to be a soldier when I was little, probably like every boy of my generation. Later on, when I attended diplomatic occasions, I began to dream of becoming a diplomat. But after years of living with so few economic resources and my parents' being excluded from power circles, I gave up that idea, too. I wondered if people of older generations, before the advent of the socialist society, were the only ones who had such choices.

But my father was serious, and he really wanted me to consider his question. He admitted that I was right about what had happened to my generation. But he tried to convince me that this was a very special period in history. He believed that the Cultural Revolution was over and that things would soon become normal. He assured me that even in a socialist or Communist society young people would always be able to make major career decisions. He told me that Karl Marx had written an article discussing this issue; apparently Marx thought it a legitimate thing to discuss with youngsters of any generation.

This convinced me. My father said that a person might not become what he wanted to be, but that he should at least have an idea of what he wanted to be. My father tried to convince me that opportunity might come at any time and that the most important thing was to be ready. He wanted me to have a good plan and to spend my time wisely. He said that to waste time was a real crime. To waste one's own time was like gradual suicide, and to waste other people's time was like murder. Since the school system did not require much reading currently and in fact did not emphasize learning at all, he asked me to read more books in my spare time than school required. He recommended that I read the biographies of Marx, Engels, Lenin, and Stalin. He assured me that these books were very readable and would be helpful to me. We had them at home, although in the frenzy of the time none of these books were publicly allowed to circulate because they were written by Soviet authors and translated into Chinese and published in China in the early 1950s. With curiosity I soon finished reading them all. Their initial impact was to reinforce my teenage tendency to rebel. I began to appreciate the rebellious characteristics of these founding fathers of European Communism, and I found a common ground between these godlike figures and myself. I learned that Lenin loved to read banned books, including the works of Marx. I loved to read banned books, too, although this time it was not Marx's works that were banned! Even though I didn't decide what career I wanted, my father's question surely opened my eyes.

IT WAS MORE THAN
JUST LEARNING ENGLISH

My father's question came at a time when the nation was gradually turning away from the radical ideology, and this was surely not a coincidence. As a parent, as well as an experienced politician, he clearly saw this political trend. The school system began to emphasize learning skills again, rather than political indoctrination. However, there were still few incentives to study. Many of us felt that working hard in school was useless because it would lead nowhere. The argument seemed true if we looked at the jobs and career patterns available to most people. My sister, for example, was a straight A student, but this did not prevent her from being sent to the countryside. Everybody in her class had to leave the city and resettle in the countryside. Later, a more flexible policy was developed. The youngest child in a family was allowed to stay in the city to provide domestic care for the parents. Even though this policy was better and more humane, it certainly did not motivate students to work harder at school.

If we look at income distribution it appears to be even more absurd. Having an education would contribute negatively to one's income. Suppose a pair of twin brothers graduated from high school in the city during 1950s or early 1960s. One of them went to college, and the other started to work, as the government provided full employment at the time. By 1970s, the latter would most likely earn more than the former. This salary system really did not provide any incentives for high school graduates in the city to pursue a higher education.

At our school, leaders really tried hard to encourage students to study. For example, they invited graduates who had done well in school and had found their learning relevant and helpful to give speeches. Their stories were posted on campus to help inspire the current students. It did work to some extent. Compared with students at other schools in the city, we were notably more enthusiastic.

The previous emphasis on indoctrination rather than skills had resulted in a growing number of students with lower and lower grades. Even though some of them were better motivated now, they definitely needed extra help to catch up. One way we tried to help them was to organize self-help tutoring teams. One academically stronger student was paired with a weaker one. In our math course, the teacher even said that each unit in the textbook was relatively independent, and that those who were behind previously could still have a chance to learn the material well.

Incentives, however, came more often from family than from school. Parents were more concerned about their children's learning than the school administration. Even during those years when the radical policy forced the school to focus on political conformity instead of learning, many parents never stopped urging their children to learn basic skills. For example, my father had always kept an eye on my activities in school. He encouraged me to participate in afterclass activities such as playing the violin and volleyball. More emphasis was given to subjects such as math and Chinese.

Although I always had As in my English class, my father soon found that what I had learned was really very limited, not more than one hundred words a semester. How could one possibly read or speak English with only a few hundred words? He decided to take the matter into his own hands. Even before I went to primary school he had taught me how to read Chinese, and before I started learning English at school he had taught me the alphabet and a few English words. Now, he began to give me extra English lessons at home. First, he wanted me to enlarge my vocabulary. Each week he taught me a dozen new words. After I learned about three hundred words, he suggested I try to read some articles and learn from context.

At the time, however, it was hard to find anything written in idiomatic English. There was only one weekly magazine published in English called *Peking Review*, but it was full of government propaganda with jargon phrases that literally made no sense at all when they were translated into English. Other than that, probably only English translations of Chairman Mao's works were available in the foreign language bookstore in Nanjing. One Sunday afternoon my father and I went to that bookstore together. He browsed there for a few minutes and didn't find anything interesting. It then occurred to him that *The Communist Manifesto* in English might serve as a good textbook for me. Although the language was a bit old-fashioned, the English was excellent and idiomatic.

Father told me that he had read the book in English when he was young. He recalled something funny and laughed. He said that he had actually learned a lot about communism through English when he was young. For that reason, he said, he should thank his English teachers, an American missionary in particular. I knew that in his time communist books were forbidden by the government. One could be put in jail or even lose one's head if detected reading them by the police. Of course, if the books were in English, few policemen could tell they were about communism. His story sounded so marvelous that I immediately liked the idea of reading *The Communist Manifesto* in English.

I had already read it in Chinese, and that helped. I started to read the English with an English-Chinese dictionary, and when I still could not understand something, I checked the Chinese version. If the English sentence structure still did not make sense to me, I waited until the weekend so Father could explain it to me. I wrote down all the new words I did not know in a tiny notebook with English words on one side of the page and the Chinese equivalents on the other. Every day I brought this notebook with me to school. During class breaks or when I was bored in class I took the notebook out and tried to memorize these words.

I soon found my English vocabulary was larger than that of some English teachers at my school. As a matter of fact, few of the teachers there could really speak English. My first teacher once told us we should write "goes," putting "es" instead of "s" after the verb. I asked her if we should do the same thing with the verb "to do" since it also ends with the letter "o." She said yes. Then I asked her if we should pronounce it as "dooz." She said: "Yes. Exactly." Apparently she had yet to learn how to pronounce that word!

Most of these teachers had only learned Russian during the 1950s and early 1960s, when China had a special relationship with the Soviet Union. After that alliance was broken, a few schools started to teach a little English. By the time I went to junior high school, English was the only foreign language taught in school although there were few teachers who could speak English.

Before I had finished reading the first section of *The Communist Manifesto*, an epoch-making event occurred and my father found something even better for me to read. After Henry Kissinger's secret trip to Beijing, it was announced that the president of the United States, Richard Nixon, was going to visit China. In February 1972, the Sino-U.S. communiqué was signed by President Nixon and Premier Zhou Enlai in Shanghai. My father noticed in the Chinese newspaper that the document was written in both Chinese and English. He thought this would be good English reading for me, because it would have to be in excellent modern English, and having it side by side with the Chinese version would also be a great help. So, for weeks we waited for the sale of the English version at our city's foreign languages bookstore. When we finally got a copy, my father even took the trouble to make a paper cover to protect it from being worn too quickly.

After Nixon's visit, there was a growing enthusiasm for learning English throughout the country. One day my English teacher told me that our school district was going to hold a competition of English recitation and I had been picked to join a few others to represent our school. I was very excited because I knew how good my English was compared with that of others and that I had a good chance of winning the championship. In preparing for the contest, I had to decide what to recite. My textbook seemed to be too easy and wouldn't be able to show my real strengths. On the other hand, there were political restrictions, and if I chose a poem originally written in English, for example, I might be criticized for attempting to spread capitalist ideas. After some thought I chose to recite an article by Chairman Mao entitled "In Memory of Dr. Norman Bethune." There couldn't be anything more acceptable than reciting an article by Chairman Mao, although my purpose was to show the real strength of my English.

Dr. Bethune was a Canadian surgeon and a member of the Canadian Communist Party. He came to China during World War II to assist the Chinese Communist army in resisting the Japanese invasion. Unfortunately, he became infected with a blood disease through accidental blood contact with one of his patients and died in China. At his memorial ceremony, Chairman Mao delivered a speech exalting his internationalism and altruism. During the Cultural Revolution, this speech and two other articles by Mao were very popular. Almost every Chinese between seven and seventy, educated or illiterate, could recite them fluently. The radicals in power stated that these articles represented the fundamentals of Mao's thoughts. Not only were these articles translated into English, but phonograph records were made with native English speakers reading them. This helped me a lot. I listened to the record again and again, until I could imitate it almost perfectly.

As I expected, most candidates at the contest could only recite a few passages of very simple English sentences from our textbooks, such as introducing oneself and one's family. When it was my turn, I recited the five-page article with an almost pure British accent. The audience was amazed, and I easily won the championship.

For a whole year, my school placed my certificate of award in a showcase on campus. This honor not only reinforced my interest in English but further motivated me to excel in general. I also discovered something in the article very different from the often interpreted theme of altruism. I found that, in the first place, Dr. Bethune was a well-educated professional and specialist. It was his knowledge and skills that made him stand out. Without them, he would not have been able to make such a great contribution to the Chinese. The moral I drew from this story was that a man had to prepare and equip himself before he could really help others.

As learning English became fashionable, other changes came to the country. A few months after China regained its seat in the United Nations in October 1971, an English textbook entitled *English 900* published by Macmillan was introduced into China. The book sold well, and of course my father bought me a copy. Months later the Voice of America began to use this book to teach English in its Chinese-language broadcasts. Although it was prohibited to tune in to foreign radio broadcasts at the time, thousands of English-learners in China became loyal listeners. My father found out what I was doing, but he didn't stop me. He just asked me to be very careful, and not to turn the radio too loud. Occasionally I would even listen to VOA's news broadcasts in Chinese that followed the English program. When I heard some interesting news related to China, I would tell my father and he seemed to be interested, too. Now it was more than just learning English. The society was gradually reopening to the outside world.

A TELEVISION CREW FROM HAWAII

Since the Communist takeover in 1949, the geography taught at school was dominated by the official line, just like all other subjects taught at school. From the 1950s on, this line basically divided the world into three parts: the socialist bloc, the capitalist bloc, and the rest of the world. The socialist bloc included the Soviet Union, China, the Eastern European countries, and a few countries in Asia. The capitalist bloc included the United States, other European countries, Australia, and New Zealand, as well as Japan. The third bloc included all the poor countries in Africa, Latin America, the Middle East, and Asia, such as India. This line didn't change until 1974 when Chairman Mao reassessed global politics and redivided the world into superpowers, developed countries, and developing countries.

When my sister started primary school in the 1950s, the children were taught to believe that two-thirds of the people in the world lived in poverty and had miserable lives. This included the great majorities of the people living in the capitalist bloc and the third bloc of the poor countries. Only the people in the socialist bloc lived a happy life. When I entered primary school in the mid-1960s, China had broken with the Soviet Union and all the Eastern European countries except Albania. We were taught to believe that even more people now lived unhappily because the Soviet bloc was no longer socialist.

During the Cultural Revolution, China became further isolated from the rest of the world, because it distanced itself from any countries close to either the Soviet Union or the capitalist bloc. Almost anything associated with a foreign country became a stigma. Those who had relatives living in other countries tried to deny the fact in order to stay out of trouble. By 1970, the only foreign leader welcomed at Beijing and thus really well known to every household in China was Sihanouk of Cambodia.

This situation changed quite dramatically after 1971. As a teenager, I was often thrilled to see dancers and singers from other socialist countries such as Albania, Romania, and North Korea. People talked a lot about their different hair and dress styles, and the word "foreign" began to have positive connotations again, especially after Nixon's visit in 1972.

The status of the three blocs also changed dramatically in the popular mind in the following years. The capitalist bloc now became the most valued and envied. It was referred to as the West, although it included countries such as Japan and Australia. The Soviet bloc remained the second, and the rest of the world was still "the poor and the backward," and no one yearned to imitate the life of those countries.

Foreign political leaders, businessmen, and tourists often found themselves surrounded by huge crowds of curious Chinese on the street. Many of the visitors reported it made them feel like pandas in a zoo. Almost every other week we had a delegation from a foreign country visiting our school. America was no longer merely a distant country on the map when we had a Hawaiian television crew on our campus. We were told that this was the first American television crew on its own, not accompanying politicians, to visit China. The Chinese government was very eager to use this as a vehicle to show the Western world how the new China looked. Both the provincial and the municipal government sent officials to accompany this group to our school.

During the morning break I was standing on the playground when the group came out of the principal's office to begin its tour of our campus. At that moment they realized that it would be helpful if someone could help them carry and move the cables connecting their television camera to their television van. A teacher came and asked me to give them a hand. I was more than happy to do so. In those days anything associated with foreigners had an aura of mystery and became a source of pride. I was excited as I dirtied my hands with the cables.

An hour later our English teacher approached me with a mysterious smile. He came with another kid to replace me in my job of holding cables, and told me there was another great task awaiting for me. The Americans wanted to have a short conversation in English with some students later in the afternoon. I had been selected along with a girl from the grade above me.

We skipped our classes and prepared seriously for the occasion in our teacher's office. We tried to guess what questions we would be asked and how we should answer them. In fact, we had hardly learned to speak anything conversational, because our textbooks contained only political slogans or Chairman Mao's quotations. We felt embarrassed and ill equipped.

Usually I went home for lunch. That day I stayed to prepare for this important event. I asked a boy from the school who was my neighbor to bring me my *English 900*. I knew it would be much more helpful than our school textbooks. When he came back with the book I wanted, he surprised me by handing me a handkerchief and a brief note from my father, who happened to be at home that day. I opened his note, which read: "Be confident and prepare well." Father knew I would often perspire a lot under pressure or stress. So he sent me a handkerchief, in case I hadn't brought one with me to school in the morning.

Around 4:00 p.m. there was a knock at our door. I knew the critical moment had come. We were led into the reception room for distinguished visitors. As I entered the room I noticed that all the window shades were down and the room was dark. More than two dozen people sat along the walls, most of whom I had never seen before. They must be either government officials or security persons.

In the center of the room there was a huge rectangular table covered by a white tablecloth and some fresh flowers. We were asked to sit down at one corner of the table. A television camera was set up at the other end. One smiling American sat opposite us. I noticed a tiny microphone, only half the size of my little finger, pinned to the dangling part of the white tablecloth. I was amazed at its small size; it brought to mind all the spy stories I had heard about the Soviet Union and the United States. That made me even more nervous, and my palms were all wet.

As soon as we sat down, someone turned the spotlight on. I could hardly see any one but the American sitting across from me. He was a middle-aged man, a little fat, and bald. He started by asking the girl: "What's your name?"

The girl didn't get it. Maybe she was too nervous. Maybe it was because he had a strong American accent. Instead of "what" he said "hwat." Also, he used "what's" instead of "what is." So the sounds we heard became "Hwats your name?" After a little pause he asked the same question again. This time he was nodding at me instead of the girl. I felt I understood him, and began to respond.

From then on, he always asked me first, and then repeated the question to the girl. So I was actually responsible for interpreting his questions. The whole conversation did not last more than twenty minutes, but the school authorities were very pleased. Afterwards, they were praised several times by various government officials for the high quality of English teaching at our school. However, I knew in my heart that my English would never have been so good without my father's help.

"NINE-POUND GRANNY"

The more English I learned from my father, the more disappointed I felt about my school education, because I realized that his school had taught much more than ours did. For example, in his junior high school, his English textbook included "Thirty Tales from Shakespeare," which sounded far more advanced than my textbook. Father surprised me even more when he told me that in some of the high schools in his days all subjects except Chinese were taught in English.

I knew he once had an American missionary teacher. At first I thought this was why his English was so good. I assumed that students in other schools that did not have American missionaries would not have comparable English proficiency. One of his stories showed me I was wrong about this.

Early one summer he transferred to a school in a different city. The new school required a placement test for each subject. Since his old school had an American missionary and the new one didn't, he thought he wouldn't need to worry about the English placement test at all. He reviewed all the other subjects except English, and passed them all but English. It turned out that the missionary had never emphasized grammar. As a result, my father had to buy a multivolume English grammar book and study the whole summer before he could pass his English placement test.

These stories made me aware of the poor quality of education my generation was receiving. I recalled that at primary school there had been a semester in which almost all classes were canceled and replaced by political indoctrination. By fifth grade, quite a few of my classmates could not even read. Even my sister often scoffed at me, for she had learned twice as much at her school as I did at mine.

Her college did not really offer a college education. In fact, among the forty-five students in her class, she was the only high school graduate. Some had attended high school but never finished before they were sent to the countryside to work with the peasants. Others had not even entered high school. One had merely finished the fourth grade. A political process put them together as a college class.

They stayed in college for two years instead of four, due to the radical policy. The radicals as well as Mao himself seemed to be very skeptical about intellectuals. They believed that the more knowledge one had, the more conservative or counterrevolutionary one became. They were afraid the students would be influenced by their conservative teachers if they stayed in college longer. In such a political environment, college students only learned the bare minimum. My sister had classes for about three months during her two years in college. The rest of the time was occupied by political and other nonacademic activities. No wonder society scoffed at these college graduates as mere primary school pupils.

By 1972, a more pragmatic policy was introduced by Premier Zhou, who was now in charge of the daily operation of the central government after the sudden and mysterious death of Marshal Lin. Our textbooks were revised with more advanced materials. More classroom time was spent on learning and less on brainwashing. Tests and examinations were given far more often. Sometimes we had three tests a day in different subjects. Once we even had citywide standard exams on each of the six major subjects: politics, Chinese, math, physics, chemistry, and English. Although we had much more homework to do than before, we preferred studying to brainwashing.

However, the change didn't last long. Another radical group, headed by Mao's wife, Jiang Qing, soon came to power. They argued that the new policy was intended to turn the clock back to the time before the Cultural Revolution. Mao seemed to be hypersensitive about this, for it was he who had launched the Cultural Revolution and he did not want to see the country return to its former ways. By the end of 1972, Mao gave his open support to his wife and other radicals by bluntly announcing that Marshal Lin had never been a radical but a conservative. The implication was that all radical policies should be carried on and all the moderate changes should be stopped.

The radicals made a shrewd political joke about the people who did not like the radical changes brought by the Cultural Revolution. They said that the people who saw deterioration instead of progress were like a stubborn old granny who could not tolerate anything new and cherished her good old days. The granny thought everything was best in her time, had deteriorated in her daughter's time, and became even worse when her granddaughter was born. "Look," the old granny said, "When I was born, I weighed nine pounds; when my daughter was born, she weighed eight pounds; now when her daughter was born, the poor baby only weighed seven pounds. It has really gone from bad to worse."

I was not an old granny, but I could share her proverbial view in terms of quality of education. I often heard people jokingly call themselves the "nine-pound grannies," and that phrase alone revealed their political attitudes. This was also the time when I began to see larger problems in the society beyond our education. Before, I had never challenged the national leaders and their leadership. When I visited my parents at their labor camps I often used a quote of Mao: "Believe in the people and believe in the Party. Every problem will be solved eventually." Now I began to think about what I was saying. Apparently I heard two different voices from the top leaders. Whom should I listen to and whom should I believe and trust?

It was the first time since the Communist takeover that people were so openly exposed to the great differences among the top Communist leaders in terms of policy, values, and even ideology. It was also a political awakening, and people began to hold their own opinions. It was definitely different from the days when my sister was in high school and everybody was so eager to conform. Only in that sense, did I disagree with the "nine-pound granny"; instead of deterioration, I saw progress.

MOTHER COMES HOME

My father stopped sending me to see my mother at her labor camp after the tall fat man's unpleasant visit to my school. I knew he was afraid of the negative consequences for me at school. All communication between Mom and the rest of the family now was through her roommate, Ms. Hu. When her husband went to see her, the kindhearted woman asked him to bring in things my mother needed on his next trip. Through him we not only sent things to my mother but also learned how she was doing.

Hu's husband was a lecturer at Nanjing University and lived in our new neighborhood. They had a three-year-old daughter. From my own experience I knew how hard it was for her to be separated from her mother. When people like my parents were detained in the Cultural Revolution, they were already middle-aged and their children were mostly teenagers. I was an exception because I was born very late. But the people who were detained now were mostly in their thirties. Their children, like Hu's daughter, were often toddlers.

These people were detained for the alleged memberships in the so-called antirevolutionary May 16th organization. In our province, the range of the persecution was particularly wide; while more than two million people were accused in the whole nation, in our province alone, about half a million people were involved. General Xu was mainly responsible for this. He was the governor of our province, as well as the commissar of the Military Regional Headquarters in Nanjing, one of eight powerful military forces in the nation. His support was critical in

Mao's effort to oust Marshal Lin, and many people viewed him as a hero in the struggle with the radicals. While his enthusiasm in eliminating the radical influence seemed to be justifiable, most victims of the current campaign were really innocent people like my mother and her roommate. With such an imbalance of power, even good intentions could result in a disaster.

Some episodes of this persecution were appalling. Once my mother was asked to attend a meeting, the purpose of which was to put more pressure on people so that they would confess their memberships in the May 16th organization. As usual, those who confessed were promised leniency, while severe punishment was meted out to those who denied wrongdoing. All the people in the labor camp were supposed to come. It was an opportunity for my mother to see my father. She looked around for him, but could not see him anywhere. Maybe he was sick, she thought. Her thoughts were interrupted by an announcement that someone was guilty of being an "active antirevolutionary," a capital offense at the time. The next thing my mother heard was that the person was sentenced to death and would be executed right away. She felt a chill run down her spine, and instinctively turned to look for my father again. She was afraid she might hear my father's name on the loud speaker. Fortunately, she didn't. The following day she heard that he was sick, and his sickness was good news.

As the number of victims of this persecution grew, society at large finally began to show some sympathy. When the persecution was over and the detained were released, each received an official statement. "While under the circumstances it was reasonable to detain you and investigate your case, we now find no solid evidence against you. You are thereby released with no prosecution." Both the persecutors and the persecuted were declared not guilty, and the case was closed without a real ending and justice was never done. What is more, the government or the Communist authority was never blamed.

Around the Chinese New Year of 1973, my mother was allowed to come home every other weekend, just like Father and others in the labor camp. We began to have a normal family life again. However, a year and a half in detention put her in a terrible shape physically. Her old heart disease worsened, and she had problems with her circulation. Her lips looked as purple as blueberries, and she was extremely weak. Yet, when she went to see Dr. Ma, one of the three doctors who had rescued her and me at my birth, he felt it was a miracle that she had survived. As a Western-style doctor, he felt he could do nothing more, but he suggested that it might be worthwhile to try some traditional Chinese medicine. He had just started to study Chinese medicine himself.

She tried Chinese medicine prescribed by several doctors. The herbs did strengthen her body, but the symptoms of her heart disease did not go away. We started to search for a doctor who knew both Western and Chinese medicine. It was then that we came to know Dr. Gu, who was recommended by some old friends who used to teach at Nanjing Agricultural University when my father had been in charge in the early 1950s.

Unlike Western pills, Chinese medicine is very hard to ingest. Instead of preprocessed small pills, often it is a combination of different dried plants, sometimes even insects. Boiled in water for hours, the medicine finally becomes a dark, thick, and extremely bitter soup. I always found it hard to drink, but Mother was so determined that she took it twice a day for a whole year, until the symptoms of her heart disease disappeared. When she saw Dr. Ma again, he could not believe his eyes. She had red lips again, just like a young, healthy woman.

The mental recovery, however, took longer. Her verbal response had become much slower, and she talked little with others. Even though we lived with five other families in one house like an extended family, she felt as if she were a stranger. To help my mother adjust to a normal family life, Father tried to socialize with others and let her play the role of a hostess. The two families we often socialized with at the time were both former faculty members at the Nanjing Agricultural University. Father suggested that we meet every month at the home of one of the three families, with each couple being host in turn. So about every three months we gave a small party, and we always invited Dr. Gu. Perhaps because all the families had some kind of Western education, each liked to cook some Western dishes to create an atmosphere. My two favorite dishes were fried bananas, and potato salad with shrimp, ham, green beans, and tomatoes.

From Father I learned that these parties were called "cocktail parties," and I also learned more about Western customs and eating habits. The sources of his stories included his dinners in European and American restaurants in Shanghai before the Communist takeover and banquets in Nanjing by or for the Russians when the Soviet Union was helping China develop its economy. Those stories often made my mouth water, and made me love the Western-style parties at our home even more. Surrounded by old friends and engaging in free and intimate conversations, my mother gradually felt comfortable again and our house once more had a homelike atmosphere.

THOUSANDS OF MILES FOR NOTHING

By 1973, the radicals headed by Mao's wife became very unpopular. This was particularly true for city residents, who were better informed than peasants in the countryside. It was even more so among the well-educated people in the city. Premier Zhou Enlai began to enjoy more popularity. Mao was no longer viewed as a demigod who never made errors. At home, my father even called him "the old man" in English, with a hardly disguised discontent and grudge in his tone. Of course, he always reminded me not to use this phrase in public. Indeed, to any sober-minded person, Mao's effort of launching the so-called Cultural Revolution seemed to be both fruitless and ridiculous. In March 1973, Mao appointed Deng Xiaoping as one of the vice premiers. Earlier in the Cultural Revolution, Deng had been labeled as the Number Two public enemy in China and purged from the Communist Party. Within five years the same hand that had pushed him down raised him up again.

Deng's comeback undoubtedly caused uneasiness and confusion. To those who had closely followed the Party line and had been promoted to important official positions in recent years, this looked ominous for their own political future. As for us, the younger generation, we all remembered those caricatures we had made ridiculing Liu Shaoqi and Deng Xiaoping. Now, one of the most ridiculed suddenly returned to great influence and power.

The political struggle between radicals and moderates within the Party was an open secret. Deng's comeback was only a part of it. Officially, the Party never admitted this inner struggle, but most people knew who was on which side. The moderates were reinforced by a growing number of former government officials who were now reassigned to positions, just like Deng. Those who had not yet been reassigned were allowed to leave the labor camps and wait for such appointments at home. Such was the case with my parents.

The new political development was popular. People had had enough of the radicals and their policies, and now they definitely wanted a change. Repositioning former officials seemed to give a signal that the Cultural Revolution was over and that the country was back to normal. People greatly resented the current officials, for they enjoyed much greater privileges than their former counterparts, so people welcomed the old folks back. It was human nature to forget, if not to forgive. The irony of a revolution based on class struggle was that the new ruling class could be much more privileged than the old one.

I thought my parents would soon return to their old positions, but that didn't happen. Their cases were complicated because they had worked as underground Communists. During the Cultural Revolution, all underground Communists were suspected of actually having been moles inside the Communist Party. It was extremely difficult for them to prove their innocence. This may sound very strange to a Westerner accustomed to the concept of presumed innocence. In China, very often it was just the opposite. Once charged you were presumed guilty until proved innocent.

In my father's case, a special investigation team had been organized. The team even had a secret code: "101," and the members traveled thousands of miles throughout China talking to everyone they could identify as being related to him. These included fellow Communists in the underground, former classmates, neighbors, relatives, friends, and acquaintances. The team even visited prisoners who had formerly worked for the Nationalist government or the Japanese puppet government to check if they knew anything about my father. However, the miles of traveling yielded nothing.

Throughout the country, thousands of these investigation teams spent an enormous amount of public money traveling millions of miles and came back with nothing. Hundreds of investigators came to my father for information about other underground Communists. Most investigators were extremely biased, and when my father told them the truth they simply would not listen to him. They only wanted him to testify against his former colleagues. They rejected what he wrote and asked him to write it again. But no matter how he revised it, he could not satisfy them, because they couldn't get what they wanted. They even threatened to punish him for not cooperating.

Occasionally, there were people who eventually yielded to such threats. But I often heard Father encourage my mother not to give in to such pressure. He felt it was his responsibility to protect these underground Communists, many of whom he recruited into the Party in the 1930s and 1940s. They had actually put their lives in danger to join the Communist Revolution, and my father felt somewhat responsible for that. Now it was particularly painful for him to see that those active in the Revolution were hurt by it in the end. Was he wrong in the first place when he had convinced them to join the Revolution? He could hardly answer that question. However, he was determined not to make their lives harder again this time.

His toughness paid off as cases were closed due to his truthful testimony and many people were assigned to new positions in the government. Even though my parents didn't get anything, they were genuinely glad to see so many of their old colleagues treated justly.

"WE, THE TRUE MARXISTS . . ."

The inner Party struggle intensified after Deng's political comeback in 1973, because Deng often fought against the radicals more vigorously than Zhou Enlai. This sometimes backfired, and it certainly did on the issue of school education. Deng emphasized learning and skills acquisition, but the radicals argued for focusing on indoctrination.

Deng's position was more popular. In fact, the traditional culture had always emphasized and even glorified education. Traditionally, schools were few and most children could not go to school. Education was almost the only vehicle of upward social mobility. For thousands of years, passing an extremely difficult academic examination was the only channel to becoming a government official, whose social and economic status was the highest among all the walks of life in China.

There were numerous stories of poor boys becoming rich and powerful this way. It was not only rich families who cared about their children's education; poor parents also tried hard to give their children a chance to be educated. This effort often meant an incredibly heavy financial burden for poor families. In return, such parents would be especially disappointed and upset to see their children fail in school. Often they would beat a child to study harder. Under the pressure, some children even committed suicide.

Unfortunately, one such incident occurred in 1973. A girl of my age in a small village in an inland province failed her English tests several times and wanted to give up studying English. Neither the school nor the parents would let her. She killed herself, leaving behind this little poem:

> I am a Chinese.
> Why should I learn English?
> Without knowing the ABC,
> I can still operate a machine.

The news made me sad, and I empathized with the poor girl. This tragedy, however, was manipulated by the radicals, who lost no time in citing this as an example of how Deng's policy hurt children. They knew how to irritate Mao by claiming Deng was going to roll back and wipe out all the achievements of the Cultural Revolution that were supposed to end the Chinese cultural tradition. With Mao's approval, the radicals soon launched a new political campaign called "Condemning Marshal Lin and Confucius." The name appeared odd, but the goal was clear. The real target was neither of the two men, who had thousands of years separating them, but Premier Zhou Enlai and other moderates.

The political wind once again turned left in 1974. This change was quickly reflected at my school. Currently, my class teacher was a middle-aged woman, and she went out of her way to follow the new trend. The course she taught was politics, the one I hated the most. It required the students to memorize long excerpts, sometimes as much as a thousand words, from the documents of the Communist Party. Once I decided not to bother to memorize them, and I only scored 59 in the exam as a result.

On a Sunday afternoon, this woman and another teacher visited my downstairs neighbor, Mr. Zhang's wife, who was also a teacher at our school and had been sick for months. Afterwards, they came upstairs, and that surprised me a little, for I rarely talked to my teacher in school. My father received them politely in our tiny sitting room, formerly the bathroom of the house now shared by six families. After exchanging greetings, the woman told my father that she was concerned that I might become a "white professional." It was a jargon used by the radicals. They argued that a person should be both willing to do and capable of doing what the Party asked him to do. This was called a "red professional." The least desirable was a capable person who did not follow the Party line, a "white professional." The woman was warning my father that I was interested in learning skills in school, but not interested in the indoctrination instruction.

My father had never bought the radical argument, and he actually approved of my behavior in school and encouraged me to focus on learning. He did not like this woman's talk at all. In fact, he became really upset when he learned from our neighbor that the woman's husband had been an underground Communist. He felt they should never follow the radicals. The nation was still in disarray because of the Cultural Revolution. People had hoped that the moderates could set the country on the right track again. Now the radicals had made a slight comeback, and people without integrity were starting to travel along with the radicals.

Fortunately, we didn't have anyone like that within the family circle. This was important, because in those days one could only speak freely within a trusted circle. If a member became a traitor, everyone else could be put in jail. For the same reason, inner-circle conversations could easily get one excited. I still vividly remember such an occasion when my third uncle's daughter, Cousin Ping, and her husband joined us in such a conversation. Ping's husband was a young aeronautic engineer. Even though it was winter time and the room was freezing cold, he perspired heavily because of his excitement.

He said that the problem of China was not its Marxist system, but rather the opposite: the system was not truly Marxist. We all agreed. Like many Chinese at the time, we all believed that the radicals were traitors to Marxism and that even Mao's leadership was hardly Marxist. Mao was certainly responsible for the disastrous Cultural Revolution. We were not sure if he had been fooled by the radicals or if he was truly responsible. No matter which, we felt that we could not hope that he would be able to get the country out of trouble. The leaders we could trust and had hope for were Premier Zhou and Deng Xiaoping. We even talked about other Communist leaders in history. We believed that Engels had helped Marx develop his theory, but Stalin destroyed the system which Lenin had established. If Lenin had lived longer and Mao had died earlier, both countries might be better off, we thought.

The door was shut tightly, and voices were kept low. The atmosphere in the room reminded me of the clandestine meetings my parents had as underground Communists. Joining such a secret conversation made me feel grown-up and mature. With a dramatic gesture, Ping's husband said resolutely, "We, the true Marxists here in this room, have to fight the radicals and rescue this nation!" What he meant by a "true Marxist" was merely a patriot with some integrity. After decades of Communist rule, the best words left to describe a good, honest man was to claim him a "true Marxist." I really didn't know that much about Marxism, but I definitely felt it was my mission, too, to rescue my nation from the radicals.

MY SISTER'S LONG JOURNEY

My sister married in the summer of 1974. It was, of course, a big event for my family. She and her fiancé had gone to the same high school and they had known each other for more than a decade. Their relationship had undergone quite a strenuous test. The political storm of the Cultural Revolution not only destroyed all social institutions but also subdued and distorted some basic human instincts such as love. Millions of Red Guards were trained to devote their love wholly to their great leader, Chairman Mao. For a short period of time, asceticism prevailed in China, almost as strongly as in medieval Europe or Victorian England.

By 1969, the ice of asceticism gradually melted, and my sister and her boyfriend began dating openly, although their fondness for each other had begun much earlier. At the time, her boyfriend was in the army, based in a neighboring province to the north, Shandong. My sister worked in the countryside for two years and then enrolled in college for two years. During those four years they could only afford to see each other once a year. Also, following the traditional Chinese culture that forbade sex before marriage, they kept a platonic relationship mainly through correspondence, unlike some other former Red Guards who lived promiscuously.

In January 1973, my sister graduated from college and began working as a teaching assistant in the Department of Chinese Language and Literature at the same college. She wanted to get married. However, my father wanted her to wait until the charges against him were cleared, so that she wouldn't have a tainted family name when she married. In his judgment, the political wind in China would soon turn in his favor. Well, he was only partially right. Although Deng returned to power within two months, as did many others, his turn didn't come for four more years. My sister didn't wait that long.

The uncleared charges against my parents not only delayed my sister's marriage, but they also had a negative impact on her career. She was an extremely hardworking person, and wherever she worked she found opportunities for advancement. However, her supervisors always hesitated because of her family background, and often postponed promotions. For example, the college wanted to offer her a position in charge of Student Affairs, but dared not to do so unless my father's case was officially closed and his membership in the Communist Party renewed. Although my mother had renewed hers, my father didn't get his membership renewed until June 1974. Only then could my sister get the job.

Also during that summer, my sister's fiancé was selected by his army unit to attend the Army Academy in Nanjing. Once he became a student, he would not be allowed to marry until graduation, so he wanted to get married before he registered. This time my father had no objections, and the wedding was set for the first of August. I was sixteen then, and learned a lot about weddings and marriage from this event.

For example, the new couple and their families were supposed to give out candy, both during and after the wedding. The minimum, according to the custom at the time, was a package of eight candies. Those who were closer to the family expected to get more, sometimes as much as a pound. Because our family had so many relatives, friends, and acquaintances, my mother had to buy 250 pounds of candy. The first thing we did in preparing for the wedding was to package these wrapped hard sweets and chewy candies.

Old customs came back, surviving the Cultural Revolution when people were not even supposed to dream about better food, more colorful clothes, or cozier housing. Now wedding ceremonies became big events in people's life again. The climax was the wedding banquet at a restaurant. The dinner usually had twelve courses, and tables had to be reserved. Each large round table could serve twelve to fifteen people. My parents reserved five tables and invited over sixty guests, since we had so many relatives and friends. All of my mother's relatives living in Nanjing came to the wedding, and this was the first time I had seen them all at one place since my grandpa's funeral.

Apparently the wedding served another function. It was a public announcement of our restored family name. In addition to the usual wedding congratulations for my sister and her husband, everybody coming to the wedding also congratulated my parents for their recent renewed memberships in the Communist Party. They all wished that my parents, especially my father, would soon be restored to their former government positions. My father seemed to have a good reason to have postponed the wedding. I could easily imagine how gloomy it would have been if it had been held before our family name was restored.

In fact, there was another banquet held for my sister's wedding in the city of Nantong. It was a smaller city on the other bank of the Yangtze River, where my sister's in-laws lived. Her father-in-law was one of the few survivors who had completed the Long March of the Red Army in the 1930s. Like my parents, this was another couple who had devoted their early lives to the Communist Revolution and had made great contributions to the Communist victory.

However, they came from a totally different background. Theirs involved generations of poor landless peasants. Neither of them had any education before they joined the Communist movement. The father was a shepherd, recruited at age of thirteen, when the Communist Red Army established its first military base in the mountains of Jiangxi Province in 1927. The army taught him how to read. He followed the army in its Long March, probably the longest military retreat in human history. When the army reestablished its headquarters in a small town named Yanan in northwestern China, he found himself in charge of the medical team of the No. 359 Brigade, a famous Communist unit at the time. At their new base he won the heart of a local peasant girl who was ten years younger. Of course, the girl was illiterate, and only learned how to read after she married him and joined the army.

In contrast, both my parents had very good educations before they joined the Communist movement. It was their educated heads, instead of empty stomachs, that drove them to Communism. By conventional wisdom, they should probably not have been involved at all. After all, my father's father was a banker and my mother's great-grandfather was one of the largest textile manufacturers in Nanjing, who had once owned a big house of over forty bedrooms. It was really amazing how the early Communist movement had attracted people from such diverse backgrounds.

My sister's in-laws did not live in Nanjing, and this created a housing problem. Most new couples could not get a housing unit from the government. They had to live with one or the other's parents for a while, usually the husband's. In my sister's case, my parents had to provide housing.

Because housing was so tight, a bedroom in the parents' house was usually the only private place for a new couple. Furnishing the room became an important issue in the wedding plan. Furniture was very expensive, and a whole set of furniture for a bedroom usually cost more than two years' salary. In most areas it was customary for the man or his parents to provide the furniture. This was quite a financial burden, and many single men could not afford it and couldn't get married at all.

On the other hand, the desire for a better material life was awakening, and young women wanted more and more pieces of furniture for their wedding. They even counted their furniture by the number of legs: four legs for the bed, four legs for the dresser, four legs for a wardrobe, and so on. There was often much gossip of whether a girl received 16 or 24, or even 32 legs.

My sister's wedding was planned in a hurry. There wasn't time to prepare furniture. Her in-laws promised to purchase four pieces of furniture after the wedding. For the moment, they had to borrow my parents' old furniture to fill my bedroom, which they temporarily used as their room. Neither my sister nor my parents cared that much about the furniture. To them, it was silly and philistine to count the number of legs in the furniture. With or without the furniture, my father wanted to thank my sister's in-laws for their longtime support of the relationship while our family still had a tarnished name. To my father, their trust and respect was more than any number of legs of furniture they could provide.

Because my sister still worked in Anhui, she and her husband still had to live separately after their marriage. Even with my parents' financial support, my sister could only come home about once a month. Her husband would join her then at our home. When they came, I had to move to my grandma's bedroom and let them have my room. After I moved back to my room when they had left, I would occasionally find some condoms under my bed. Family planning was already enforced in China then, although each couple was still allowed to have two children. For many couples, especially those living in the cities, this was not a problem. For economic reasons and concerns about their children's future, many elected to have only one or two children. Among many government policies enforced in China, family planning was never the worst nor the most unpopular one, although it seemed to have received the most attention in the West for many years. After I came to the United States in 1987 I often received such unexpected sympathy: "I don't blame you for coming here, because your government doesn't allow you to have children." I often felt awkward and didn't know how to respond to such well-meaning but ignorant sentiments. When primary concerns in life such as food and housing were barely taken care of, the right to have more children was hardly a priority. A stable marriage was often an achievement in itself.

"GOOD WILL BE REWARDED WITH GOOD, AND EVIL WITH EVIL"

My father was now relieved of all the physical labor at the labor camp, and simply waited at home for his new assignment. It was a big change in his life. For years, he had been doing tasks that required extraordinary physical strength, such as carrying as much as 250 pounds of human excrement at a time with another person, or lifting a 200-pound sack of rice by himself. Fortunately, he never hurt his back or injured himself otherwise. He had a strong body, for he had had good physical training in high school and college, and continued to do exercises every day. At the age of sixty, he was physically stronger than I was at sixteen. In the summer, I was often ashamed to go out with him in shorts and a T-shirt, for I looked pathetically pale and weak.

Having time on his hands, Father started doing many different things. Of course, he spent more time with the family, and made even more friends than before. He read a lot, and did a few odd jobs fixing this and that in the house. He seemed to enjoy this kind of manual work, and, in fact, he was the only person capable of house maintenance in our family.

However, the most unusual thing he did at the time was to help repair and restore an old printing press in Nanjing that specialized in printing Buddhist scriptures. The printing press had been built by a local Buddhist named Yang at the beginning of the century. During the first half of the century, the press reprinted various rare Buddhist classics that otherwise would have been lost.

Like many other religious establishments in China, this one was kept intact until the Cultural Revolution. When the Communists took over China in 1949, for political reasons they preserved many temples and churches, whether they were Buddhist, Taoist, Islamic, Protestant, or Catholic. The idea was to appeal to more people and encourage their support of the new government. These sites were also considered a part of our culture, and those places often became tourist sites and business attractions. For years, people could still openly admit their religious beliefs and have places to go for religious practice.

For example, there was a Buddhist temple near the residential compound where we first lived. It was just a few yards from the wall gate my father had built, which helped to bring more visitors. The temple was on the top of a hill, an excellent spot for seeing the sunrise. Appropriately it was named the "Cock Crow Temple." Dozens of Buddhist nuns lived there, and their vegetarian restaurant was very popular, especially among professors and students, who often had breakfast or afternoon tea there while chatting and enjoying a beautiful sunrise or sunset.

I remember being taken there by my parents or other relatives as a child. The last time I was there was on a Buddhist holiday just a couple of months before the Cultural Revolution. I was only eight years old. During an evening walk Father took me there. He probably already had some sense of the forthcoming political storm and its possible consequences for religion. I remember his saying that I might not see so many people there again.

That evening I was most impressed by an old woman. She had bound feet like my grandma, but she was about twice my grandma's size. With joss sticks in her hands she was climbing on her knees. There were hundreds of stone steps leading to the temple, and she was trying to climb all the way on her knees! I could not understand and asked my father. He told me it was a way to express her piety as a Buddhist. That looked quite foolish to me, but Father said I should respect her strong will.

During the Cultural Revolution, both the temple and the printing press were destroyed by the Red Guards. Five years later, even the walls of the temple were burned to the ground by an accidental fire, when the site was occupied by a small factory producing electronic components. In 1974, Premier Zhou Enlai decided to restore some Buddhist establishments so that China could claim to the rest of the world that the Communist Party was tolerant of religion. He summoned Mr. Zhao, the national leader of the Buddhist organization in China, and asked him to take on this task.

Mr. Zhao and my father had known each other for decades. They had worked closely running the refugee camps during the Japanese occupation of Shanghai in the late 1930s. I always called him Uncle Zhao as if he were my father's elder brother. On his next visit to Nanjing, I heard him and Father talk about restoring the Buddhist printing press in Nanjing.

At the time, few government officials had the courage and enthusiasm to involve themselves in restoring Buddhist establishments. Although the political wind had shifted, many still felt sensitive about religion and did not want to fall victim of another radical attack.

Uncle Zhao was glad to find supporters in Nanjing. One of them was a man named Shi who used to be in charge of religious affairs in the municipal government. Even before Uncle Zhao's visit, Shi had once come to our house soliciting my parents' support for restoring the printing press. In his conversation with my mother he said, "I know you both suffered a lot during the Cultural Revolution, and I probably should not get your husband involved. But since his support carries more weight, I came to knock on your door anyway." Before Shi finished speaking, my father entered the room. He shook Shi's hand warmly and assured him that he did the right thing for the nation. Lots of Buddhist classics needed to be preserved, Father said, not only for the sake of our generation but also for our children.

The next day, Father and Shi got on their bikes and visited the old site of the printing press, trying to estimate the damage and the cost of repair. It turned out to be not so bad, and they were very excited about their discovery. Now that they had word from the premier through Uncle Zhao, they felt even more enthusiastic. In further discussions with Uncle Zhao, Father helped him identify some key personnel in the provincial government who might be supportive. Finally, Uncle Zhao was able to mobilize enough political support to obtain funds for restoring the printing press.

Although Father was enthusiastic about preserving Buddhist culture, he was not a Buddhist. In fact, he did not believe in any kind of god, and was an atheist. This was in accordance with the orthodox Communist doctrine. The entire generation brought up in China after the Communist takeover was atheist. The powerful propaganda of the Communist government effectively reduced the number of religious believers.

However, Father thought that religious beliefs and activities should be allowed, and he didn't think they would hurt the Communist system. Instead, he felt confident that the majority of the population would remain atheist. Once I heard him comment on the Albanian Communist leader Enver Hoxha, who claimed that religion had been finally eliminated from Albania, because the Communist government there had banned it. Shaking his head, he laughed and asked: "How could things be so simple? I think the Albanian leader was only deluding himself."

Treating religion as a part of the culture, Father always told me to respect different religions. When I was little, he mostly referred me to Buddhism. As the years passed and I started to learn English, he began to tell me more about the Bible and encouraged me to read it. From him I first learned the Chinese words for Psalms, Proverbs, and Song of Solomon. When I was at college, he even gave me an English Bible as a gift. He believed there was some ideological and philosophical richness in religion that we should not ignore. To him, ignoring our rich cultural heritage was foolish.

I think we did get some strength from Buddhism during the hard times. There was a Chinese proverb originating from Buddhism: "Good will be rewarded with good, and evil with evil. It is not that there is no reward, but the time has not come yet. When the time comes, everything will have its reward, good or evil." The former foreign minister Chen Yi used to quote this proverb in many of his public speeches before the Cultural Revolution. At home, Father often imitated Chen's strong Sichuan accent and used the proverb to cheer us up. Now, seeing my parents being cleared of false charges and my sister getting a big promotion and happily married, I thought to myself: "If good will be rewarded with good, maybe that time has come."

CHAPTER 6

LETTERS THAT HELPED OTHERS

Making friends came naturally to my father and he enjoyed helping people. Now that he had more time on his hands, he made even more friends and often tried to help them. The most remarkable friendship was with a former rebel leader named Jin. This young man graduated from high school in 1964, two years before the Cultural Revolution began. Because of the limited enrollment of colleges and universities, he could not acquire a higher education. There were many young people like him in the city, and my father tried to help them by expanding a city-run teacher-training institute into a two-year community college. At the time, English teachers were urgently neeeded, because schools had just started to replace Russian with English. China broke its tie with the Soviet Union in the early 1960s and English, rather than Russian, became the foreign language of preference. The new community college started with a first class of twenty students all majoring in English, and Jin was one of them.

They were expected to be assigned teaching jobs upon their graduation. Unfortunately, when Jin was about to graduate in 1966, the Cultural Revolution began, and in the chaos none of the students received a diploma. The authorities at the college level were paralyzed, and the local government could not put the graduates on the city's payroll as promised. Frustrated and upset, Jin organized his classmates to fight for their rights. Since my father was the founder of this community college, Jin and other student representatives went to Suzhou to see him. These young people called themselves rebels and held public meetings denouncing my father as a "capitalist-roader." During the meetings they made him admit that the city government of Nanjing had promised to give them their diplomas and jobs. They even took him back to Nanjing to hold similar public meetings to gain sympathy and support.

This awkward situation made an unusual basis for friendship, but during the process my father and Jin became very good friends. Afterwards, my father wrote at least twenty letters on Jin's behalf to various officials in local government, and persistently took care of the issue until it was eventually solved ten years later when Jin became a faculty member at the community college. I often heard Jin express his gratitude to my father, and my father would smile and say: "Only by fighting can people really know each other." It was a traditional Chinese saying and could be translated as: "No discord, no concord."

Another friendship my father developed was with a couple of single women. One of them was a math teacher at my school who had once taught my class as a substitute. Her teaching fascinated the whole class because she was such a master of the subject. She amazed us by quickly developing sets of problems as she stood at the blackboard to replace the ones in our textbook. The other woman used to be a volleyball player and coach, and was a very skilled organizer of sports events at the city's Department of Sports, which my father supervised before he went to Suzhou as deputy mayor. Like many other city residents, she was forced to leave the city and relocated in the countryside during the Cultural Revolution. Now that China's door to the outside world was reopened, the city was preparing to host an increasing number of visiting sports teams from the West. The Department of Sports needed her organizing skills and wanted her back. However, it took too much bureaucratic effort to reregister her as a city resident, so the department only offered her a temporary position. Very tentatively she asked my father if he could help her reregister as a city resident and make her job permanent, knowing that now many of his colleagues were back in power in the local government. My father immediately agreed to write letters for her to some officials in her department, urging them to take the necessary steps to solve her problem.

She lived with the math teacher, and their house was only five minutes walk from ours. I often saw them walking together hand in hand. Neither of them was married, but they shared one apartment. Such a relationship was quite unusual in China and I was very curious about it. When I asked my father, he said they could just be two single women staying together, but it might be possible that they were a homosexual couple. I had never heard that word before and did not understand it. My father explained it to me this way. Unlike most people who loved a person of the opposite sex, a few people tended to choose a person of the same sex as a partner. It was rare but it did happen, and they were often not socially acceptable. He said that I might be too young to understand this, and warned me not to use the word "homosexual" casually, as it might be offensive. He then asked me whether the woman teacher was good at teaching, and I told him that our whole class loved her. "Forget what I have just said about homosexuality," he said, and dropped the topic. However, looking back today, I can't help wondering where he came by such a liberal view on homosexuality. It was such a taboo in China, and even many people of my generation had strong prejudices against this uncommon human behavior.

Early one summer morning on the traditional Chinese holiday called the Dragon-Boat Festival, my father sent me to the women's apartment. It was customary to eat special rice dumplings wrapped in reed leaves, and in my family we usually made more than one hundred. My father asked me to pack up a dozen to take to the women. He said they probably would not cook this food as most traditional families did. If we gave them some dumplings it would make it feel more like a holiday. So I did what my father asked, and was warmly welcomed at their house, although they were both a little surprised and the woman from the sports department even seemed a bit embarrassed. It was she who had asked my father to help her. It was common for people who asked for help to give gifts to the people from whom they asked help, not the other way around. Perhaps she heard that my father had always refused to accept gifts from people asking for help when he was in power, so she never tried to send him any. However, she certainly did not expect to receive a gift from him! It touched her deeply to realize how kind my father was.

With so many of his former colleagues back in power, my father's influence in the local government was increasing. Again, we began to have many visitors at home, and most of them were the people who had previously worked for him. I had seen many of them as a child. They came with the hope that my father might be able to help them move back to the city. The technical school that he had founded in the 1950s was dissolved during the Cultural Revolution, and all the faculty members were forced to leave the city. Now they often came to visit my father, hoping he could help them find jobs and city registration cards. These people usually brought local produce from the countryside that they gave to my father as gifts. At first, he tried to refuse, but such refusals were awkward because it was not practical to ask these people to take perishable foods back with them. Yet accepting gifts was against his principles, and he had to find a better way to deal with it.

Since the early days of the Communist Party, members were taught not to take things without some kind of repayment. I learned many legendary stories of this principle from my school textbooks. For example, one story was about a teenage Red Army man who had been hungry for days, hiding from Chiang Kai-shek's troops. One evening he felt his hunger was driving him crazy, and decided to steal into a peasant's field to dig up some potatoes. He left a few coins with a note which said: "Dear fellow: Because I was so hungry I took some of your potatoes without your permission. Please accept the few coins I left in your field as a compensation." He signed it "A little Red Army Man." Other stories described how the Communist troops liberated a village from Japanese occupation and never accepted any gifts from the villagers, even though the villagers wanted to give them something to express their thanks. In contrast, if Chiang Kai-shek's troops drove the Japanese away they would search the villagers' houses for chickens and other food, telling the villagers that they should be grateful to the troops who freed them from the Japanese. As a child, I learned good from bad through these stories.

This kind of practical discipline had certainly helped the Communists earn respect and gain support from the people, and eventually helped them come to power. However, after the Communist takeover in 1949, many officials became corrupt. They accepted gifts, or even demanded bribes from the people who needed their help or service. With a one-party system, power corrupted with incredible speed. After decades of rule by the Communist Party this became a serious social problem. In fact, corruption was the main reason millions of demonstrators went to the streets in all the major cities in the spring of 1989.

Seeing the danger of corruption, my father was determined not to accept gifts from the people who came to him for help. Yet it was hard to persuade the visitors to return home, their gifts still with them! Finally, he had a better idea: he accepted the gifts, but insisted on giving something in return. In most cases he gave one visitor's gift to the next. He told each visitor that his or her gift would be accepted only if the visitor took something back in exchange. In this way, our home served as a trading post, and on an average weekend more than a dozen items changed hands.

By writing letters asking officials to help solve people's problems, my father gained even more influence in the city, although he did not have any official position. At first, he simply asked personal favors of his former colleagues, but gradually he became a liaison among them. One department director might not know another, and would feel uncomfortable asking the other one to do something. They both knew my father well, and he could write asking them to help each other. Once these officials had to turn to my father for help, he could in turn ask them to help more of those who had no power at all. In fact, in large part his letters benefited people who did not have power but had problems that needed to be addressed by the government. Most of them were victims of the Cultural Revolution or other political persecutions that took place under Communist rule. Because he always gave priority to those who had been wronged and had suffered a great deal in the past, he began to be looked upon by many people as a Robin Hood figure in our city.

As a matter of principle, he never wrote letters for his family members or relatives unless he was convinced that we had been wronged or unfairly treated in the first place. This made him quite different from many other officials who used their power to help their spouses and children or relatives. This happened so frequently that it became a serious problem in the late 1970s and 1980s. The general population was quite angry at this abuse, and in fact that was another reason triggering demonstrations in 1989. Frankly, there were moments when I wished that my father would do more for me and our family. However, I could quite understand why he adhered to his principle, and for that I respected him. It was not that he loved his family less but he loved his country more.

However, based on a few cited cases where high-ranking Communist officials subordinated their family interest to public interest, some critics in the West charged that the Communist Party made these officials less human by requiring them to behave contrary to family interest. Although nepotism has been condemned in the West in general, these critics, driven by anti-Communist ideology, were less willing to credit these Communists with noble behavior. They interpreted the opposite behavior as parental love. Nothing could be more ridiculously out of touch with reality! Whenever I read this kind of misinformed and misleading comments in Western media, I vowed I would write something someday to set the record straight.

My father's observance of his principle didn't make him less human. Both traditional Chinese culture and the Communist Party Charter required that public interest be put above individual interest. We were not to blame the Communist Party for requiring its members to behave nobly. The Chinese people respected and loved their leaders who lived up to such high moral principles. They wished to see more of this.

It was the selfish misuse of this so-called parental love on the part of so many powerholding officials that enraged the general population. In their positions, officials could easily sacrifice the public interest for their children's interest. For example, many of them took advantage of their power to arrange to have their children go abroad to college with money from the Chinese government or other funds that should have gone to more qualified candidates. Sending their own children to the schools abroad, and then, in 1989 killing the children of others on the street! That was what this parental love of the high-ranking Communist officials produced.

The moral principle of putting public interest above individual or family interest was not wrong. It was universally true that sacrificing personal interest for the public one was considered noble. The problem with a one-party system, however, is that it is unrealistic and impossible to expect every official to behave with such high moral principles, since we know that power corrupts and unchecked power corrupts even more. Few leaders could live up to this principle. It is necessary to have a democratic system with a balance of power and due legal process. If a society does not have effective enforcement to make its leaders abide by the law but lets them be restrained only by their own consciences or morality, such a society is almost doomed to fail!

NOT READY TO MAKE THE PLEDGE

After my parents renewed their Party memberships in 1974, I was often approached by the Communist Youth League at school asking me to apply for a membership. Had this happened a year before, I would have been thrilled. The League was founded in the early years of the Communist movement in the 1920s to include people between fifteen and eighteen years old, because the Communist Party required its members to be eighteen or older. The youths of that time, like my father, joined the Communist movement by first joining the League and then, when they were old enough, the Party. They pledged in more than words to devote their lives to the Communist cause of building an egalitarian society. However, between the Communist takeover in 1949 and the Cultural Revolution in 1966, membership in the League as well as in the Party gradually came to represent social status more than dedicated purpose. While a Party membership was often a necessary step toward having a really successful career, to be a League member simply meant to be recognized as a good child. One had to excel in school in order to be a member, and my sister was given that honor in 1962.

Family background also played an important role. It was much easier for those who came from "revolutionary" families to become members. Those students whose parents were land or property owners or capitalists before the Communist takeover, especially those who had worked for Chiang Kai-shek's government, had a more difficult time being accepted. The organization required them to do more and do it better than other students before it extended its membership to them. Sometimes it was simply impossible. For example, because his father had been labeled a rightist, my cousin Mei was never accepted, although his grades were tops in his class. That was a painful experience for him.

After the seven-year interruption caused by the Cultural Revolution, the Communist Youth League began to recruit again in 1973. However, because the charges against my parents had not been cleared yet, I was not even considered a candidate. It hurt my feelings and I felt that I should not have been discriminated against for my family background. In 1974 things were quite different. Yet by then I had doubts.

First, I no longer felt it was such an honor to be a member of the League. In both the League and the Party, I saw many whom I did not respect at all. In fact, I felt there were at least as many wrong-minded persons as there were good ones inside these Communist organizations. At the top level, the radicals who were ruining the country were, of course, Party members. Looking around me, many people I respected were not Party members, while many members were not at all impressive. This was also true in the case of the League. As a whole, I didn't think it was a group I would feel proud to belong to. I was not sure if I wanted to join a Communist organization at all.

Second, it bothered me that it became a general practice for anyone who wanted to be a member to write confessions from time to time, although the charter of the organization didn't require it. To me, confessing was a religious practice. In China, there was a very bad image associated with it because of the novel *The Gadfly* by Ethel Lilian Voynich. The hero in the book, a young revolutionary, was betrayed by his

Catholic priest, and his confession led to his arrest and execution. This novel was a best-seller in China in the early 1960s. It was banned during the Cultural Revolution, like all other foreign novels. By the early 1970s, the novel circulated among teenagers again as a favorite book, even though there was no official approval. One lesson I drew from it was that I should never confess my inner secrets to anyone.

In each of these confessions, the applicant was supposed to confess that he or she had some "wrong thoughts," and the organization would assign a member to "help" the applicant "correct" his or her thinking. In a later confession, the applicant was supposed to report any progress being made in terms of correcting the "wrong thoughts." Of course, he or she had to admit having some other "wrong thoughts." After a few cycles of confessions like this, he or she would have built up a record and would eventually be accepted as a member. In many cases, the whole process was simply a fake. It was hypocritical, and I didn't like it at all.

However, I felt pressured, at home as well as at school, to apply. Both my parents often expressed their concerns that I was not a League member. It was a kind of natural parental concern, just as any mother would feel concerned if her thirty-year-old daughter still was unmarried. A mother did not need to explain why her daughter should marry, but she just expected and even demanded that her daughter conform to social norms. Even friends of my parents would often pressure me. One of them was the former principal, now "restored" as the deputy principal, of my school. Every time he came to visit our house he would urge me to join the Communist Youth League. I often heard him say my father had given him the best advice and help he had in his life when he introduced him to the Communist Party. In return he felt responsible to see me do well at school and have a bright future. He believed one necessary step in assuring this was to join the Communist League and then the Party as soon as one could. After the deputy principal left our house my mother would usually say, "I think the principal was right. You should apply to join the League." My father would not say anything that direct, but he would remind me that ours was a "revolutionary" family and all of his siblings had joined the Party.

It was difficult for me to discuss this issue with my parents. I felt there were at least three complications. First, if I told them that the Communist organization was not good enough for me to belong to, they would probably be outraged. I knew that, although they had lost their trust in certain leaders, they had not lost their faith in the Party as a whole. It always seemed amazing to me that those who had joined the

Party before the Communist takeover could maintain such faith in the Party, even after they had personally suffered from it, especially during the Cultural Revolution. For example, when I entered the school the deputy principal was still a target of the current political persecution and we were organized to blame him for everything. That was how he was treated by the Party only a couple of years ago, and now he was encouraging me to join the Communist League! I did not understand him or my own parents.

Second, although I was grateful to the deputy principal for his concern, what he said also bothered me, because it sounded as if I should be motivated to join the League for my personal interest and advantage rather than the public interest. This was different from what it was supposed to be. When my father joined the Communist Party early in his life, he had done so for exactly the reason he stated in his pledge when he was formally accepted into the organization: to build a universal egalitarian society, as the Communist theory promised, for the interests of the majority of the people. However, after the Communist takeover in 1949, the underlying logic for anyone to join a Communist organization had changed to include considerations of personal interest and private gain. This remained a challenge to the Party, and even today it has not found a satisfactory way to handle this issue.

Third, I would feel ashamed if I told them I was not yet ready to devote my life to an altruistic, idealistic cause. That would make me look selfish. I admired those who really believed in the pledge, but I did not feel ready to take it myself. Although I soon gave in to the pressure and applied for the membership in the League, I was often haunted by the guilt of not being ready to make a noble pledge.

MILLIONS ARISE AFTER ONE MAN'S DEATH

I graduated from high school in the summer of 1975 when I was seventeen years old. I wasn't forced to leave the city and settle in the countryside as my sister had been. The government policy had been changed and now allowed one family member to stay and provide domestic care for their aging parents, an adult child's responsibility in China. This more humane plan was warmly welcomed by city residents. Since my sister was still working in Anhui, I was to be assigned a job in the city.

It usually took about a year for the local government to actually find jobs for people like me. I knew I would have some time to myself, and it felt great. I spent most of my time reading foreign literary works that had been translated into Chinese. Among them were books by Chaucer, Shakespeare, Dickens, the Brontës, Galsworthy, Balzac, Hugo, Stendhal, Flaubert, Maupassant, Tolstoy, Dostoevski, Turgenev, Goethe, and Hawthorne. Some of them were translated before the Communist takeover in 1949, but many were translated after, and almost all of them were reprinted after 1949. Indeed, China hadn't been completely isolated from Western culture until the Cultural Revolution. In 1975, most of these books were still banned. Fortunately, my sister had access to them in the library at her university. Every month when she came home, she brought about a dozen books for me to read.

I particularly enjoyed novels that depicted political power struggles, for they helped me understand the current ones in Beijing. As the premier, Zhou Enlai was trying to keep the economy going. Yet the radicals reproached him for neglecting political indoctrination. They did not care if the unattended crops grew into fruitless weeds. In fact, the absurd radical argument in the controlled media was that China would be better off with socialist weeds than capitalist grains.

It was no wonder that national productivity hit a record low. People's daily lives became harder. At the local markets, there was less and less to buy. Often my father and I had to ride our bikes for miles to the outskirts of the city to buy vegetables from the peasants. This cost us two to five times more, but we had no choice, for the local markets didn't sell these vegetables any more. The higher cost of food made life difficult for city residents. Housing was subsidized, but food cost 60 percent of one's income. The new price hike was painfully felt by every household.

Ignoring reality, the radical-controlled media kept up its propaganda. The comment heard most often in those days was: "The revolutionary situation is getting better and better, day by day." The word "revolutionary" had long been used simply as a positive adjective to be placed before virtually any noun. All they were saying was: "Today is better than yesterday." But, having experienced the deteriorating living standards, who would agree with such an obvious lie? To many, the word "revolution" had long since lost its positive meaning. I, for example, often asked family members and trusted friends: If a revolution doesn't bring more food to the table, what is so good about it?

While the silent majority put all its hopes in the premier, the news of his death on January 8, 1976, shocked every household, especially in the cities where the residents were better informed. They had been watching the inner Party struggle very closely because they knew how much it affected their lives. To many, Zhou's death took away their last hope.

For quite a long time, Zhou presented the image of a man who had sacrificed personal and family interest for the public good. There were numerous stories about how he had lived an extremely thrifty life, in strong contrast to many other officials, especially the radicals. To the millions of Chinese, the contradiction between Zhou and the radicals was not a power struggle or an ideological conflict. It was a conflict of human character: a battle between good and evil, between honesty and hypocrisy, between nobility and viciousness, between morality and corruption, and between justice and injustice.

To understand this personification of characters, one has to understand a little more history, both that of the Communist Party and of China, itself. In the Party, Zhou was the Number Two Communist for years before Mao became the ultimate leader in the mid-1930s. Yet, after the Communist takeover in 1949, Mao first picked Liu as his successor, and then replaced him with Lin during the Cultural Revolution. Zhou did not gain the second highest position until his last days. Zhou handled this with a humble air of great calmness, which looked noble and gentlemanlike according to traditional Chinese culture. Zhou's modesty helped his popularity and many people considered him the personification of nobility.

There is an old Chinese saying that depicts the relationship between an emperor and his prime minister: "To accompany a king is like accompanying a tiger." The injustice and cruelty of authoritarianism in the long history of China were reflected in classic Chinese literature. There were numerous stories of how a cruel and suspicious emperor wronged some of his loyal officials and even the prime minister. An emperor might imprison, torture, and even behead them at will. The influence of this literature often drove ordinary persons to sympathize with unfortunate officials. As a result, people easily understood the difficulties Zhou had in dealing with Mao, and sympathized with him.

When the news of Zhou's death came, hundreds of millions of people cried openly, despite the cultural tradition that to shed tears in public showed a shameful weakness. My sister was eight months pregnant when the premier died. She cried all the way home on the train from Anhui. She knew it was very bad to be emotionally upset at this stage of her pregnancy, yet she could not contain herself. Most people on the train were crying, too. Whenever my sister tried to stop, she heard someone near her cry loudly, and this made her begin to cry again.

The news of Zhou's death was broadcast by both radio and television. Few households had television sets at the time, but many people wanted to have a last glimpse of Zhou before his body was cremated. They went to either their own workplace or a workplace in their neighborhood to watch television. The closest place we could go was the Astronomy Department of Nanjing University, which had an 18-inch black-and-white television set. For almost a whole week, every member of the six families in our residence went there, including my seventy-six-year-old bound-foot grandma. To accommodate a large audience of about 200 people, the television set was moved outdoors each evening. The whole audience cried as they watched.

Besides this universal mourning of Zhou's death was the people's genuine concern about the nation's future, to which everyone's individual interests were tied. Tears became an expression of each individual's political position, not just sympathy with Zhou, but also a hatred of the radicals. Fairly soon, an order came from Beijing banning all mourning activities. One could not even cry! Don't try using the dead to beat the living, the radicals said. By the living, they were referring to Mao, whose absence from Zhou's funeral had further disappointed and irritated people.

For almost two months, sparkling tension silently grew between the authorities and the angry masses. Many continued to cry privately. They tried other ways of expressing their feelings. One weekend, a middle-aged college lecturer came to our house. He also brought his wife and four adult children. My father let them in, and our little sitting room soon became crowded. No sooner had they sat down than the man started to say that they came to see my father simply because he looked so much like Zhou. Then he asked his wife and children to take a long, good look at my father. We were all surprised and embarrassed, because Zhou was such a prominent figure. We also felt uncomfortable because Zhou was dead now. Yet we understood.

Locally, this political tension created a tough situation for managers and government officials, who were squeezed in the middle. They had to carry out the ban. Yet it was very unpopular. Some officials took the ban more seriously than others, and really upset people. Many people came to our house to complain about those local officials. The man most criticized was in charge of the Department of Culture in the municipal government. On one occasion, he had rudely taken away and destroyed the dried flower wreaths people made for the late premier. That didn't surprise me, however, because I knew him quite well. This was the same person who had caused great trouble for my father in the labor camp, almost driving him to suicide.

The tensions were mounting. On March 5, a radical-controlled newspaper in Shanghai outraged people even more by suggesting that the late premier was a public enemy. People in Nanjing were the first to take their anger to the streets. Overnight, dozens of posters appeared in public places to repeal the ban and call for the punishment to those who dared to tarnish the late premier's name. Tens of thousands of people went to the streets to read these posters.

That night I took my bike and rode downtown to join the huge crowds. It was difficult to get close to the posters. When I finally reached one I heard someone in the crowd yell:

"Could someone in the front read it aloud so that we could all hear it?"

"That's a great idea," many people echoed.

A blue-collar worker in his twenties came out of the crowd. I heard him say:

"If you all want me to read aloud, I will do it."

"Read aloud! Read aloud!" The crowd yelled. The man then started to read.

Sometimes he had to pause because the streetlight was not bright enough. Someone suggested that he use a flashlight.

"Who has a flashlight?" "Who has a flashlight?" The words were repeated until someone said: "I have one." An even younger man stepped up. With the help of the flashlight the man read more fluently. The readings ended with slogans for the people to follow and repeat. The man read these in an even louder voice and the whole crowd joined in. We shouted as loudly as we could, and our voices burst out through the darkness and echoed in the freezing March air. I felt warmed up by the excitement as I joined in the yelling.

The following day more posters appeared on the streets of Nanjing. Some college students even put posters on the trains leaving for Beijing and Shanghai. That immediately resulted in an order from Beijing, labeling this as a counterrevolutionary incident and asking the local government to crack down. That evening I biked downtown again. There were even more people in the square, but I also saw a lot of armed policemen standing around. I knew there would be a serious confrontation sooner or later, but I didn't anticipate what was about to happen in Beijing.

In early April there is a traditional Chinese festival to mourn the dead. That year, millions of people went to Tiananmen Square to mourn Premier Zhou. They put a lot of wreaths of flowers on the square, usually five feet high. There were also thousands of elegies posted in the square. Readers copied them by hand and mailed them to their families and friends, sometimes thousands of miles away from Beijing. My cousin Ping mailed quite a few to us.

The mourning activity became a very powerful public statement. In its twenty-seven years of rule, the Communist authority had never been so challenged. On the evening of April 5, 1976, thousands of people were brutally beaten and arrested. The peaceful gathering in the square was described as an uprising similar to the Hungarian Incident in 1956. Two days later, the would-be successor to the late premier, Deng Xiaoping, was blamed for the uprising of millions of people. He was immediately removed from all his official positions. A relatively unknown figure, Hua Guofeng, was promoted to replace Deng. A sweeping arrest followed in every corner of the country. This was the famous "Tiananmen Incident" of 1976 that shocked millions of people and awakened many more.

Who could anticipate then that in 1989, only thirteen years later, there would be another Tiananmen Incident? Instead of being a scapegoat and losing his office as he had in 1976, this time Deng was the one who gave the order. History is written with extremely bitter irony!

LIFE GOES ON

Despite the Tiananmen Incident in April 1976, irreversible changes were taking place everywhere in China. After China reopened its doors to the outside world, the Chinese government signed several contracts with foreign companies to build factories and plants. One of them was a big petrochemical plant located on the outskirts of Nanjing. The construction of the factory had to proceed on schedule, and not even the political storm in Beijing could slow it down.

A faculty member at the Department of Foreign Languages and Literatures at Nanjing University served as an interpreter in the negotiations for the project. He was one of the people whom my father had helped by writing letters on his behalf. He suggested that I volunteer to do some translation work for the project to practice my English. Both my father and I liked the idea.

The project had just started and all the drawings, blueprints, specifications, and documents needed to be translated into Chinese. A team of about ten people was put together, headed by a chemical engineer named Fan. Other team members were from faculties at universities and colleges in Nanjing. There were so many materials to be translated that it was more work than a few people could manage.

It hadn't been easy to gather these people together and it was more difficult to get additional help. In the first place, few people knew English, but it was even harder to transfer those who did to work on this project. China's human resource system at the time was so rigid that each worker was actually bound to a specific place of work. Most leaders at each workplace regarded the number of employees at their work site as an indication of their power and they did not easily let anyone go. There was a tremendous amount of paperwork and political bargaining for the government to maneuver and redistribute its workforce. For example, in order for a teacher at the Department of Foreign Languages and Literatures at Nanjing University to work on this project, the project leaders had to write proposals to the municipal government because the project was under the supervision of the municipal government. In turn, the municipal government had to write proposals to the provincial government because the university was under the supervision of the provincial government. As a matter of fact, the university was directed by the Higher Education Department of the provincial government and the project was led by the Chemical Industry Department of the municipal government. That presented two more layers of bureaucracy. The transfer would require approval from the director of the Chemical Industry Department of the Nanjing municipal government, the mayor's office, the governor's office, the director of the provincial Department of Higher Education, the president of Nanjing University, and even the chair of the Department of the Foreign Languages and Literatures at the university. It is not hard to imagine how difficult this would be. In fewer than thirty years of Communist rule, the once-dreamed-of efficiency of a centrally planned economy had deteriorated into an obstructive bureaucracy. Despite its authoritarianism, the government lacked the flexibility to organize a good production team.

Under the circumstances, Mr. Fan was more than happy to have me on the team as a volunteer. Besides, he turned out to be an acquaintance of my father. He had been the chief chemical engineer of the Department of Chemical Industry at the municipal government of Nanjing before the Cultural Revolution and my father and he had been colleagues. During the Cultural Revolution, they worked at the same labor camp. I felt close to him for another reason. Like my second uncle in Shanghai, Mr. Fan had been labeled a "rightist" in 1957 and persecuted for many years. It was my impression that most of the so-called rightists persecuted in 1957 were the best intellectuals in the nation. Indeed, Fan graduated from MIT in the 1930s and was one of those well-trained professionals who remained in China after the Communist takeover in 1949. His English was quite good, and his knowledge was profound. The two months I worked with him reinforced my impression about rightists in general.

While working as a volunteer with this translation team, I waited for the government to assign me a job. I would have liked to be assigned to work at this state-owned chemical plant, but this was impossible. Theoretically, there were two types of ownership for enterprises then in China: state-owned and co-op. In reality, both types were run by the government. The only difference was that the employees in the latter usually had lower wages and fewer benefits. So, everyone preferred to work in a state-owned enterprise. Yet the government couldn't satisfy everyone. For fairness, it set a policy that said that only if one's siblings were all working as peasants and not on the payroll system, could one be entitled to such a job. Since my sister was no longer working as a peasant, I wasn't eligible.

Before I had time to feel sorry for myself, a natural disaster occurred. A terrible earthquake took place on July 28, 1976, obliterating the entire city of Tangshan in northern China. Among the one million residents, a quarter died and another 160,000 were badly injured. Tens of thousands of soldiers were sent to rescue the survivors. Many soldiers dug with their bare hands for people and bodies buried in the debris. Once again the People's Liberation Army affirmed its image as an army of the people. Westerners might have a negative image of a Communist army, but most of the Chinese saw it differently. In a natural disaster, people counted on the army to come to their rescue. In fact, who could have thought that such a trusted and friendly army would shoot at the demonstrators in Beijing in 1989?

The rescue efforts in Tangshan were remarkably efficient. Within a few days, over 20,000 medical professionals were sent to the area. Only twenty days after the earthquake, traffic in the inner city was running again and some businesses reopened. The incident seemed to prove that, in dealing with a crisis, an authoritarian society had strengths that a democratic society might not have. The centrally planned economy had actually showed some remarkable strengths in the early years of the Communist rule. As time passed, however, all that remained was a paradox: the system still had strengths in a crisis, but it was weak and cumbersome in peacetime, and could not organize production efficiently, as happened at the new chemical factory in Nanjing, where there were not even enough translators for the project.

The earthquake in Tangshan also made the radicals more unpopular. The nation was concerned about the survivors. But the radicals didn't care about them at all. They even reproached the current premier, Hua

Guofeng, for caring less about the more "important" issue, which, according to them, was castigating Deng. Such nonsense outraged the people and further separated them from the radicals.

To many Chinese, 1976 was a catastrophic year. First, they lost their premier in January. Then they lost the chairman of the People's Congress, Marshal Zhu De, on July 6. Next, a quarter of a million people lost their lives in the big earthquake on July 28. Historically, there were many stories about how natural disasters came before the death of an emperor or the end of a dynasty. When the earthquake occurred in Tangshan, rumors soon spread that this was an omen of Mao's death. It didn't take long to confirm people's foreboding. Mao died on September 9, and left the ultimate power in the hands of a relatively unknown figure, Hua Guofeng.

In a sense, Mao had been a great leader, because he had inspired many people. Yet many people only remembered the disasters he had caused. The prevailing feeling throughout the nation at his death was more of concern than sorrow. Most people worried that the radicals headed by Mao's wife would soon take over. Although a fairly large number of people grieved over his death, I actually thought he had lived at least one year too long. I wished that Mao had died before Zhou so that Deng would have had a chance and the nation would not be ruined by the radicals. This was not personal rancor. As Shakespeare wrote, "It was not that I loved Caesar less, but that I loved Rome more."

The country was saved, however, by an unexpected coup d'état on October 6, 1976. In an abrupt action, Hua Guofeng arrested all the four archradicals, Mao's wife and three men. When the news came from Beijing to Nanjing, tens of thousands of people went to the streets to celebrate the fall of the "Gang of Four." From what I saw on television, this mood prevailed throughout the entire nation.

People really had a remarkable way to celebrate the fall of the Gang of Four. One day my father received a dinner invitation from an old friend: "Please come and join us to celebrate the elimination of the 'sideways-walkers.'" In Chinese, to walk sideways and block others' path is a metaphor for bullying. Because crabs walked sideways and autumn was the season to eat crabs, this friend invited my father to a crab dinner, using crabs to symbolize the radicals who had bullied people for so many years. That year people had crabs for dinner a lot. Each time they would specify three male and one female crabs, for that's what the Gang of Four consisted of. I had more than a dozen crab dinners that fall, and each time the joy was double-edged.

As I recall, the whole nation had never been so excited. People felt a great relief of being "liberated." In fact, the word "Liberation" had long been used to refer to the Communist takeover in 1949, and now people started to refer to the fall of the radicals as the "Second Liberation." The use of this term now showed that the fall of the radicals was seen to parallel the events of 1949. The Western media often reported the excitement as a sign of an anti-Communist mood in China. Well, this was not an accurate interpretation. On the contrary, popular confidence in Communism was never so strong, and the upbeat mood was second only to the time immediately after the Communist takeover. To many, life could go on with great expectations.

MY FIRST JOB

A month after the fall of the Gang of Four I became an employee in an electronics factory. About fifty other high school graduates were hired at the same time. The history of the factory reflected the economic development of the past two decades. In the late 1950s, the factory had only twenty employees, and it produced folded paper boxes. Within twenty years it transformed itself into a manufacturer of electronics with more than 600 employees. One of our products was oscilloscopes. The technology revolution of the twentieth century had a global impact. National politics might affect a nation's rank in the world economy, but all nations experienced technological advance. Communism or not, radicals or moderates, nothing could stop the trend and power of modernization.

Yet people were not always prepared for such dramatic changes. For example, at my factory, most of its employees were middle-aged women with little education. The arrival of fifty high school graduates was timely. In great demand, we were soon promoted from the assembly line to positions that required more education and knowledge.

The difference in education, age, and sex, however, did not block my communication with these middle-aged, illiterate women. As a matter of fact, I soon found myself getting close to them. They all lived in the south end of the city where my grandparents used to live, and they spoke with a strong local accent, which I could easily speak with because I'd learned it from my grandparents. The ease between us soon made these women tell me their life stories. Many of them had been fans of the theater group that my mother had run. Some of the actresses they admired were frequent guests at our home. They told me that they used to wait in long lines to get tickets for the performance, sometimes even during thunderstorms. From those stories, I learned more about my mother and her work.

Shortly after I had started working in the factory, my mother was appointed to manage a theater/cinema with 1,300 seats. Her theater group had dissolved during the Cultural Revolution, and this was a managerial position similar to her old job. Movies were in high demand in those days. During the Cultural Revolution, many movies were banned. Now with the Gang of Four arrested, people expected to see those movies again. However, the authorities seemed fairly reluctant to lift the ban. The new premier, Hua Guofeng, made it clear that he would not reverse Chairman Mao's policies implemented since the Cultural Revolution. He actually did make some changes; he gave greater priority to economic development. Yet he was hesitant to give up ideological control. Only under the pressure of the moderates, those who had been restored to the positions they had held in the government before the Cultural Revolution, did Hua gradually reverse the radical policies.

A movie called *Dreams in a Red Chamber* was caught in the middle of this transitional process. The story was based on a superb classical novel written 200 years ago. It was staged in the form of a local opera, the same type that my mother's group had performed. The film was actually a recast of the stage performance, like those of Placido Domingo. Although there was a high market demand for showing this movie, the ban wasn't officially lifted. As a compromise, cinemas were allowed to show the movie, but tickets were not for sale publicly. Only organizations could buy them. This created pressure on the leaders in each workplace, and the task was often passed to unions, which were actually quasi-government agencies in China. All employees were automatically members of the union and union leaders were appointed government officials. The chairman of the union in my factory was a woman. She called me in one morning and asked me to help her. Tickets were in great demand. Some cinemas were even selling tickets for shows scheduled months later. This woman must have heard about my mother's new job and wanted to use this connection. She said I could take a day off as paid leave. Then she gave me a check and told me not to return until I had the tickets. Under such pressure, I had to ask my mother to do her best to get 600 tickets for me as quickly as possible. The next morning when I entered the factory with the tickets in my hand I was hailed as a hero.

I wasn't happy about it, however. Something seemed wrong and it bothered me. I soon knew what it was. This incident made it very clear to me that personal influence and connections were critically important to getting things done. Not only did an individual need connections in order to advance, but an institution needed connections to achieve its goals. This created enormous opportunities for corruption and nepotism. Increasingly, our society became an invisible, entangled network that overrode the straightforward, transparent structure established after the Communist takeover. To a large exent, the effectiveness and efficiency of the centrally planned economy was based on this structure. If a soldier in an army needed connections to get a better weapon, such an army would be weak and unlikely to win. Now, with an increasingly entangled network, how could the Communist system work? I felt this was a serious problem.

At the time, however, my thoughts for solving the problem were to look backward. I hoped that we could somehow reestablish the social order that was in place before the Cultural Revolution. In the late 1970s, most people felt the same way, including some leading intellectuals and thinkers. We were trying to "restore the glorious tradition" that we thought had been ruined by the radicals. Gradually, however, such a "lost glorious tradition" was demystified. For example, before the Cultural Revolution, we had such horrible persecutions as the "anti-rightist campaign" in 1957. Even before the Communist takeover, things were not quite right in the Communist guerrilla bases. Eventually, it became clear to us that there really wasn't a time in Communist history that could truly serve as a model. It took us, however, a few years to realize this.

OVER TWO HUNDRED BILLION HOURS WASTED

In 1977, a year after the fall of the Gang of Four, the Chinese government decided to give a salary increase to about 40 percent of its employees. The raise of about seven yuan a month (approximately three dollars according to the current exchange rate) was not insignificant: the average salary of a worker then was only thirty to forty yuan a month. This was the first time that so many people were given a raise. Everybody was eager to be included.

In our factory, the 40 percent quota was distributed evenly among all the divisions and units. The selection process involved three steps. First, each person gave a speech at a group meeting explaining why he or she should be selected. Second, the group collectively evaluated each one's work over the past years to select those who most deserved the raise.

Finally, the factory authorities balanced the raises among the different groups to make sure there was no apparent unfairness.

As an apprentice, I was excluded from this raise, but I was included in the selection process. This provided me with a good opportunity to observe how individuals fought for their own interest. In contrast to the usually friendly atmosphere at the workplace, these group meetings generated very tense feelings. Since it was a zero-sum game, everybody became a rival.

Most of these workers could only read a little, but none knew how to spell or write. Yet, at the group meeting, each had a prepared speech in hand, which must have been written by a spouse or a child. There seemed to be a uniform pattern to all the speeches. The first point was that one had closely followed the Party's leadership. The evidence cited most often was consistent attendance at the political study sessions. Only one man stood out and said anything different. He said that he seldom attended those sessions when the Gang of Four was in power, and therefore had been less influenced by their absurd theories. This now made him more politically correct. To be absent in political study sessions was usually viewed as negative and was often punished, but now he was asking to be given credit for it! The man was in his thirties and usually very quiet. His speech quite surprised me. I later learned that he was in fact a graduate of the technical school my father had founded in the late 1950s.

This man made an excellent point. At each workplace since the late 1960s, Wednesday afternoons were set aside for political studies aimed at indoctrination. No business was transacted, and even hospitals did not accept patients except for emergencies. For almost ten years, the Chinese had wasted their time this way. Although it only affected the cities, that was at least 10 percent of a population of one billion. If each person wasted four hours a week, that amounted to over 200 billion hours wasted during those ten years! This practice was initiated by the radicals, but it continued after their fall until 1977, when Deng Xiaoping made his second political comeback with the support of the same military that had convinced and probably compelled Hua to arrest the radicals. In his speech addressed to the Chinese National Academy of Sciences, Deng argued that scientists needed to work on their research, and most of their time should be spent this way, and political study sessions should be minimized. Deng's speech had a domino effect. Within months, hours spent on political studies were cut to the minimum at every workplace. In those days, Deng was indeed widely supported and admired by the people.

Looking back, it seems very strange that such a huge waste could have been permitted. My observation was that the radicals began with a sound argument. They said that time spent on some nonproductive activities could actually increase production. This might be true to a certain extent. Yet once it went too far, it became absurd. In fact, that was my father's view. At home, he often quoted Lenin: "Half a step too far, truth becomes absurdity." I agree. It applies to situations in Russia, China, and also America. I believe those who remember McCarthyism will agree with me.

BACK TO WORK AGAIN AT THE AGE OF SIXTY-THREE

In 1977 my father was still waiting for his appointment to return to work. He had waited for years. Although the Gang of Four had been out of power for months, he still didn't have a job. This awkward situation made our family very uncomfortable.

It gradually became clear that there were serious reasons that kept him from being assigned to a new job. The personnel department wouldn't tell us what they were but someone leaked it out. In the 1950s my father's diligent work on the old city wall had offended the ignorant mayor so much that he put some very negative comments in my father's dossier, which cast a shadow on my father's career even before the Cultural Revolution. Many of his former colleagues in the municipal government of Nanjing had later become deputy ministers, ministers, and even vice-premiers of China. Because Mayor Ke had died before the Cultural Revolution, he never exposed himself fully as other radicals did. Otherwise it would have been the Gang of Five instead of the Gang of Four who were arrested in October 1976, and his words would not have haunted my father's career.

Privately, my mother often complained that my father had not been fairly treated inside the Party. Yet my father always stopped her. He said that in the first place he did not join the Revolution to get any official positions. Second, he had survived many revolutionary martyrs who had lost their lives even before the Communists came to power. Third, it could be worse; some had suffered much more after the Communist takeover.

The first notorious case of injustice after the Communist takeover happened before 1957. It involved two prominent Communist Party members, Pan Hannian and Yang Fan. The latter had worked with my father in Shanghai in 1937 as an underground Communist. With a third person, Mr. Wang, they established again an underground Communist group among journalists and writers in Shanghai, three years after the underground Communist headquarters had been forced to retreat to a guerrilla base in Jiangxi Province in 1934. After the Communist takeover in 1949, Pan became deputy mayor of Shanghai and Yang became the police chief of the city. Yet, in the mid-1950s, both men were charged as spies inside the Communist Party and were sentenced to prison. Only Yang survived jail. Nearly thirty years later when he was released my father visited him in his home. The poor man could barely recognize my father.

Wang's story was even more horrible. While my father was sent to Nanjing to open a new frontier for the Party in 1940, Wang was sent to join a Communist guerrilla force in Zhejiang Province. There he was wrongly accused as an enemy of the Communist Revolution, and executed by his fellow Communists in 1941.

Whenever my mother complained about the unfair way my father was treated, he always asked her to think about these two men. Although he didn't complain as my mother did, I could see that in his heart he was hurt. Two years at home made him feel abandoned by society. Even though he was given the same salary he collected during the years when he was in power, he felt uncomfortable and unhappy. Sometimes he would become upset and quarrel with me or my mother or even my grandmother over very trivial matters. We all understood what was making him lose his temper.

To overcome these feelings, he tried to make more friends and wrote letters trying to help others. Sometimes he had dozens of visitors each day and had to write letters for at least ten of them. All these letters had to be hand-written. In China, one's handwriting or calligraphy was very important. It was more than a communication tool; it was also a social asset or liability. As inherited from the traditional Chinese culture, attractive handwriting reflected one's level of education, intelligence, and thus social status. It was even seen as an indication of personal integrity and character. My father's handwriting was very beautiful. Few government officials could write as well as he did. In fact, his handwriting won him much respect from intellectuals and professionals in both academic and cultural circles. When my sister was a student at the university in Anhui, my father's letters to her raised her popularity among her professors. They noticed the beautiful handwriting on the envelopes. Curious and impressed, they asked her who those letters were from. When they learned that the handwriting was her father's, they looked at her differently; she was no longer the daughter of a bureaucrat, but of a well-educated intellectual.

Even though my father did not have a job, there were a lot of people in Nanjing who wished he did. Many administrators remembered him as a capable leader and wanted to see him provide the kind of leadership they felt was lacking in the current municipal government. Many professors in the metropolitan area hoped that he would be nominated for president of their schools. These faculty members often came to our house to tell hilariously funny stories about their administrators. One story was about a university president who made a fool of himself while stumbling in a public speech apparently drafted by his secretary. "Damn it," he said in public, "I don't even know this word!"

There was often conflict between administrators and faculty members. However, when my father was the principal at a technical school in the late 1950s, both administrators and faculty members respected and loved him. To the faculty members, he was a well-educated intellectual, and his English was even better than theirs. To the administrators, his management skills were remarkable. The school had more than 300 administrators, faculty, and staff members at the time. According to one administrator, my father knew them all, and their families as well.

A faculty member recalled this story in the memoir he wrote of my father. Graduating from Nankai University, the young man came to work in the school in 1954. In his first winter vacation he went to his home town and fell sick. To his great surprise, my father wrote him a sympathy letter just a few days before the Chinese New Year. Knowing his poor health and financial condition, my father even sent this young teacher five Chinese yuan out of his own pocket, which was almost a weekly salary for the young man. Having been a poor orphan brought up by his uncle and grandma, the man had seldom experienced this kind of parental love. He was moved to tears when reading my father's letter. Cherishing it so much, he saved the letter for forty years and still has it today.

Eventually in the autumn of 1977 my father was assigned a new job as deputy president of the Nanjing Aeronautic Engineering University. It was not as high a position as many people wished him to take, but it was a start. Now at the age of sixty-three, he felt both ready and eager to devote the rest of his life to public service.

NEW STUDENTS: THE HOPE OF THE NATION

After cutting back on the political study sessions, Deng Xiaoping initiated another reform in the summer of 1977. This was in higher education. Since the Cultural Revolution in 1966, universities had stopped recruiting regular four-year students. The students recruited in the 1970s could only stay in school for two or three years. The radicals argued that too much knowledge was a dangerous thing and it could contaminate the students' minds politically. The process of recruiting was also problematic. It was largely a political one and candidates' academic strengths were seldom taken into consideration. As result, some of the students recruited during those years had never finished primary school. Deng Xiaoping suggested that universities offer a four-year higher education, and that the enrollment process consider academic competence the primary criterion. He argued that only in this way would our nation be able to produce first-rate scientists and intellectuals who could help modernize China. It was a very popular idea and soon became a policy.

Many young people in our factory started preparing for the entrance exams immediately. However, it looked as if I would have to wait another year before becoming eligible. The new policy had not yet overridden an existing requirement that a high school graduate had to work for at least two years before beginning higher education. By early October, however, news came from Beijing that this requirement was dropped. Anybody with a high school or equivalent diploma was eligible to sit for the entrance exam. This news came as a total surprise to me, but I was determined to take the opportunity. I knew the exam would be very competitive. For eleven years the regular enrollment had been interrupted, and twelve years of high school graduates had accumulated. Now they were all eligible for the exam.

In our province, exams were to be given twice; first a citywide standard exam and then a provincial standard exam for those who had passed the first one. Each exam would take two-and-a-half days, and cover all the subjects taught in high school. The first exam was scheduled to be held at the end of November. I had only about fifty days to study, and I still had to work in the factory every day. There was little time to prepare. My family gave me the best support they could offer. I did not have to do my housework, and could spend the entire evening reviewing my textbooks. Late in the evenings, my mother or grandmother would even cook something special for me, so that I wouldn't be hungry when I stayed up late. I had never felt the warmth of family so much, and I knew how important it was, and appreciated it very much.

I was also fortunate to have many good tutors. A math teacher living in our neighborhood helped me with algebra. My friend Lin's mother, another math teacher at my school, helped me review geometry and trigonometry. My sister helped me with Chinese, politics, history, and geography. She collected all kinds of preparation materials and mailed them to me. Both my father and Mr. Jin helped me with my English. My father was a bit out of touch with my textbooks now, and Mr. Jin had a better sense of the parts that were most likely to be tested. With so much help, in less than two months I reviewed all I had learned in more than four years at school. I also learned things that I should have learned but was never taught.

My father tried to help me in another area. Before the exams, candidates were required to specify which universities they wished to attend and what they wanted to study. My father and I had a long discussion about this choice. I was interested in many areas, including electronics and English. Finally, for two reasons, we decided that I should pursue an English major. First, my English was already much better than that of most of my peers, so I had a considerable competitive advantage. Second, with a good command of English, I might have a better chance to study abroad in the future. As for universities, my father wanted me to get into a local one. He said I could always come home for food and laundry and have more time to concentrate on my studies.

With all this help and support, I did very well in both exams and was accepted by the Department of Foreign Languages at the Nanjing Teachers' University. I started my first semester in February 1978. Like all other university dorms, ours was very crowded. It was similar to barracks at a military base or a ward in a prison. Eight students lived in a room of 150 square feet. With four bunk beds, two desks, and four benches, there was little room to move. There were only two bathrooms on each floor of the building, shared by 160 students living in twenty rooms on each floor! There was no closet in the room. The only place for personal belongings was under the beds. The two students who shared a bunk could each put a luggage bag under the bed they shared, and that was about it. As for books, one had to stack them along the wall side on the bed, and sleep on the rest of the bed.

The first roommate I met was named Shao. When I arrived he was listening to his old-fashioned radio, which was almost as big as an antique Victorian table clock. Apparently he was from a poor family, and couldn't afford a new radio. He explained later that it was through the English learning programs on the radio that he managed to learn enough English to pass the entrance exams. I not only felt sympathetic, but respected what he had achieved despite his limited background. In his entire county, he was the only one who made his way to a four-year university that year. I was proud of him and we soon became very close friends.

Later he told me a lot of stories about his life that amazed me and helped me learn more about the hardships in the countryside. For example, in the countryside where he came from there were no toilets. Most families in his village would just dig a huge hole in the ground in their back yard and place a huge vat in it to use as a toilet. Each family used the manure stored in the vat to fertilize their vegetable gardens. One needed to be very careful not to fall into the vat. Once Shao had an unfortunate accident. He came back from a friend's house on a dark, cloudy night. It was very late and he decided to take a short cut by someone's house. It was very dark and he could not see even his own hands stretched out in front of him. All of a sudden, he stumbled and fell into the huge vat of manure. In no time his clothes were soaked in the wet manure and he had quite a struggle to climb out of the vat. When he finally arrived home stinking, even his mother and sister could not help bursting out laughing when they had realized what had happened to him.

Shao was not the only person in my class who came from the countryside. The more contacts I had with these classmates, the more I realized the kind of hardships my sister must have undergone during her two years in the countryside in Anhui. She was lucky to have been able to leave so soon. Many of her classmates had stayed in the countryside for ten years. For them, entering the university now was their first opportunity to leave the countryside. Others stayed even longer, some marrying local peasants and never returning.

For these reasons, our class was really diverse. Some had just graduated from high school, and some had already worked for almost ten years in the countryside. Some even had school-age children. Although the diversity came as a result of many individual tragedies, I felt that I personally benefited from it. It was an excellent opportunity to learn from different experiences.

Because it was the first time in twelve years that students were selected by academic competence instead of politics, the quality of the new students became a source of national pride. We were often referred to as the Cohort '77 students in China, for that was the year we passed our admission exams. It was generally acknowledged that we were the hope of China. Despite our differences we all felt we belonged to the same group and believed that we were going to play an important role in China's future.

Having a great mission made us unusually hardworking. Motivation was never a problem among us. In fact, the authorities were soon concerned that we spent too much time studying and had too few hours of sleep. Concerned about our health, they discouraged us from long hours of studying. They even made rules to force us to leave our classroom before 10:00 p.m. In the dorm, lights had to be off between 11:00 p.m. and 6:00 a.m., so that we would get at least seven hours of sleep. Rules were rules and had to be followed, but we soon found creative ways to get around them. For example, in our dorm room we decided to practice our spoken English after 11:00 p.m. for at least an hour. Sometimes we even carried on past midnight. It turned out to be a very good way to practice speaking English. The darkness in the room covered our shyness and embarrassment as we all stammered, trying to find the right English words. We also found alternative lights for our reading. For example, someone leaned against a lamp post to read under the street light. Some got up early, reading under the first rays of the morning sun. My bunkmate buried himself in his quilt and read with the help of his flashlight.

Looking back, I am touched by the high morale at the university. In fact, only four years later, this already sounded like a legend to my own students when I became a college teacher and told them the story. They could hardly believe that we were so conscientious and hardworking. But it was true! Our high spirits coincided with the generally optimistic mood of the nation. After the downfall of the radicals and with Deng gradually assuming more and more political power and implementing popular policy changes, most people believed that China would have a great future. They also believed that everyone was going to have a fair share in this new way of life.

CHAPTER 7

"I WANT TO RIGHT THIS WRONG!"

My father was back in public service again. After an eleven-year interruption, he felt he had lost much precious time and had to work extraordinarily hard to catch up. His was a feeling shared by a whole generation of executive administrators and intellectuals. These were people like my father and Mr. Fan, the chemical engineer, who had been forced to do manual labor instead of their professional jobs for a decade. Once back in responsible positions again, these middle-aged people were happy and enthusiastic about their work. They often felt they were young again. In fact, many of them used the phrase "second spring" to describe this new period in their lives.

On weekdays my father spent at least twelve hours at work. Every morning a few minutes after 6:30, an old Benz made in the 1940s waited for him in front of our house. We wouldn't see him again until after 7:00 p.m. On Sundays our house became his office again, as it had been a decade before. Even my role didn't change too much: I still served every guest a cup of tea. However, instead of being a small kid who was eager to serve but could hardly hold the cups steady, I now understood what was happening. At the dinner table, we often had conversations about what was going on in the nation as well as what was happening in each of our lives. Through those conversations I came to know more about my father's work. He liked to tell us about the major problems he faced at work and ask our opinions before he made any decisions. He especially wanted us to debate and argue with him. I thus became a participant in his decision-making process. He called this "domestic democracy." Of course, he wouldn't always do what we urged him to do. In fact, it made him happier if we opposed his ideas and his decision later proved to be correct.

One challenge he had was to manage the university as if it were a city or a mini-society. Many of his initiatives went beyond the usual responsibility of the deputy president of a university. I often heard him say that he would like to concentrate on academic and professional issues rather than social issues. However, he felt he had to deal with them all. One big issue at the time was that faculty members were often distracted from their work because of housework and inconvenience in their daily lives. To solve the problem, my father negotiated with the local government to open a convenience store near the campus. He also helped several key faculty members find jobs for their spouses at a closer location, so the spouses could take care of their families, freeing the faculty for their jobs. Due to lack of space, a local high school often refused to accept children whose parents were working at the university. My father had to persuade the high school authorities to take these children. He achieved that by offering some university facilities to the school.

My father's main concern, of course, was the students. At lunch time, he tried to go to the students' cafeteria as often as possible so that he could have more contact with them. At my own university I never saw administrators in our cafeteria. My father's style distinguished him from most other executive administrators. By keeping in touch with the people at the grassroots level, he could make some wise and popular decisions. For example, after collecting a fair amount of information from the faculty and the students, he decided to initiate a curriculum change. The current higher education system was very much like the Soviet model, where most courses were compulsory and there were almost no elective courses. My father preferred the Western model that gave students more flexibility in choosing courses. He thought that would help students become more independent and creative. His idea of having more elective courses was well received by both students and faculty.

He also volunteered to teach an evening course in basic English to administrators. Most of them had not received a college education. In addition to giving them an opportunity for formal study, my father hoped that, by taking the class, the administrators would understand the difficulties of intellectual work and have more respect for the faculty members. Most of the administrators were Party members and had held powerful positions for years. From their perspective, the faculty members were not only less important, but had much easier jobs. At least their lives looked easier. This misconception increased the conflicts between faculty and administrators. The faculty members only came to campus when they had classes and they did not have to come to work and stay on campus between 9:00 a.m. and 5:00 p.m., which were the administrators' hours. In his position as a well-educated administrator, my father tried his best to promote better communication and understanding between the two groups.

Only a few months after he took this job he gained a reputation on the campus as an "expert," someone who really knew about higher education. This was quite an accomplishment because people usually did not have much confidence in the executive administrators and viewed them as ignorant powerholders. It was true that leaders of an organization or institute were seldom knowledgeable about the profession. This was a big problem under Communist rule. The Party often put someone in charge of a hospital who did not have any medical training or knowledge, or someone in charge of a university who had never graduated from a university. This situation was probably more understandable shortly after the Communist takeover, because at the time they didn't have enough Party members who had appropriate training and background. The Party tried to solve the problem in two ways. One was to urge Party members in leading positions to learn as much about the profession as they needed and thus to transform themselves from laymen to experts. The other was to extend Party membership to professionals so that they could take up the leadership. However, this effort failed. First, the Party never had enough trust in professionals to recruit a large number and put them in charge. Second, few Party members had the motivation or qualifications to become professionals. As a result, almost three decades after the Communist takeover, it was still, in many cases, the ignorant bureaucrats who were in charge of the highly educated professionals.

Behind this issue was prejudice against intellectuals in general. In China the word "intellectual" included almost anyone with a college education. With their knowledge and capacity for reasoning, "intellectuals" often became a road block to authoritarianism. When the authorities felt their power was threatened, they could be ruthless. The first notorious case involving intellectuals occurred in 1955 when a prominent literary critic, Hu Feng, disagreed with Mao on a fundamental issue of literary criticism. Hu did not believe that literature should always serve a political purpose. He wrote a long essay on this subject and asked for an open debate. In response, Mao denounced him in a major newspaper as leading an "anti-Communist clique," and changed the issue from an academic one into a political one. In the consequent persecution Hu and dozens of people associated with him were jailed. Nationwide, over 2,000 people were involved and persecuted.

The political persecution against intellectuals happened time and again, both in the anti-rightist campaign in 1957 and during the Cultural Revolution. In 1971, the radicals even drafted an official document denouncing almost anyone with a higher education as being deeply influenced by capitalist or "counterrevolutionary" ideas and in need of brainwashing. After the radicals fell from power, although the new leadership in Beijing affirmed that people with higher education were innocent, these people still were often the targets of discrimination in their daily lives, especially by the human resources departments in each workplace. Under the Communist system, these departments held all the power because they were in charge of all promotions and salaries. Most people heading these departments had been supporters of the radicals or so indoctrinated in the radical ideology that they could hardly think in any other way. This became a barrier in the current effort to mitigate the damage caused by radical policies.

Shortly after his appointment, my father encountered such a case. It so happened that Hu Feng's eldest son worked at my father's university. Simply because he was Hu Feng's son he was denied proper salary raises and benefits for many years. Seeing the nation was heading in a new direction, he thought he might have a better chance. He wrote a letter requesting that the university authorities address the injustice that he was experiencing. Having examined Hu's dossier, my father felt there was no reason not to help him. Yet, when he asked the official from the human resources department to carry out the task, the man reminded my father that this was Hu Feng's son. "Yes, I know," my father said. The man seemed to be ignoring him and repeated: "He is Hu Feng's son." My father smiled and assured him: "I heard you. Please just do what I said, and I will be responsible for it." The man repeated again: "He is Hu Feng's son," and added in a raised voice: "Hu Feng is still in jail." "So what?" My father also raised his voice. "Hu Feng is Hu Feng. His son is his son. They are not the same person. We shouldn't hurt a person simply because his father is in jail. Let's correct this injustice. I'm willing to be responsible whatever the consequences. Let me put it simply. I want to right this wrong! Don't you understand?" There was not only anger in his voice, but also a sense of justice and bravery. I could still feel it when he told us what had happened. We all applauded him heartily and felt that some justice had been achieved. Surely he knew that he was not just helping Hu's son. He was also making a personal statement about his attitude toward Hu Feng's case, and he wished that someday, someone could right that wrong as well.

THE FORBIDDEN FRUIT

The Chinese education system was modeled after that of the Soviet Union. Even as a college student, I was put in a classroom group of fixed size and makeup. The seventy new students in our department were divided into three groups of about twenty-three each, based upon our scores on the entrance exams. Each group had all its classes together. My section scored highest and was academically strongest, and our courses were accelerated. Even so, I was soon bored by most of the work. I wanted to read more, but our textbooks did not provide us much reading. This was because they were compiled under the influence of a currently popular linguistic theory called Communicative Method. It emphasized listening and speaking rather than reading and writing. I did not like this, and started to search for alternative books. At the library I found a set of textbooks used in colleges before the Cultural Revolution. It contained many interesting stories, and I enjoyed reading the texts after class. Gradually I found myself spending more time on these books than I was on the required classwork.

I occasionally needed someone to help me understand the text of my extra readings. I asked Mr. Jin for assistance. Although he had tutored me while I was preparing for the entrance exam, he was not very useful now because his own English was limited. My father could not give me much help either, because he was too busy. However, he did introduce me to two well-known English professors at Nanjing University. They were both trained in the West. Professor Chen had a Ph.D. in literature from Yale University. He had been the head of the Department of Foreign Languages and Literatures at Nanjing University for many years. Professor Guo was an expert in English etymology and one of the few scholars in China who knew both Greek and Latin as well as English.

I was thrilled with the opportunity to know these two prominent professors. Both of them respected my father very much. However, I soon found that if I wanted to have them as my mentors I had to earn that right. I had to do my homework well and to show my intelligence.

There was no nonsense about it. They wouldn't waste their time on someone who was not motivated or did not have the talent to learn the material, even though they respected my father. Every other week I visited one of them and had a conversation for a couple of hours. This was quite similar to the tutor system at Oxford University. After a couple of months I found that both of them liked me and became more involved in my studies. They gave me the moral support I needed to disregard the current methodology used in college and to attempt to read more English on my own. With their help and encouragement, the scope of my reading grew rapidly.

Fairly soon I realized that as a result of my reading I was becoming more interested in the ideas I encountered than in the English language I was supposed to be learning. As I became more familiar with those ideas, I became more critical of our society and the political system. My change of mind was sometimes reflected in the classroom. Our textbook had a story about the power of money in capitalist countries. In the mid-term exam, we were expected to discuss the limitations of money and capitalism. However, my statement was wildly unorthodox. I first admitted that it was indeed a bad thing that money was everything in capitalist countries. Yet I went on to argue that in socialist countries, such as the Soviet Union, power became everything. Those who held the highest government positions were able to get everything they wanted. Then I asked: "Isn't that as bad, or maybe even worse?"

My question was too bold and it shocked my teacher. He immediately reported it to the department authorities. They talked with me and asked me if I was referring to China. Of course, I denied it, although I had China in mind when I wrote the comment. "Which countries were you referring to when you used 'countries' instead of 'country'?" asked the Party Secretary of our department. I knew I was caught. Suddenly it occurred to me that Eastern European countries such as Bulgaria and Hungary were also socialist. So I said what I meant was those Eastern European countries. They accepted this answer. Since the Soviet Union and the Eastern European countries were labeled "revisionists" by the orthodox Chinese Communists, it was acceptable to criticize them, just like any capitalist countries in the West. I was not hurt too much by this incident, except that my score on the exam was lowered a little.

I became even more enthusiastic about reading English books that were not on the school's recommended list, although ever since I was a teenager I had read books that were forbidden. The reason was quite simple: forbidden fruit always tasted better. I also searched for books to which others had no access. That created an excitement for reading as well. A woman writer and retired faculty member in my department named Yang quenched my thirst by lending me many books she received from friends abroad. I still remember some of my favorite books that I borrowed from her, such as *The Diary of Anne Frank* and a biography of the famous French sculptor Rodin. The joy of reading these books was twofold: I was not only interested in the content, I was also excited by the fact that I had access to them.

Among the books I read in English during my college years were some classics in psychology. As a branch of science, psychology had been underdeveloped in China for decades. Only a few Soviet psychologists and their theories, such as Pavlov and his theory about conditioned reflex, were allowed to be taught. All Western psychologists were ignored, and their theories were labeled pseudoscientific or false. In 1977, when we were asked to select a major before entering college, psychology was not even available as a choice, because there wasn't a psychology department in any university. In my university, for example, the Department of Psychology had been dissolved years ago and all the faculty members had been transferred to teach in the Department of Education. However, beginning in the late 1970s, psychology became a valid area of academic interest. Names of Western psychologists such as Sigmund Freud became really well known. Between 1978 and 1984, almost every periodical and popular magazines in China published articles about Freud. Just mentioning his name during a conversation would convey that the speaker was a learned or well-informed person.

Students and faculty were hungry for psychological literature, but few books were available. For example, Freud's works could not be found in any libraries. Of course, they had not been translated into Chinese yet, but English versions were not available either. My access to them was both accidental and remarkable. We had a family friend who was a reference librarian in our city's library, which was the third largest library in China. Together we went through all the index cards by author, title, and subject, but we could not find any books by Freud. One day he remembered that there were a couple of drawers of index cards that had never been open to the public. They were cards for a few thousand books that the library inherited from a small Japanese library during the Japanese occupation of Nanjing in the late 1930s and early 1940s. These books had not been in circulation since the Japanese surrender in 1945. On a Sunday morning when he was the only person working in that part of the library, he let me sneak into a dark room where those index cards were located. He showed me the boxes of the cards buried in dust. Our search turned out to be fruitful and astounding. We found cards for *A General Introduction to Psycho-Analysis* and *The Interpretation of Dreams* by Sigmund Freud, and also for the seven-volume *Studies in the Psychology of Sex* by Havelock Ellis. Just a glimpse of the title assured me that this was a topic that was really taboo. As a twenty-one-year-old, I could feel my heart pump harder. The excitement of tasting the forbidden fruit was already there, even before I actually got my hands on those books. We came out of the dark room and the librarian told me to wait outside while he went to search for the books. I waited only a few minutes, but it seemed like hours. When he finally returned with *A General Introduction to Psycho-Analysis* and the first volume of the *Studies in the Psychology of Sex*, I almost yelled "Hooray!" There was about half an inch of dust on the top of each book. I took out the record cards and the last dates stamped on them were in 1945! That made me the first reader in thirty-four years!

Although this experience was unique, the thirst for knowledge was nationwide. It took a few years for the academic world to rediscover and digest the "forbidden fruit." In fact, the whole nation was devouring previously proscribed Western culture. Coincidentally, the biblical story of the forbidden fruit became very popular again. People like my father had certainly read it before, but now it was our turn to enjoy it. After a decade of prohibition and even intentional destruction of knowledge, especially the body of knowledge that came from Western culture, the metaphor was even more poignant and powerful. For better or worse, history has reached a point of no return. The incorporation of Western culture into Chinese culture became just as irreversible as what had happened in the Garden of Eden.

A CHILLY SPRING

The spring of 1978 was a warm one. Many of those who had been wronged in political persecutions rehabilitated themselves. Even those who had been persecuted as "rightists" early in 1957 had a chance to appeal their cases. Encouraged by the new political wind and personally urged by his younger brother in Beijing, my second uncle in Shanghai went to Beijing to appeal his case to the personnel office in the central government. The man in charge of the entire personnel system was Hu Yaobang, who had recently been returned to the center of power himself. Hu was an outspoken man with a very open mind. In 1953 when Hu was the chairman of the Communist Youth League, my uncle was the League leader in Shanghai, directly reporting to Hu. Having this trace of an old connection, my uncle arrived in Beijing with some confidence and hope. He went to the personnel office, delivered his appeal, and asked to meet with Hu. Three days later he was told that Hu had an answer for him: "The appeal was received and there was no need to meet at this point. Our office will take care of the case." The executive secretary assured my uncle that he would receive a formal letter within a month. The letter did come, and my uncle was very impressed by the efficiency of Hu's office. Before the end of the year, he was assigned a position in the Shanghai government at a level equivalent to the one he had held twenty years before.

Many others also benefited from Hu. A directive came from Beijing admitting that many "rightists" in 1957 were actually wronged by Mao. It asked that these people be reinstated in their careers. Thousands of people were reinstated, many with direct help from Hu. Although Hu had played an important role in clearing his case, my uncle didn't have a chance to see him again until April 1981. That year, my uncle attended a high-level meeting of party leaders in Beijing. At the time, Hu had recently been promoted to the position of Deputy General Secretary of the Party. At dinner time, my uncle handed a note to a security person, requesting a meeting with Hu. In his note he said he hadn't seen Hu for twenty-seven years and missed him very much. By 8:00 p.m., he was told that Hu would meet him at 9:00. Again, my uncle was very impressed by Hu's efficiency. When the two men finally met, Hu stretched out his hand long before my uncle could hold it, and said, "You have suffered, I know. But now it's all over, and you are back at work again. That's good, very good." They shook hands as old friends, and my uncle was moved to tears.

Hu's confidence in the current Party leadership assured my uncle that what he had suffered would never happen again. Of course he trusted Hu, and he had good reason to. Yet no one could know that within six years Hu would be first promoted to General Secretary and then ousted from this position. This demonstrated the real danger in  our society. The fundamental problem with the system was not government regulations or policies. The problem was that people were never assured of their rights. Anyone could become a victim overnight, Party members and nonmembers alike. One could be hurt when remote from politics. One could be hurt when at the center of power. The former president Liu Shaoqi was jailed and tortured and starved to death in 1969. No matter how hopeful the current political situation appeared, one could hardly trust the system. Those who did were inevitably rewarded with bitter disappointments.

After the fall of the radicals in October 1976, many educated people liked to quote Shelley to reassure themselves that the darkest days of the radicals' rule were over: "If winter comes, can spring be far behind?" Unfortunately, the spring of 1979 was wintry cold, politically. In fact, almost every other year in the following decade there was a similar shift of political winds. Each new gust brought a sense of terror that threatened people's normal lives.

The first chilly spring came in 1979 after a really warm winter. Back in the middle of 1978, an article was published in a journal for internal circulation at the Central Party Academy, an institute providing continuing education in Marxism for high-ranking Communist officials. The author argued that any truth had to be tested by practice. If practice or reality demonstrated that a theory were wrong, it should be abandoned. Any theory might be wrong and anyone could make mistakes, including authorities in the government, and it was foolish to be dogmatic about any doctrine.

In the following months, this article was reprinted in all the major newspapers in China. The article was backed by Deng as a challenge to Hua Guofeng, who was currently both the Party chairman and the premier of the nation. As Mao's successor Hua adhered to whatever Mao had said and held it as a truism. This article encouraged the whole nation to reconsider the basis of this dogmatism. By advocating that a person should be free from the old framework of thought, it encouraged people to become independent and creative again. It was a daring move to set up a new principle in the post-Maoist period and it unleashed enormous energy from the billion Chinese individuals who wanted to pursue a better life.

Encouraged by this thaw in the political atmosphere, a movement for freedom and democracy soon spread from Beijing to other parts of the nation, especially on university and college campuses. At my university, many of the country's outspoken intellectuals were invited to come and give speeches. Students issued their own periodicals. Several of my classmates translated some short essays and poems from English and printed a collection entitled *Rocks from Other Mountains*. The inspiration for the title came from a Chinese myth. Like Prometheus who stole the fire from heaven to benefit human beings, these young students wanted to embrace Western ideas to solve Chinese problems. By late fall 1978, many young people in Beijing posted their articles with daring new thoughts on a downtown wall. It came to be known as the "Democracy Wall" because many of these articles demanded greater individual freedom and democracy. One prominent argument was that to achieve "modernization in agriculture, industry, science and technology, and the national defense," which were claimed to be the national goals by the Communist authorities, another goal must be set. That was the modernization of the political system.

The word "democracy" was very popular and was widely used at that time. For example, when Deng addressed a central Party meeting in December 1978, even he used the word "democracy" quite often and he stressed that "democracy is an important preliminary condition to the emancipation of one's mind." A couple of months later, however, the political wind suddenly shifted. Now that he had consolidated his power base and undermined Hua's position, Deng curbed his demand for democracy and jailed several authors of articles on the Democracy Wall. These young authors became the first victims after the revitalization of communism that came after the Cultural Revolution. Ironically, the incident was more closely monitored by Western media and concerned activists than by Chinese living in China, where its impact was only gradually felt.

Weeks had passed before I even heard of the trial in Beijing when a chief contributor of the articles on the Democracy Wall was sent to jail for fifteen years. A few days later, when I encountered my friend Yang, who had loaned me so many English books, she shared a marvelous memory. Several decades before she had seen a play performed as an opera in Sichuan Province, where Deng was born. The play was about a persecuted prince in exile, a story somewhat similar to Shakespeare's *Hamlet*. With support from the people, the exiled prince finally killed his political enemies and came to power. Players in Chinese operas often wear symbolically colored masks, red for good people and white for bad ones. One unique feature of this provincial Sichuan opera was that the players sometimes changed their masks from scene to scene. What was remarkable in this play was that the prince wore a red mask throughout the entire play, until the curtain was raised for the curtain calls. At that moment, the audience suddenly found their beloved prince wearing a white mask! The woman told me that she really appreciated the implicit meaning in this dramatic change of masks, although it sent an uncomfortable chill down her spine. When she told me this story, I felt that chill too, but we both had a good laugh and felt it would be perfect timing for a political satire if someone dared to stage this play again.

On reflection, I felt that the real issue was even greater than whether good or bad people were in charge. For thousands of years, leaders often thought that they must eliminate their political rivals if they wanted to stay in power. They beheaded or imprisoned their rivals, treating them as captives in war. Modern democracy or the civilization that Tocqueville hailed was never established in China, even though the Communist Party had claimed that it wanted to build such a democracy. With that in mind, despite all the negative aspects of the presidential elections in the United States, we became envious of the peaceful transfer of political power every four or eight years.

PEOPLE FIRST

In early 1979, a border war broke out between Vietnam and China. It is not yet clear why that happened. For months the Chinese media told stories about the Vietnamese government's persecution of Chinese people living in Vietnam. We were told that thousands of them had been deported by the Vietnamese government. They were sent to sea, where many of them were robbed or raped by ruthless pirates. Only the survivors reached the Chinese shore. To millions of Chinese, these stories were infuriating. For more than a decade the Chinese government had supported the Vietnamese in their war against the United States. The Chinese people paid dearly for this. While thousands of Chinese were starving at home, a tremendous amount of food, clothes, and arms had been transported to Vietnam as free aid. Nothing could compare with the sense of betrayal and hatred for this Vietnamese ingratitude. Some sarcastic people even said that we should not have supported Vietnam in the first place, and that it was because of our own stupidity that we were suffering this outrage.

I did not hear my father comment on this, but I felt he too was upset. In addition to his general concern about the Chinese being persecuted in Vietnam, the whole event seemed to mock his own life. In the early 1960s when China was supporting Vietnam against the United States, he was both professionally and emotionally involved. As a local government official in charge of public relations, he was responsible for mobilizing public support for Vietnam. Almost every week he gave public speeches addressing the issue, and his eloquence was so impressive that many people became his friends after listening to his talks. At home, he often showed me a map of Vietnam with surrounding nations such as Cambodia, Laos, and China, and taught me geography. The map we used was a colored one, with solid red indicating the territory occupied by the Communists, and grids in red lines representing areas where Communist guerrillas were very active. Each week, we updated our map according to the news we heard from the radio. Every time a city or town came under Communist control we cheered for the victory of the Vietnamese people and celebrated their defeating the American imperialists. My sister often asked how soon Vietnam would be liberated from imperialist aggression. My father always cited the eight-year war of resistance against the Japanese between 1938 and 1945 as an example. He said that, difficult as it was, the final victory would be ours. In this case, he said the victory would belong to the Vietnamese and the Chinese people. One of the most popular plays my mother's theater group performed at the time was called *The Children of Uncle Ho Chi Minh*. I saw that play many times and always enjoyed it. As children we grew up in an environment that supported the Vietnamese against U.S. aggression, and the adults actually contributed their time and energy to the support of Vietnam. A couple of years later some Red Guards even volunteered to cross the border to join the Vietnamese army, although the Chinese government did not actually encourage them to go so far. Only one decade after that, however, a war broke out between Vietnam and China. All the efforts seemed to boomerang. No wonder many people felt betrayed when the border war between Vietnam and China began.

Once the war broke out, a strong patriotic feeling prevailed among the general public, and sincere good will and support were generated for the combat forces in the battlefield. We knew that armies throughout the country, including units from our province, were sent to the front. It surprised my family, however, when my father's youngest brother wrote from Beijing saying that he was going too.

My uncle was an army colonel and before the Cultural Revolution he had served in the national headquarters of the armored corps of the People's Liberation Army as a deputy director of the Political Department. In the armed forces, each headquarters consisted of three departments: the Department of General Staff, the Political Department, and the Logistics Department. As a deputy director of the Political Department in the national headquarters, he was one of the youngest officers to hold such a high-ranking position in China. His seemingly smooth career path was interrupted by the Cultural Revolution when he was sent to a labor camp for army officers in an inland province. There he was asked to tend horses for seven years. In an accident, a horse broke three of his ribs. Miraculously, he survived and remained quite healthy.

Like many others, he expected to be assigned a new position after the radicals fell from power. However, due to personal politics, he was ignored and not renominated to an official position until the war broke out. The news of the war stimulated his soldier's heart. He wrote a letter to the highest military authorities volunteering to go to the front. In his letter he said that he was still young (only fifty-eight years old!) and in very good physical shape. He said he was not asking for any power but that he just wanted to go to the front to serve his country again. Moved by his sincerity, the authorities sent him to Vietnam as a special military observer. Thus, by the time we received his letter he probably had arrived at the front in south China. We could not respond to him in time, but we all wished him well and felt proud of him for having such courage and spirit.

He sent us letters telling what he had observed at the front. Some of his stories were outrageous. For example, the Chinese army often found military supplies in the hands of the Vietnamese troops that were actually made in China. The arms, trucks, and even sacks of rice that were now in the Vietnamese army had been made or produced in China and sent to Vietnam as a gift to support the Vietnamese during its war against the United States. Now, these became military supplies for the Vietnamese army in their war against China. History is often full of ironies!

Despite heavy casualties in the front, my uncle returned safely to Beijing a few months later. Coincidentally, my father joined him in Beijing at the time. Between January and August 1980, my father was sent to study in the Central Party Academy in Beijing, a school that trains high-ranking officials in Marxist theory. My uncle, just returned from the border war with Vietnam, also enrolled in the academy. Their brother, my second uncle living in Shanghai, was also invited, although in the end he did not join them. Even without him, two brothers of their age studying together in that institute was remarkable and our whole family became very excited about it. What made me even more excited was that I could visit Beijing now, because I could stay in the academy's inexpensive guesthouse at night and tour the city by day.

When school closed in July, I set out for the capital. My best friend, Lin, came with me. We planned to stay for ten days. Like many other tourists, we soon realized that ten days were not enough. We had to be very selective in choosing what to see. The first place we dropped from our list was Mao's Memorial Hall, where his body was kept for visitors to pay their tribute. I had never seen him while he was alive and I did not much care to see his body now. Like many youth of the day, I began to have more disdain than respect for this former giant. It was only four years since his death in 1976, but a growing number of people were beginning to realize what a disservice this man had done to the nation during the last ten years of his life.

At the time, however, the Communist authorities were not yet ready to admit this and officially denounce the Cultural Revolution launched by Mao. Many officials kept silent and did not criticize the Cultural Revolution openly, even though most of them had been victimized by it. Although it was politically safer to keep silent, my father often failed to do so. During a meeting with an American delegation, his outspokenness even shocked an American woman. When she noticed that Father could speak some English she started to talk to him directly without an interpreter. "What do you think about the Cultural Revolution?" the woman asked. He responded, "A disaster!" The woman was taken aback by his blunt answer. "What?" The woman had to ask again to confirm what she had just heard. "I said it's a disaster," my father continued, "but it's over, and we are moving ahead again." Of course, the reason he did not hesitate to make such a comment was because he felt confident that his criticism would be justified by the revitalization of the Communist Party. At the time, this seemed fairly reasonable.

Although we dropped Mao's Memorial Hall from our list, we did want to see the building next to it, the Great Meeting Hall of the People. It was a place similar to the Capitol in Washington, D.C., in the sense that the Chinese People's Congress always had its sessions there. We heard that it had recently been opened to the public and we wanted to see it. One morning we took the bus from the Central Party Academy to Tiananmen Square where the Meeting Hall was located. To our surprise and disappointment, we saw a sign on the ticket booth that said: "Closed to the public today because of scheduled foreign visitors." We went back again the next morning. Again, to our surprise and frustration, we found a similar sign: "Closed to the public because of visiting overseas Chinese."

The third morning we went there again, and this time we were finally allowed to enter. Once inside, the guards yelled at the crowds in a very rude manner and within minutes I decided that we did not belong there and that this hall did not belong to the people either, despite its name. Lin was just about to take a picture when a guard came over and almost confiscated his camera. He said photos were not allowed, although we could not see any signs indicating this. I sighed to my friend and we both felt a bitter irony. As citizens of Communist-ruled China, we were treated as third-class citizens in our own land, simply because none of us had a Westerner's high-boned nose and pale skin, or dressed well like the rich overseas Chinese!

During his stay in the Central Party Academy, my father wrote several articles comparing Marxist theory with the reality he had faced since the Communist takeover. He showed me his manuscripts and I liked them a great deal. One of them was later published in the major newspaper in our province. The article was entitled "Always Keep in Mind That Our Party's Ultimate Goal Was to Serve the People" and that was its main point. Our government claimed to be of the people, for the people, and by the people. Although this idea became famous through Lincoln's speech, it was first accepted by Dr. Sun Yat-sen after the 1911 Revolution and then by the Chinese Communist Party as its own goal in its early days. In fact, "To serve the people" was one of the best-known quotes from the late Chairman Mao. My father certainly tried to live up to the moral principle of caring for others more than for oneself. During the famine in the early 1960s, he asked our family to save whatever we could from our own plates and gave the extra *liang-piao* (the certificate for rationed food) to his chauffeur, whose teenage sons were often more hungry than we were. I still remember the grateful smiles on the faces of that driver and his wife, who was a teacher at my kindergarten.

However, my father realized that sometimes a government official could face an awkward dilemma. The orders coming from the authorities might conflict with the interest of the people. Should the official follow the orders or listen to people's demands? My father advocated that the official should keep in mind that our Party's ultimate goal was to serve the people and therefore he should do whatever was in the best interests of the people. Even though he might offend his boss and hurt his career, he would get moral support from the people and they would be grateful to him. Eventually the Party would recognize his decisions were correct and give him the credit he deserved.

I understood his point because he seemed to be practicing this principle all his life. He did eventually get a few rewards. For example, as a deputy president at his university, he often made decisions that were warmly welcomed by the people but not always pleasing to his direct supervisor the president or to some bureaucrats in the Higher Education Committee of the provincial government. It was lucky for him that this time the people's voice did count and the central government in Beijing soon nominated him to be president of the university in 1979, two years after he had started to work there. For most of his life, however, he had not been so fortunate and he lost many career opportunities because he stuck to this principle.

Another example was his decision to build the wall gate, instead of tunneling holes through the wall as Mayor Ke asked him to do. Sometimes it even required subtle skills to achieve the goals. During the "anti-rightist campaign" in 1957, for example, my father was the principal of a technical school, and orders came down to label whoever had criticized the Communist Party in the previous year as "rightists." In his position, my father made the best effort to minimize the damage of such persecution, although that was a very dangerous thing to do. He could be labeled a "rightist" himself simply because he had not labeled enough other people as "rightists." He understood that if he were labeled a "rightist," not only would he lose his job, more people in the school would be persecuted, because whoever succeeded him would be a person more willing to carry out orders. So, to be practical, he used all his skills trying to handle the situation cautiously. In this way, he managed to maintain his position as the head of the school and to protect as many people as possible at the same time. A few years later, when the political wind shifted in a moderate direction, he lost no time in doing his best to make justice prevail. At the time, he was working in the municipal government in charge of culture, education, health care, and sports. Within this jurisdiction there were 1,013 people who had been labeled "rightists" in 1957. Between 1961 and 1962, he spent a huge amount of time reexamining each case and he officially declared 1,002 out of those 1,013 persons innocent!

When a new wave of persecutions started, there would be official documents that defined the target of the campaign. There was always a difference among officials in their use of these official documents. Some would interpret the official definitions of "public enemies" very broadly and maximize the number of "enemies." Others would use them conservatively and minimize the scope of the persecution. To a large extent, the size of each persecution depended on the actual mix of these two types of officials. People would be lucky if they worked for a "good" boss; if they happened to work for a "bad" one, they would be very vulnerable. Exactly for this reason, many victims tended to think that their tragedies simply resulted from the ill luck of working for the wrong person. It was easy for them to overlook the fact that it was the system more than individual officials that had caused all of their troubles. There was something seriously wrong with Communism. I wasn't sure if the theory was wrong, or if we had been damaged by malpractice. It had certainly rewarded those who cared less about the people and punished those who put people first. Yet my father was not the least regretful about the choice he had made.

"DEMOCRACY LOST"

In January 1981, five months after my father graduated from the Central Party Academy, he was assigned a new job. This time he was asked to go back to work in the municipal government of Nanjing, in charge of the same department where he had worked before the Cultural Revolution. This new assignment was partly a response to popular demand. People working within the jurisdiction of this department had voiced their desire for stronger leadership, and many specifically asked for my father. Considering my father was a university president now, the authorities had to make their job offer more attractive by assigning him to a position at the municipal leadership level instead of to one of its departments. So, in addition to putting him in charge of that department, they nominated my father as a deputy chairman of the standing committee of the People's Congress of the City of Nanjing.

The People's Congress had been a part of the political structure since the Communist takeover in 1949. The Communists came to power with wide support from the Chinese people, and one of their appeals was their promise to establish a political system more democratic than the old Nationalist government. Modeled on other modern democracies, a political structure was set up with four parallel organizations and institutions: the Communist Party, the People's Congress, the People's Government, and the People's Political Advisory Conference. This parallel structure existed at all levels of the administration, the central, the provincial, the municipal, and the county. The People's Government was the executive branch. The People's Congress and the People's Political Advisory Conference were somewhat like the two houses in the British system or the Senate and the House of Representatives in the United States, although only the People's Congress was supposed to be a legislative body and to make laws. In reality, however, there was never a balanced power structure, and the Communist Party was always the dominant power overseeing the other three. The function of the People's Political Advisory Conference was the murkiest. When the Communists took over in 1949, all the political parties existing at the time were legally allowed to continue, and each was represented in the People's Political Advisory Conference. The Communist Party therefore claimed that it had kept its promise of democracy. However, in the years after, it turned out that this body served only as window-dressing and that the other political parties really existed just for show. The Communist Party never shared power with them, and the number of new members other political parties could recruit was strictly controlled. Even this limited form of democracy was eliminated during the Cultural Revolution.

In 1980, the revitalized Communist leadership returned to their earlier position regarding a limited form of democracy. At all levels of administration, this parallel power structure was reestablished. According to the procedure, my father's nomination to be a deputy chairman had to be approved by vote of the standing committee of the People's Congress. There would be one chairman and eight deputy chairmen for the standing committee of the People's Congress of Nanjing. Among the ten candidates nominated by the Communist Party, there was one who would not be elected. When my father explained the voting process to us, we felt both excited and a little nervous. We were excited because we all liked this democratic process, however limited it was. With voting it would become clear who among the Communist officials was popular and who was not. If we had always had this kind of democratic process, my father would have had a more successful political career. We were concerned, however, that because he had not been working in the municipality for the past fifteen years, his name might not be that familiar to people. We were a little nervous that he might not be able to get enough votes.

"What happens if you lose the election? It will be a demotion for you if you end up holding that department head position alone. How can you face that, Daddy?" my sister asked with a very concerned voice. "Well, that won't happen. If it does, I will simply accept the people's decision. You know, it's really not that important to have such an official title as a deputy chairman. I will just focus on my work in the department. That's what this is all about. I came back to work in the municipal government because people wanted to have a stronger leadership in that department. They have trust in me because of my past record." My father always had such an indifferent attitude toward changes in his career. At home, my mother often teased him and called him an "old fool." That day she called him "old fool" again, and we all had a good laugh about it. Yet in our hearts we respected him even more for his noble spirit. In fact, we should have had more confidence in him, for when election day came he won an overwhelming victory. Many people even wrote in his name for deputy mayor, although he was not a candidate for that position. These people thought the standing committee of the People's Congress was only a "rubber stamp" and they wanted to see my father in a position with some real power.

Cheered by the votes, we were really glad that this voting system was coming back. This system was not at all strange to me. The first day I went to primary school we were told to elect a student in our class as the student monitor. On the grassroots level in the rural areas, the tradition of voting was maintained faithfully, even during the Cultural Revolution in the late 1960s. In the isolated mountain village where my sister had lived and worked with the local peasants, the villagers held an annual meeting every winter to elect the village leader for the next year. Most of these villagers were illiterate and their attitude toward politics was usually lukewarm. When political meetings were held, mainly as a way for the government to inform the villagers of its recent policy changes and to ask them to obey all the orders, villagers often found reasons not to attend. Each household would send only one member to the meeting. However, when the annual election was held, every adult member from each household came. They took this vote seriously and wanted to elect the person they trusted the most.

As a matter of fact, it was the Communists who had introduced voting to the remote rural villages they occupied in the 1930s and 1940s. The Communists had advocated democracy, promised democracy, and even implemented democracy in their occupied rural areas, and that greatly helped them win the support from the peasants and their families, which was about 90 percent of the Chinese population. Carrying the banner of democracy helped the Communists overthrow the previous Nationalist government led by Chiang Kai-shek. This was not often understood in the West. Most Westerners thought of Communism and democracy as mutually exclusive systems, but in China, democracy had once been embraced by the Communists, and democracy was both a method and a part of their goal. They used the appeal of democracy to mobilize more support to overthrow the Nationalist government and they promised there would be real democracy after they came to power. However, after the Communists gained power, the glimmers of democracy gradually disappeared and even the concept of democracy was nearly abandoned.

In the Communist lexicon, there has been an odd phrase, "democratic and centralized system," which defined a situation where leadership was democratically selected but that functioned with centralized authority thereafter. In the history of the Communist Party Mao took over the leadership of the Communist Party in the mid-1930s in a kind of democratic process. At the time, the Soviet-supported leaders dogmatically obeyed Soviet instructions and failed to understand the reality in China. Their leadership caused a great military loss to the Red Army and resulted in the 7,000-mile retreat known as the Long March. In an emergency meeting during this long march, a dozen top Chinese Communist leaders chose Mao by a marginal vote to replace the military leadership. During the next years, Mao won over the effective leadership within the Communist Party by his astounding military strategy. His successes led to an unchallenged leadership for more than a decade, and to the final victory over Chiang Kai-shek's government in 1949. After so many years under Mao's unchallenged leadership, the phrase "democratic and centralized system" lost its original meaning. Democratic process disappeared and only centralized authority was left. The word "democratic" was often used to describe a leadership style rather than a political process. When a leader seemed to be willing to listen to different opinions, he was praised for being "democratic." Even this positive connotation of the word "democracy" was often dropped, however, and thus the word was only used negatively and was generally associated with an attempt to overthrow the Communist government.

All of this was so dramatically different from those early years in the 1950s and before. In the early 1950s, Communist propaganda blamed imperialism, especially the American imperialists, for all the wars around the world. The Communists claimed to be peace lovers and democracy builders, and this was reflected in the songs composed during those days. It was ironic that when the Korean War broke out, both China and the United States claimed to enter the war for exactly the same reason! In their own words, they both came to the war to defend world peace and democracy. Decades later, however, the word *democracy* almost disappeared from the Communist doctrine. Today, the Chinese government claims to be a peace lover but no longer claims to be a defender of democracy. Within half a century, the Communist position on democracy had been turned upside down.

Since the 1911 Revolution led by Sun Yat-sen, democracy has inspired people in each progressive social movement in China. Yet each time a new social order was established, democracy was soon abandoned. So many times we thought we had finally obtained democracy, but every time it was lost again. I often wondered why. Many years later I sat in the classrooms in the United States taking courses in American civilization and learned that President Washington declined to run for a third term. Suddenly I felt that was the greatest thing Washington had ever done. It is much easier to find a victorious general than to find a successful statesman willing to give up power voluntarily. Although history could not be replayed, I suspect China today would be quite different if some of its leaders had truly done as Washington did. Recalling John Milton's *Paradise Lost* and *Paradise Regained*, I wondered if some great poet of our time would write "Democracy Lost" and "Democracy Regained" to describe twentieth-century Chinese history. Like "paradise," "democracy" was certainly lost in China, although some might argue that it had never existed. When will it be regained? That still remains the question.

BITTER LOVE

During the two years my father worked at the Nanjing Aeronautic Engineering University, our family continued to live with the five families in that one-family residence. Like most other workplaces with a large number of employees, the university was supposed to provide its employees with housing. However, the university did not have any housing available when my father started to work there. He did not want to push the university to provide housing, because he knew that housing was tight and that many faculty members were living in very crowded conditions. Shortly after he returned to work in the municipal government of Nanjing, we were provided with a house by the city. With his new title as the deputy chairman of the Standing Committee of the People's Congress in the city, he was entitled to have a single-family house inside the municipal employee residential compound where we had lived in the 1960s. Again, however, there was no single-family house available at the time. The housing department found one for us outside the residential compound instead. It was a few blocks away from the compound, adjacent to a neighborhood of low-income residents. There was a fairly large courtyard surrounding it, although the house itself was small. But at least each of us had a room now, and this was quite a luxury according to Chinese housing standards. Although my room was tiny, only about sixty square feet, I was quite happy.

Even though our new house was not quite as good as the single-family houses inside the residential compound, occupying such a roomy residence right next to a low-income neighborhood often made us feel guilty. In this poor neighborhood, families of two or three generations with seven to ten people had to live together in two or three rooms. Most of these people were blue-collar workers. Their workplaces usually could not provide housing, as big institutions such as universities or the municipal government did. They had to rent from the limited housing stock on the market, which usually consisted of shabby little sheds owned by different housing bureaus in the city. The last time I had been to this neighborhood was in the late 1960s when I visited the rice-grinding mill operated by the family of a former classmate at my primary school. I remembered how poor she was then, and I could see that poverty still remained in this neighborhood.

The more poverty I saw around me, the more I looked forward to seeing the new leaders in Beijing move China ahead so that a growing economy would eliminate such poverty. However, my confidence in the new leadership was greatly reduced when I felt a new political wind sweeping China again in the spring and summer of 1981. It was triggered by a movie called *Bitter Love*, which was never allowed to be publicly screened. Critics backed by the authorities went public through the government-controlled media and criticized the screenwriter, Bai Hua, as unpatriotic. The tone of the criticism sounded just like that of the radicals under whom this nation had suffered for over ten years. Bai was criticized for portraying too much poverty and injustice. One particularly controversial line came at the end of the movie, when the hero asked himself, having suffered for more than two decades after he was labeled a "rightist" in 1957: "Surely I love my country, but who loves me?"

The critics insisted that if someone were a true patriot he should never ask what the country can do for him but only what he can do for the country. It sounded somewhat like John Kennedy's words, but in practice it used patriotism as an excuse to deny and forbid any criticism of the mismanagement by the Communist government. Most people felt sympathetic with the screenwriter, and the public was quite sick and tired of such opportunistic criticism, too. In fact, Bai Hua was no less patriotic than any of his critics, and he had joined the Communist army in the late 1940s. It was out of patriotism that such a provocative question arose. In one of his earlier plays he asserted that we should all feel guilty if we couldn't make the Communist system work today, because it meant that we were letting those who had lost their lives for the Communist victory in 1949 die in vain. His movie *Bitter Love* described how the failures of the regime let people down and left those who had once been patriotic feeling cheated and bitterly betrayed.

Although Bai Hua's *Bitter Love* was a fictional story, I knew numerous examples of true patriots who had had to taste such a bitterness. My father was an example, and his long-time friend Professor Qian was another. Qian was one of those professors with whom my parents had often alternated giving Western-style parties. Qian was an American-educated engineer. In 1948, he graduated from a college in Iowa with a master's degree and found a good job. A year later, his daughter was born in the United States. When the Communists took over in 1949 he—just like many other young intellectuals overseas at that time—was inspired by the birth of a new China. Many such men and women abandoned their careers and returned to China with patriotic devotion. Despite the American government's effort to encourage them to stay as permanent residents, Qian and his wife returned to China in 1951 with their Chinese-born son and American-born daughter. The new Chinese government gave them a warm welcome. Qian began to teach in the Nanjing Agricultural University and was in charge of researching production of modern agricultural machinery for the new China. Two years later, my father was put in charge of that institute, and the two families became neighbors and close friends, sharing a two-family house. Both Qian and my father were patriots trying to make the new China a powerful nation. However, the new China did not work out as promised. Thirty years after this social experiment that had inspired and involved over half a billion people, Communism failed to deliver either economic prosperity or a broader democracy. Ironically, those who had put their faith in it and devoted their lives to it were often punished and persecuted as enemies of the Communist system, especially during the Cultural Revolution.

Professor Qian died of pancreatic cancer in 1985. On his death bed, one of his last wishes was to drink a cup of Coca-Cola, a beverage he had often consumed in the United States thirty years earlier. Unfortunately, only the privileged few in China had access to the soft drink, and his little wish was never fulfilled. A great number of genuine patriots experienced such "bitter love." In the end they were each to feel the betrayal of their ideals for the country that they had loved so dearly.

The criticism of *Bitter Love* soon became a new political campaign and public persecution, as literary criticism backed by Communist authorities always did. This time, the target of the politically motivated criticism soon shifted from the individual movie to a so-called ideological trend of liberalism. The word "liberalism" was really misused. It had nothing to do with the concept of liberalism as it is understood in the West. What it meant was a simple human desire for more freedom. After years of extremely strict ideological control, people began to have a little more freedom to pursue different personal goals. Some began to try different styles of dress; others developed different tastes in music. A few even explored different philosophies and studied them as an academic interest. To the hardline Communist authoritarians, even a little freedom—a little "liberalism"—was too much. They considered it to be a negative impact of Western influence and viewed it as a direct threat to Communist rule.

I would not have been surprised to hear that this call for a curb on the "ideological trend of liberalism" came from some of the most hardline Communist leaders. However, I was very disappointed when I learned that this new political campaign was backed by Deng Xiaoping. Despite his crushing of the Democracy Wall in Beijing in early 1979, most people still respected him as a great leader and reformer, and even acknowledged that the posters on the Democracy Wall might have gone too far. This time it was different, because his antagonists were not just a group of unknown youths, but some prominent writers. In a secret speech circulated among a small circle of top leaders, Deng not only criticized Bai Hua, the author of *Bitter Love*, but also blamed a handful of other leading intellectuals for contributing to the "trend of liberalism." On the list was an old man, Ba Jin, probably the most prominent Chinese novelist of this century alive today. I first heard the rumor from Yang with whom I once had a conversation about Deng and the changing of theatrical masks in a local opera shortly after the Democracy Wall incident. If what she said was true, it seemed almost certain that Ba Jin was going to be one of the targets of the imminent persecution. At first, I could not believe this could be true, but I heard the rumor again from another, more reliable and authoritative source, our family friend Uncle Zhao.

My father and his brothers had known Uncle Zhao since the 1930s when they were working together operating the refugee camps during the Japanese occupation of Shanghai. As one of the deputy chairmen of the People's Political Advisory Conference of China, Uncle Zhao was now a top national leader. He happened to be in Nanjing at that time on a diplomatic errand, accompanying a high-level Japanese Buddhist delegation visiting China. My parents and I visited him at his hotel. Our conversation soon turned to political topics and we were all concerned about the coming political storm and worried about the nation's future. From that conversation I confirmed that what I had heard from Yang was basically accurate. I still vividly remember the heavy atmosphere and the long silence after our conversation came to a dead end. Everyone in that hotel room fully understood what this meant to the future of the nation. It would change its agenda from economic development to ideological disputes again. We had already lost one decade to the Cultural Revolution and could not afford to lose another!

What seemed to be most disappointing was that this time Deng was on the wrong side. Most people still had high expectations of him. To some degree, Deng was our new hero. As a national leader, Mao once enjoyed unprecedentedly high popularity among the Chinese. In the eyes of people my sister's age, he had been an almost divine figure through the 1960s. Because of the disasters he had brought about during the 1970s, this image had gradually become negative. As Mao's reputation dramatically declined, Deng's image became increasingly positive. People often have admiration and love for their national leaders, and many Chinese had such feelings toward Deng in the late 1970s and early 1980s. However, as history often proved, such politicians can prove to be unworthy of such love. They let their supporters down and made them feel bitter at their misplaced loyalty.

Although this is a universal phenomenon, the degree of such bitterness was quite different. In a modern democratic state, people might easily adjust their feelings by casting their votes for the opponent in the next election. However, in an authoritarian society, people do not have such an opportunity. Because of this, they are often very excited when they think they have a great leader, although eventually and almost inevitably they will be deeply disillusioned. There seems to be an irony or paradox here. National leaders in an authoritarian society often enjoyed greater popularity and public mandates than their counterparts in a democratic society. In the United States, on the one hand, a president might be elected by a slim majority, and a large number of the citizens do not vote at all. Thus, his election represents only a small proportion of public support. On the other hand, leaders like Mao or Deng had almost the entire nation supporting them. They were hailed as heroes, although they might soon cause the whole country to suffer. My heart was deeply touched when I found a similar idea conveyed in a movie named *Mayor Chen Yi.* The screenwriter, Sha Yexin, was another provocative contemporary writer. In the movie, he let the prominent outspoken Communist mayor make a wonderful comment on the Third Symphony of Beethoven: "History can be very ironic. You see, this music was meant to be dedicated to a hero [Napoleon]. Yet, by the time the music was finally composed, the hero was not a hero anymore!" I was thrilled when I heard these words. I felt I shared something with the author, although he didn't know me at all. I was only a young member of the audience sitting in the darkness of a movie theater, whereas he was a well-established playwright. Yet, different as we were in terms of fame and social status, we both experienced and shared that same feeling of a misplaced and embittered love.

CHAPTER 8

TO BE, OR NOT TO BE

I graduated from Nanjing Teachers' University in January 1982. This was the first time in sixteen years that Chinese students had completed four years of higher education. The last such graduates were those who entered college in 1962. Those who began between 1963 and 1965 did not finish because of the interruption of the Cultural Revolution. No students were recruited for four-year colleges until the end of 1977, and the nation had to wait another four years to see the graduates. We were really in unprecedented demand when we graduated in 1982. That year, the Chinese government also decided to adopt the degree system, and we became the first to receive bachelor's degrees since the Communist takeover in 1949!

I started to teach at a college in Nanjing in February 1982, and I was happy about my new job. Since early childhood I had heard about my father's experience as a teacher, and the respect he had for the occupation made me like it too. In his view, a good teacher always had a strong positive influence on his or her students, and that could really make a difference in the world. Coincidentally, every member of my family was or had been a teacher. Not only my father, but also my sister had taught, and my mother used to teach Chinese in the high school that my sister later attended. My brother-in-law had joined the faculty of the Army Academy in Nanjing after he graduated. My father said that our family was a family of teachers and he often teased me by asking me if I was going to bring another teacher into the family through marriage.

My first assignment was to teach Extensive English Reading for a class of over forty students. This had been my favorite course as a student, because it provided me with more reading than any other course. I had long believed that there were advantages to learning English that were greater than just the ability to speak another language. English was a tool that could open our minds for perceiving things we would not otherwise be able to see. I knew my father had read Lamb's *Tales from Shakespeare* in English in high school and I think that had some impact on his outlook on the world thereafter. In college, I had learned much more through English than I had learned about English. Now as a teacher, I wanted my students to benefit as well.

One morning I wrote a quote from Shakespeare on the blackboard:

> To be, or not to be: that is the question:
> Whether 'tis nobler in the mind to suffer
> The slings and arrows of outrageous fortune,
> Or to take arms against a sea of troubles,
> And by opposing end them.

The quote was already well known in China in translation, largely due to Lawrence Olivier's *Hamlet*, a very popular movie. Olivier's part was read by a celebrated Chinese actor. Movie translation was a professional business in China, and each year a few foreign movies were selected to be dubbed in Chinese by professionals. They did it so skillfully that when the audience heard the Chinese, they often felt it was coming right from the mouth of the foreign actors on the screen. The perfect dubbing could make the audience forget that the person they saw on the screen was not actually speaking Chinese.

However, even the best translation lost a great deal of the original meaning, especially when the originals were such thoughtful works as Shakespeare's. I wanted my students to learn from the original. I started by asking them a seemingly simple question: "Does it appear to you that it is always nobler 'to take arms against a sea of troubles' than 'to suffer the slings and arrows of outrageous fortune'?" They all nodded their heads, because our school education since childhood had always taught us that it was brave and virtuous to fight against something wrong and it was cowardly and shameful to suffer or compromise. "If that were the case, was Hamlet, or Shakespeare, asking a stupid question?" My students were silent, and many of them buried their faces in their books and were afraid that I would ask them a further question. I knew my question had puzzled and probably even surprised them. As a matter of fact, I was puzzled too when I was asking myself the same question while preparing for the class. Instinctively, I knew that somewhere in our value system we also respected the capability of suffering and enduring and viewed it as noble, but I just could not find a good example to illustrate this point until I recalled the name of the late Premier Zhou.

When the premier died in 1976 millions of people mourned his death. One of the reasons was that people believed he had suffered and endured many wrongs. In recent Chinese history, his role was unique. Richard Nixon had some insight on it when he wrote in his memoir: "Without Mao the Chinese Revolution would never have caught fire. Without Zhou it would have burned out and only the ashes would remain."[1] Zhou never disagreed openly with Mao, but he had his own way of mitigating and controlling the damage that Mao's policies had caused. Many people had benefited or at least they believed they had benefited from Zhou's way of handling things. Believing that Zhou had suffered for their sake, people felt grateful to him and thought of him as a great and noble man.

Zhou's perceived nobility was very different from that of another prominent Chinese Communist leader, Marshal Peng. The former defense minister had a brave and open disagreement with Mao. Witnessing famine and chaos caused mainly by Mao's radical policy of pushing collective farming in the late 1950s, Peng wrote a long report and sent it to the top circle of the Party leadership. He disagreed with Mao and appealed for an immediate halt to this policy. Outraged by Peng's opposition, Mao condemned him as a public enemy and had him removed from his office immediately. Only after Mao's death was Peng's reputation officially rehabilitated by the Communist authorities at the end of 1978.

Both Zhou and Peng enjoyed much honor and popularity. Yet the difference between the two was so great that it seemed difficult to reconcile the opposite principles that each had stood for. If Peng was brave, was Zhou a coward? If Zhou was wise, was Peng foolish? If both were noble, which one was nobler? To me, Shakespeare's question was amazingly appropriate for our current situation, except that he had raised

1. Richard Nixon, *Leaders* (New York: Warner Books, 1982), 248.

this question hundreds of years before. From their smiling faces I knew my students appreciated my personal reflection.

In my own mind, however, the reflection did not stop here. I began to realize that the same question was applicable to my family circle as well. On the one hand, my second uncle was expelled from the Communist Party in the late 1950s for his outspoken disagreement with the notorious Mayor Ke. Like Marshal Peng's, his deeds had an outwardly heroic character. On the other hand, my father seemed to have reacted more cautiously to avoid political ostracism, and by staying in power, he had more opportunities to control the damage of many political persecutions. Within his jurisdiction, the numbers of people persecuted were minimized. Many had escaped disaster because of him, and they felt grateful to him. In a final moral judgment, who was nobler? My father, or his brother?

Even at a personal level, I wondered if it was nobler to speak my criticism of our political system and to be put into prison as a dissident, or to keep a painful silence and use the limited freedom I had in my classroom to cultivate independent thinking among my students. Which was nobler? "To be, or not to be: that is the question." Time has not yet passed Shakespeare by, and the question he put forward is still meaningful today.

THE ANSWER IS BLOWING IN THE WIND

Although our political system did not change much, the economic system did. Many changes occurred, beginning in 1979, and the first happened in a little village in Anhui Province. When the peasants took the initiative to divide public land into small pieces and assign each family the responsibility for its own plot, the death knell of collective farming was sounded. In the new covenant, each family had its quota of grains to produce for the government but if a family could produce more, it could keep it and sell it for profit. This covenant gave the peasants more incentive to work the land and it produced fruitful results. A couple of years later, the central government openly supported this reform and rapid economic reform began to sweep the nation.

In the cities, small private enterprises started to grow and a more flexible market was created. Even the employees of state-owned enterprises could take on second jobs. One booming market was continuing education, and evening classes mushroomed in the large cities. College teachers were in high demand, especially English teachers. In my department, almost every faculty member had evening classes to teach and earned a little extra income. I joined the wave and enjoyed the benefits. Because I did not have classes every day at my own college, sometimes I also taught off-campus classes during the day. I co-taught a class of engineers at a large state-owned plant that produced electric generators. The factory sold products abroad and had frequent contacts with the West. Each year a few professionals took a trip abroad to learn techniques to improve the products. To qualify for such a trip, one had to pass an English proficiency test. Most of the engineers were in their forties and had only learned a little Russian in school. Now they had started learning English. The factory organized a class of about forty people to have on-the-job English training for six months.

My students were highly motivated because everyone wanted an opportunity to go abroad. One of the attractions of going abroad was the opportunity to purchase some merchandise usually not available or affordable in the domestic market. To most Chinese, this was the best or the only opportunity to purchase high-quality modern household supplies and electronics such as color televisions and refrigerators. For a time, going abroad became an obsession for millions of Chinese, and this reflected people's lack of faith in their own country. Despite the revitalization of the Communist Party after the radicals had been phased out, people grew increasingly dissatisfied with the pace of the reform. People now had an opportunity to compare their standard of living with that of the rest of the world. Formerly their only perspective was comparing today with yesterday. The Communist government loved this comparison, because it helped persuade people that they were better off than they had been and so should be satisfied.

Once people had a new perspective, however, things looked quite different. For decades, the Communist government had kept information about the West from its citizens. When millions of Chinese saw pictures of Hong Kong, Tokyo, and New York, they were overwhelmed. Instead of slums in metropolitan cities depicted in Charles Dickens's novels, people saw high-rise office buildings with shining glass walls, thousands of cars on multiple-lane highways, and neon lights flashing on the skylines of big cities. Inevitably, people would ask the tough question that the Communist government could hardly answer: Why had this taken place in the capitalist countries? People became more frustrated when they realized that this would not happen soon in China. The best and most realistic hope was to go abroad, either on a short visit or as a permanent immigrant. To millions of Chinese, that seemed to be the only chance to enjoy modern civilization.

There were few ways for Chinese to live abroad. International marriage was one of them. Earlier, in the 1970s, Chinese were not even allowed to marry foreigners. A few who were defiant had been put in jail. By the 1980s, the regime gradually loosened its control on this matter, and more and more international marriages took place in China. However, not everyone could find a foreign lover. Another way was to apply for immigration through relatives living overseas. Unfortunately, not many could find overseas relatives either. In my entire extended family, for example, there was only one cousin of my mother who we believed was living in Taiwan. He had been in the air force of the Nationalist government of Chiang Kai-shek and had fled to Taiwan before the Communist takeover. Even his parents were not sure if he was still alive.

A third and more common way was to try to study abroad. Since the late 1970s, the Chinese government had allowed students to study abroad, and had even sponsored universities and research institutes to send a few selected young professionals abroad. The rationale was that these people would learn English and the technical know-how to help modernize China. Although my college was not a major institute, it had the opportunity to send at least one faculty member to Australia. How much I wished to become the next candidate!

I worked very hard to earn that chance. Within a year, my efforts seemed to bear fruit. The student evaluation showed that I was one of the most popular faculty members, and many professional associations accepted me as a member. One day after I returned from an academic conference, I was summoned to the office of the chancellor. With a benign smile on his face, he began to ask about my parents' health and my parent-caring responsibilities. Our conversation seemed quite pointless to me at first, until he asked me if I could be away from home for a while to pursue further studies. Instantly I knew what he was talking about. He must have been considering me as the next candidate to go to Australia! Without any hesitation I told him that both my parents would love to see me have such an opportunity.

I was excited and could hardly contain myself. After I left his office I could feel my heart beating very fast. I immediately went to see my department head to confirm the news. Like the chancellor, he did not say anything definite, except to advise me to start preparing for such an opportunity. I understood why they were so cautious; this was a sensitive issue and any nominated candidate would instantly become the envy of the entire faculty.

When I announced the news at home, everyone rejoiced. My sister seemed even more excited than I. As usual, my father cautioned me not to be too excited. He even asked me to take extra care in crossing busy city streets. He did not want me to have an accident as a result of my euphoric mood.

In the following days, my excitement grew as many colleagues came to congratulate me. During the next political study session on Wednesday afternoon when the whole faculty convened at the auditorium, I was deeply engrossed in my own thoughts about my trip to Australia and did not hear anything spoken at the meeting. I was brought to my senses again when a colleague came up to me during the break. I didn't like the woman at all, and the way she talked to people always made me uneasy. There was too much unnatural familiarity in her tone. Her father-in-law was a high-ranking official in the provincial government. In fact, he had been an underground Communist under the leadership of my father. After the Communist takeover, her father-in-law had more promotions and ended up holding more important government positions than my father. There had been numerous rumors about the woman using the influence of her family for personal gain. Her appearance in front of me now and especially her jeering tone seemed an evil omen to me. With a wicked smile on her face she said: "I heard that you had *once* been considered a candidate to go abroad. Wasn't that true?" I noticed her emphasis on the word "once." Did that mean there was a new decision being made and I was no longer the candidate? My God, she must have used her power to replace me as a candidate! I was totally lost and didn't know how to respond.

After the meeting I rushed to see the department head to find out what was going on. Again, he didn't say anything definite, but hinted that some decisions were made at levels beyond the school authorities. He said that at least I had been summoned to talk with the chancellor. I knew what he was trying to say. He wanted me to believe that both he and the chancellor had intended to select me, but at a higher level, that is, the Bureau of Higher Education of the provincial government, some other decision had been made and I was dropped in favor of another candidate. He added that things were changing all the time and nothing was final yet. He even suggested that if that woman could change things by using her family background I should try to change it back by using my family background. But I knew that was hopeless. My father wouldn't do anything of the kind, and would not be able to do it effectively, either. In fact, he did write a letter for me to the director of the bureau, requesting a fair decision in choosing the candidate to study abroad. Of course, that wasn't the most effective way, and I lost my opportunity. Months later, the woman went to Australia.

I was terribly upset by this incident, and so was Mr. Jin, the enemy-turned-into-a-friend of my father. During the Cultural Revolution, Jin had organized public meetings denouncing my father as a public enemy. However, when he got to know my father, Jin became a close personal friend. Jin was now a faculty member in a college. On one occasion when he met with an official from the Bureau of Higher Education of the provincial government, Jin challenged the bureau's decision. Jin said: "I was really puzzled by your decision. Wasn't it obvious that there were stronger candidates who deserved such an opportunity?" The official hesitated for a moment, and then replied: "Yes, you are quite right. Because her English was not so good, we decided to send her abroad to study." Jin could hardly believe his ears. He also had hoped to be sent to study abroad someday, and had worked very hard toward that goal. Now he was told bluntly that only if his English were poor would he have the opportunity to study abroad. What shameless nonsense! As it was a rare chance to go abroad, it would only be fair for candidates to be selected on merit, not incompetence.

It was this kind of shameless abuse of power that made people livid and feel hopeless living under the Communist system. By now, power abuse proliferated in every aspect of people's life. I first noticed this problem when I was working as an apprentice in the factory years before. When the economic reform successfully lifted the lid of rigid authoritarian controls, it also aggravated abuses of power. Within a decade, it became almost impossible to get anything done without personal connections. You needed this network to find a job, and you needed it to have a new or better housing unit. Sometimes even positions that did not seem to be powerful at all might become overwhelmingly powerful. You could be frustrated when you couldn't find a space for your child in a daycare center, but if you happened to know the director of a daycare center, a nice spot would be waiting for you. It was the same situation when you wanted to get your children into a better school. The golden rule of this society became: where there was a personal connection there would be a way. You simply need such connections to live and survive in this society. Of course, you needed them even more if you wanted to leave this society and to go abroad. You hated the system when it worked against you, and you rejoiced when you benefited from it. You cursed it; you loved it. You tasted its bounty, and you became an addict. This trading on connections became a social disease. It was destroying characters like a drug, and it was growing and spreading throughout society. Could we ever get rid of it? The answer seemed to be blowing in the wind.

CHALLENGE BEHIND DEATH

While I was still trying to recover from the frustration and hurt of not being chosen to go to Australia, another painful piece of news came, and this time it was from my family circle. My father's sister died of pancreatic cancer late in the summer of 1983.

I had only seen my aunt twice in my life, but her image was unforget-table. She and her family lived in an inland province named Hunan, where Chairman Mao was born. Because the cost of traveling was high and incomes were low, people seldom traveled to another province, unless it was a business journey sponsored by an employer. I had never been to that part of the country. One of my aunt's two daughters had visited us during the early years of the Cultural Revolution when travel-ing was free for the young. She stayed at our house for only one night and she was a quiet person and didn't say more than a dozen words during the entire evening. I learned very little from her about my aunt.

My aunt's life was different from that of her brothers and she became a theater artist instead of a politician. As early as her years in high school in Nanjing, she was influenced by my father and participated in the student movement against the Japanese occupation of northern China. On the eve of the Japanese invasion of Shanghai in 1937, she and her three brothers gathered in Shanghai to participate in the anti-Japanese movement. That was the last time the four siblings had been together, and they waited for forty-five years before coming together again when the three brothers came to see their dying sister.

When the war broke out in Shanghai, the brothers stayed in Shang-hai with the resistance movement, but they sent their sister back to Nanjing to take care of their mother. She took her mother and retreated further inland to Hunan Province. At the time, the Communist Party and Chiang Kai-shek's government formed a coalition to resist the Japanese, and Zhou Enlai became a cabinet member in Chiang's gov-ernment in charge of cultural affairs and wartime mobilization. Ten theater groups were organized to help wartime mobilization. My aunt joined one of them as an actress and married one of the actors. Al-though the theater groups were financially supported by Chiang's gov-ernment, most of them were actually under Communist influence. In fact, my aunt's husband was a Communist Party member. The couple remained in the theater throughout their lives, first as actors and later as directors. Though not politicians anymore, the couple had a hard time during the Cultural Revolution because they once worked for Chiang's government. The rebels treated them as Chiang's agents and tortured them both mentally and physically. Even today I do not know exactly what happened to them during those years. It was very painful for them to recall the horror and I never asked my aunt about it.

I met my aunt in the spring of 1980 when she came to Nanjing on a business trip and stayed at our house for a week. At the time my father was studying at the Central Party Academy in Beijing, and both my mother and sister had to work during the day. I had time to be with my aunt because I was at college and only needed to go to campus when I had classes. We took long walks in the streets and chatted about almost anything we could think of.

The first thing I noticed was her temperament. She looked more like a scholar than an artist, with more tranquility and reflection in her than passion and eloquence. She came to Nanjing to do some research for a playscript she was writing. I found that no matter what else she was doing she was also deep in thought about her writing. Anything she saw or talked about seemed to touch an artistic nerve in her and she would become instantly inspired.

It seemed to me that she was always living in her artistic world, yet she told me a story about her husband that seemed to show that he was even more isolated in his world of art. Once she told her husband that they needed a new comforter for the family. He went to several shops but came home empty-handed. "I couldn't find a comforter in any of the shops," he said. Of course not! We both laughed when she told me this story. In China, a comforter was not a final product sold in the market. You need to make your comforter yourself. The outside cover was usually a piece of colorful cloth, of either cotton or silk. The inside cover was usually plain white cotton cloth because that was cheaper and more comfortable. A string-net stuffed with cotton is stitched inside the cover sheets to make a comforter. My aunt's husband had never taken care of housekeeping. He always saw these three pieces together as a comforter. As a husband, he used it every night at home. As a director, he ordered one to be put on the stage whenever he needed it. When his wife sent him to the shops he was looking for a ready-made comforter, and of course he could not find one.

As professionals, my aunt and her husband had a simpler lifestyle than her brothers, who were officials. They had a smaller apartment of poorer quality. They had never been provided with a car and a chauffer. Nor had they been given rationed special food. They had never had access to the best doctors and facilities. In short, they had not enjoyed as many privileges as their brothers. This pattern of distributing wealth based on political power had roots in Chinese history. For thousands of years, the most powerful, wealthy, privileged, and desirable occupation was to be a government official. Anyone who was ambitious enough to climb the social ladder knew that the only way up was to study classical literature and pass the annual examination and be nominated as a government official. The whole purpose of going to school was to become an official. This tradition stifled the creativity of many generations. In the time of Marco Polo, Europeans viewed China as a highly advanced society. By the nineteenth century, despite its ancient fame for invention, China had become a nation less developed than European countries. Even the radical social revolution of communism did not change this social structure. Real success was still measured by one's mobility in the ranks of officials or administrators.

As a theater professional, my aunt did not have the best health care in the city, and that was one of the reasons her cancer was diagnosed so late. By the time it was detected, she could not eat like a normal person. In the spring of 1983, her doctor told her husband that she could only expect to live three more months.

When her brothers heard the terrible news they were first shocked, and then they began to feel guilty that they had not taken better care of their sister. She was not living in a major city, but in an inland province where health care was much less advanced, and she was not an official. They had left her behind for so many years they hadn't realized how much difference it had made to her. Once realizing this, they decided to move her from the inland province of Hunan to the best hospital with the best health care they could find. They all agreed that Shanghai was the best place for her. Of course, Beijing had the best facilities and doctors, but there were too many privileged groups. In addition, the uncle who lived there, my father's youngest brother, had not been assigned a job; he wouldn't have access to the kind of health care my aunt needed. Nanjing was a secondary city and its medical resources were not as good as either Beijing or Shanghai. Also, because of his age, my father was no longer holding the position as director in his department. He remained deputy chairman in the standing committee of the city's People's Congress, but that did not give him the same clout he had previously enjoyed to gain access for his sister to the best health care. My second uncle in Shanghai, however, had recently been nominated director of the human resources department in Shanghai. In that powerful position he was in charge of promotion of almost all the officials in Shanghai. With his help, my aunt was soon transferred from Hunan into the best hospital in Shanghai.

Despite all the efforts of her brothers, my aunt did not survive. She died in Shanghai at the age of sixty-four. Her body was cremated in Shanghai and her ashes were returned to Hunan by her husband and two daughters. Her husband told a friend when he would be returning in order to get a ride home from the railway station. To his surprise, over 300 people came to the station to pay a tribute to his late wife. He was moved to tears to see that so many people had loved her so much. When my father received the letter from him telling about the scene at the railway station, his eyes were wet, too. I heard him say: "My sister left this world too early, but she had an honorable death. She also left me and my brothers a challenge. I wonder if we will get as much love from the people as she did when we leave this world." Today, I think I could say that both he and his sister left the world with as much love as they had wished and deserved. Yet, to me, a bigger challenge remains: Can we do anything about our social structure, so that an artist like my aunt might have a better chance of surviving?

TWO WORLDS

Life is sometimes so unpredictable! Instead of going south and studying in Australia, in the beginning of 1984 I was sent to the far north, to teach at a college on the border between China and Siberia in the Soviet Union. It was a mountainous area with huge forests. In fact, one of the two major lumber concerns in China was there. At a time when most young professionals in China dreamed about going abroad and living in cities with high-rise office towers, a retreat from city life to a place with no buildings higher than five stories seemed like a journey into oblivion.

The reason for this trip was hilarious. English teachers were in greater shortage in that area than in large cities such as Nanjing. The college I went to had only one English teacher, but eighty students majoring in English. Every institute in our province needed lumber for construction. Therefore, an exchange program was set up in 1982 between this college and my college in Nanjing. For two years, my college sent one faculty member each semester to teach, and in return, the college in the north provided my college with lumber. My college had already sent three teachers and I was the last one to fulfill the contract. I thus became a part of a lumber trade.

In the beginning of February, I took the train north. After a three-day journey I finally arrived at the college in Heilongjiang Province. I had never experienced such cold in my life. The temperature was −28° centigrade. However, I was told that the worst part of the winter was over already. I soon found out that if I had come one week earlier, I would have witnessed much colder weather with the temperature $-40°$ centigrade.

With such temperatures, few vegetables could be grown locally. Every day, the cafeteria of the college offered the same two vegetables on the menu: potatoes and Chinese cabbage. They were last year's crops kept stored underground. Green pepper was served only on Sundays. I stayed there till early summer, but I didn't taste a fourth vegetable in the cafeteria until late June, two weeks before I finished my job. In mid-May we still had heavy snow storms. When I left, the girls in my class had not yet changed to skirts. They told me that they had only about ten days to wear skirts each year.

I left the place in early July. Instead of going straight home I decided to visit all the major cities in northeastern China and then to take the sea route to Shanghai before I finally went back to Nanjing. I had carefully planned this trip even before I left Nanjing for the north. As a part of the deal, the college in the north reimbursed me for all the fares. They provided me with my first opportunity to travel through almost half of China.

Traveling was not easy in China. Tickets were often very difficult to buy and hotel accommodations were usually expensive. As a part of the preparation for the trip, I tried to find at least one contact person in each of the cities I planned to visit. With a name of a contact person in my pocket, I could at least have someone to stay with or to help me find a place to stay. Also, they might be helpful in getting tickets to my next destination.

The third city I stopped at was Shenyang, perhaps better known in the West as Mukden. Here, I did not know a single person. Yet the contact person I happened to have was one of the most powerful men in the city. He was the military commander-in-chief of the province and the deputy commander-in-chief of the three northeastern provinces that used to be called Manchuria.

If I could have found another contact person, I wouldn't have bothered such a prominent figure. Before I left home I had visited someone who held a similar position in my province during the Chinese New Year holiday season. He and my father had been classmates at the Central Party Academy in 1980 and his son had been a classmate of my sister in high school. Because I knew hardly anyone in the northeastern provinces, I asked him if he could introduce me to someone in case I had an emergency. He wrote down a couple of names for me on a piece of paper, and told me to feel free to get help from them. Realizing they were quite prominent figures, I carefully folded the slip of paper with their names on it and put it in my wallet.

I arrived in Shenyang in the late afternoon. The military commander had already been informed of my coming. He and his family lived in a fancy hotel belonging to the military forces. Usually, his guests were men in military uniforms and they arrived in cars with chauffeurs. When I showed up on foot in my plain clothes and told the gatekeeper that I was expected by so and so, he was clearly surprised. He made a phone call and soon an orderly was sent to the gate to pick me up. In no time I was shown into the parlor of the military commander's residence. He and his family were just about to have dinner and he invited me to join them and sent for his personal secretary to take care of me for the rest of my stay.

After dinner his secretary came and led me into an adjacent unit in the hotel. It was the unit for his orderly and I was going to stay with him for the night. Later that night the orderly told me that our next-door neighbor was an army commander. As an officer in charge of a whole army, he was only one level lower in rank than my host. Yet he occupied only a unit the size of the orderly of my host in this fancy hotel. I had heard before about the big difference among officers in terms of their privileges. One level higher in rank meant many more privileges. Still, I was amazed to see that the difference could be so huge.

The secretary told me that the next morning I should go to the cafeteria in the hotel for breakfast and meals. He then checked with my schedule and asked me if I had any requests. I told him that I planned to have two days of sightseeing in the city and I wanted to get a train ticket to Dalian on the third morning.

The secretary left me for a while and then returned with something I didn't expect. He told me that I was in town at an awkward time. The commander and his family were leaving the city on the same date I planned to leave, and they were too occupied to take proper care of a guest. The good news was they were going south to the same city as I. The commander would have a whole compartment of the train reserved for himself and his family, so they could easily give me a ride in their private compartment. I was astounded that the commander and his family could have such a privilege, and also overwhelmed by the offer. However, I felt that I would be more comfortable to be alone, rather than with this group of ostentatious people. Besides, I was already reimbursed for my traveling cost, and I did not need to accept this offer. I asked the secretary to help me get an ordinary one-way ticket to Dalian, which I believed would not be a problem for him at all.

I was right. He left me for a moment and came back again confirming that I would get my ticket the next morning. He surprised me once again. He told me that I would be provided with a car and a chauffeur "only twice" during my stay, and apologized for not being able to let me use the car more often. He asked me how I would like to use the car. I was totally overwhelmed by this special treatment and it took me a minute to put myself together. I told him that I wanted a ride to and from the museum of the Forbidden Palace, a site similar to the Forbidden City in Beijing, and then a ride to the train station when I left for Dalian.

I was given the rides and enjoyed a wonderful and unexpectedly comfortable tour in this major northern city. I did not really think that the military commander had intended to treat me as a distinguished guest, or that he made any special effort to take care of me. However, just getting a little help from such a person meant a lot of comfort and convenience and even privilege. What I enjoyed at his home was in extreme contrast to my subsequent adventures on the way home.

My contact person in Dalian was an acquaintance of my sister, a young man in charge of student affairs at a small local college. He put me in the student guest hall at the college, where I shared a room with an old man, a visiting parent of a student. Again, I asked my contact person to help me buy the traveling ticket. This time I needed a ship ticket from Dalian to Shanghai. If I didn't get his help, I would have to wait in long queues at the ticket office for at least two nights and two days to get a ticket for a voyage in two weeks. Even with his help, I had to wait an entire week before he could finally get me an "unclassified" ticket for a voyage three days later.

I knew there were five classes of tickets for a passenger ship in China, but I had never heard of an "unclassified" ticket. The first class was a special section never open to the public. Second-class tickets offered a cabin with a double bed. With a third-class ticket, one had to share the cabin with three other passengers. Eight passengers shared a fourth-class cabin, and with a fifth-class ticket a passenger had a seat instead of a bed. I couldn't imagine what could be worse than that until I boarded the ship.

When I showed my ticket to the ship assistant standing on board, he led me to a huge room below the decks and right above the engine room. It was empty. There were no seats, not even a chair. The steel floor had not been painted for a long time, and the worn places revealed different colors of paint. There were no windows and the heat coming from the combustion made the place so hot that it was almost like a sauna. Passengers with unclassified tickets were supposed to stay here and sleep on the floor. I stood in the middle of the room and looked around. The place was so awful that it seemed suited only for animals. The slave ships from Africa to America 200 years ago might have looked better. At least from what I saw in an American movie based on the novel *Roots*, it seemed to be so. After having just spent a couple of days in the military commander's fancy residential hotel, I felt the bleakness even more sharply.

Looking at my fellow passengers and their unhappy, sweat-stained faces and exhausted bodies, I could understand why my father began to embrace Communism and wanted to establish an egalitarian society when he was a teenager. The irony was, however, there were still two sharply different worlds thirty-five years after the Communist takeover.

"I HAVE NO OTHER CHOICE, BECAUSE I'M THE COMMISSAR!"

Twice in his life my father's youngest brother almost became a general, but he never did. The first time it was because he was too young, and the second time it was because he was too old. The highest rank he held was a senior colonel. He was one of the youngest officers holding that military rank in the entire army in the 1950s. The Cultural Revolution in 1966 interrupted his career when he was forty-five years old and was just about to be promoted to brigadier general. Two decades later, he retired from the army. He would have been granted the rank of major general if he had retired a couple of years later when the system of military rank was reestablished in 1988.

I didn't have much contact with him in my childhood because he lived in Beijing and traveling was neither convenient nor affordable at the time. Later, when Cousin Ping, his daughter from his first marriage, visited us in Nanjing, she often talked about him. Ping was raised by my parents until she was ten years old. After my uncle remarried, he brought Ping back to Beijing to live with him. Ping was not happy with her stepmother. From Ping, we heard of more problems than strengths in that family. Although Ping loved her father, the impression she gave me was that her father was quite different from mine. He was much more authoritarian and seemed to be an army commander even at home. Observing our family life, one of his sons once commented that my father behaved more like my elder brother than my father.

My uncle became a frequent visitor at our house after he was assigned a new job in late 1983. The highest authorities of the Chinese military force decided to expand the Army Academy in Nanjing into a West Point–like institute. To reinforce the leadership of the institute, they appointed my uncle as political commissar and put him in charge of the entire academy. It was big news for our extended family. In addition to his promotion, we had other things to be happy about. My father and his brothers had never worked and lived in the same city since the Communist takeover. Now the three brothers were close to each other, two in Nanjing and one in Shanghai, only 200 miles away. After their sister's death, the brothers began to realize their advancing years and wanted to spend more time together.

My father was the tallest among the three and his youngest brother was the shortest. In terms of social status, however, the youngest was the highest. My father had never held official positions as high as his younger brothers had. The brothers did not look quite alike, but their voices were almost indistinguishable. Whenever either of my uncles came to visit, our neighbors, who overheard their voices, often wondered why my father talked so loud to himself.

It was not common to find such brothers; each one had gotten where he was based on his merits, and no nepotism was involved. In fact, the three brothers had three different family names, and few people knew that they were brothers. This was because they had all changed their names during the years of war and underground Communist activity in the 1930s and 1940s to cover their true identity. Only my father eventually returned to his original name.

To those who knew they were brothers, the three had different strengths. A long-time friend, Uncle Zhao, had an insightful comment comparing the three. He had worked with all of them in the refugee camps in Shanghai during the Japanese occupation in the late 1930s, and was now the top Buddhist leader in China. He said the eldest brother was the most honest and honorable, the second one was the most intelligent and ingenious, and the youngest was the most ardent and adept.

One afternoon my third uncle came to our house with a very serious look on his face. After everyone sat down in our sitting room with some apparent uneasiness, he began to explain. At the time, my brother-in-law was undergoing a reeducation process. Years before, he graduated from the Army Academy in Nanjing. However, like all the universities in China during the 1970s, the quality of its education was really questionable and their graduates were ill prepared. When the academy expanded into a higher level institute in 1983, the authorities decided to reenroll and retrain its young faculty members along with its new students. My brother-in-law joined the classes and by 1985 he was about to graduate again. At the time, a second war broke out between Vietnam and China. In fact, the border war between the two countries had never stopped. However, this was the second time the fight escalated into an all-out war and both sides mobilized more forces. An order came from Beijing to select 20 percent of the academy's graduating students to join the combat force at the front as regimental and battalion commanders. After my uncle gave his mobilization speech, 50 percent of the graduates volunteered to go to the front, and my brother-in-law was among them. As a leader, my uncle felt obliged to select my brother-in-law for this dangerous task. He came to our family to announce his decision and solicit my parents' understanding and support.

It was a very sensitive issue and the whole society was watching to see if high-ranking Communist officials were willing to send their own children and relatives to the front. It almost became a moral test for these families. A novel and a movie based on it portraying two families in this situation won a huge readership and audience. One family sent its only child to the front, and the son died in a battle. The other family tried to avoid sending its son to the front but failed. The son went to the front anyway, witnessed the cruelty of the war, and survived. He felt guilty and regretted what his family had tried to do. It was a very touching story and the readers and audience were greatly moved. However, the consensus was that most officials tried to avoid sending their own children to the front, and it was really difficult to find a one who was willing to sacrifice his own family members.

Under the circumstances my uncle felt that morally he was required to let my brother-in-law go to the front. Before he went on with any further explanations, my father interrupted him. He closed his eyes for a moment and said: "You don't need to say any more. You are perfectly right, and we all understand you and support your decision. We have all experienced the danger of death. All we can do is to tell the young people to be both brave and cautious at the same time. They have to take care of themselves. My only suggestion is that we now go and visit his father."

That night when my sister and her husband came home I could see her eyes were still red from weeping. My father pulled me aside and said: "Tomorrow, you should take both your sister and brother-in-law out for a dinner in a nice restaurant." He had not spoken with such an authoritarian tone since I was a child. I understood what he was doing. He wanted to express his emotion, even though he did not want to admit his feelings openly. That was typical of the people in his generation.

In the days before my brother-in-law left for the front, the atmosphere at home was particularly quiet. Everybody tried to be cheerful, yet no one knew exactly how. The following six months while he was at the front were even harder for the family. Fortunately, he came back without injury. He told us how close he had been to death. The first night he arrived at the front, even before he reached the regiment he was supposed to lead, he and his classmates stayed at a shelter with a group of graduates from another army academy near Beijing. During the night, two people from the other academy went out to urinate and were killed by stray shells. The cruelty of the war was no less severe than that of the Vietnam War where the Americans were involved, although this time it was a fight between two Communist countries. It was once estimated that, along the border between the two countries, there are about one million mines buried by the Chinese alone. It would be an immense task to clear all of them. The irony of history was apparent here, especially for my sister's generation. They grew up being urged to support Vietnam against the United States in the war. Now my brother-in-law had to fight the Vietnamese.

Despite the historical irony, moral values should be consistent. We cannot belittle the braveness and patriotism of those who had endangered their lives and went to war. The difference between nobility and unworthiness in human character remains, no matter how much the circumstances may change. It was unfair to belittle those Communist Party members as Party loyalists who actually lived up to the high morality the Party charter had required. It was even more ridiculous to give credit to those unethical officials simply because their deeds were actually hurting a Communist government. A good man is a good man, as a poem by Scottish poet Robert Burns says: "A man's a man for a' that."

During a relaxed conversation at our house after my brother-in-law had returned home safely, my uncle told my sister, with a smile on his face: "I knew you were going to hate me for the rest of your life if your husband had not come home safely. Your mother would probably not have forgiven me either. In fact, I would probably not have been welcomed at this house again. But I did what I had to do. I had no other choice, because I was the commissar!"

"PURIFYING THE PARTY": AN IMPOSSIBLE TASK

A prominent Chinese political dissident once commented at Harvard University that the problem in China was that the Chinese Communist Party was such a big basket that almost all the worst as well as the best eggs were inside at the same time. It was a very insightful observation. The Communist Party had embraced so many people that there were not enough influential voices left to muster up the political strength, either organized or unorganized, to counter or replace the Communist Party as the dominant political force. You had to belong to the Party in order to be listened to at all. For too many years, both the most respected and the most loathed persons in society were in the Communist Party. Even the top Party leaders did not know how to make the Party work.

After the radicals fell from power in 1976, there was a momentary resurgence of popular confidence in the Communist Party. Yet very soon it was in trouble again. People hated the radicals in power for two reasons. One was that they placed such emphasis on ideological correctness and they ignored the domestic economy. The other was that they abused the power and the privileges they enjoyed. Once the radicals were removed from power, the new Party leadership began to make the national economy a top priority. While they were quite successful in this, they failed to take care of other issues such as power abuse and the privileges given to officials. Although Mao's handpicked successor, Hua Guofeng, smashed the radical group called the Gang of Four, he was reluctant to remove the radical ideology approved and advocated by Mao. In Deng's struggle against Hua, he needed support from the officials who had been put back in power to replace the radicals. By the time Deng replaced Hua as the most authoritative man in China, these officials' abuse of their reclaimed power was even more infuriating than that of the radicals.

Especially problematic were the children of these officials. During the Cultural Revolution, many of them had suffered a great deal because of their denounced parents. Once in power again, their parents often felt guilty for causing trouble for the children. Many officials tried to make amends by spoiling them, and the results were devastating. The most notorious case happened in Shanghai where a group of youngsters committed group rapes. Many of their crimes took place in their parents' luxurious residences or second houses. This behavior angered many people.

As a son of a high-ranking official, I often felt animosity from people who did not really know me or my father. On one hand, I understood it was because people tended to generalize that all officials were power abusers and that their families were enjoying privileges. On the other hand, I had to be very careful in making acquaintances and friends because some people might try to be friendly with me simply for my family connections. I always tried to hide my family background, so people would neither be unfairly hostile toward me nor approach me for their own gain.

Those who really knew me, such as Yang the writer, often helped hide my family background. At her house I sometimes met other visitors. Yang would seldom explain my family background when she introduced me to her other visitors, although traditionally people would usually like to mention their family background in introductions. She knew this would make me feel more comfortable. Only when she was sure that the other visitors also knew my father and his character, would she mention that I was his son. Occasionally she made the mistake of introducing me as my father's son to a visitor who actually did not know my father. When she realized her mistake, she would always say something positive about our character and reputation. When this happened, I always felt sad. What a strange prejudice I had to fight! These experiences helped me understand *A Tale of Two Cities* by Dickens. The innocent descendants of the largely corrupt French noble class could hardly escape the sad fate of becoming the victims of a plebeian revolution. More than once I told my sister that I feared that we might become innocent victims of a coming revolution.

In October 1983, the Party authorities finally decided to launch a political campaign to discipline its members and purify the organization. It was not an easy task. In fact, it turned out to be impossible. There were several critical factors that made this effort doomed to fail. First, by now political campaigns had a very negative image in people's minds. Numerous campaigns punctuated the period from the Communist takeover in 1949 to the end of Mao's era in the late 1970s, the Cultural Revolution being the most extreme. Realizing the difficulty in organizing a campaign, the authorities specified from the very beginning that the focus of the new campaign would be to change minds, and not to persecute persons. Indeed, the word "campaign" was deliberately avoided. Nevertheless, people instinctively feared it.

Second, the targets of the campaign were set so poorly that it seemed ridiculous from the very beginning. Instead of disciplining Party members who abused power and enjoyed unfair privilege, the campaign was aimed at an entirely different group, the former Red Guards and those who were involved during the early days of the Cultural Revolution. Although a few of them remained in power, most anger was not directed at them. Besides, many of them had experienced a self-awakening during the later years of the Cultural Revolution. They realized its absurdity and began to oppose the radical policies of the late Maoist era. Many were involved in the earlier Tiananmen Incident in 1976, mourning the death of Premier Zhou Enlai and voicing their political support for Deng. The irony here was apparent. By launching this new political campaign, Deng was actually hurting his political supporters.

For example, my sister had been a Red Guard in high school in the early months of the Cultural Revolution. Soon after my parents became labeled as "public enemies," she began to realize the foolishness of the Cultural Revolution as well as her own involvement in it. In the early 1970s she opposed the radical policies. In 1976, she joined those who mourned the death of Zhou and she was a part of Deng's political constituency that eventually helped end the Maoist era. In the late 1970s and early 1980s, she turned into such a fan of Deng that she would argue for literally hours with anyone who tried to belittle Deng or sympathize with Hua Guofeng. With support from loyalists like her, Deng had an easy victory and became the most powerful man in China. Yet my sister now fell a victim in the new political campaign. Numerous investigations were carried out to check her history. Starting as a fan of Deng, she was now hurt by Deng's own foolishness. This was the second time she tasted the strong disappointments, and even a little bitterness of misplaced trust, in a national leader. First it was Mao, and now Deng.

There seemed to be some personal reasons behind the new mistake made by the top leaders. Many of them still vividly remembered the tortues they had suffered from the Red Guard movement. In fact, Deng's eldest son barely survived that storm and his legs had been permanently disabled. With personal emotions involved, these senior leaders could hardly see the other side of the story, that is, that it was Mao who had launched the Cultural Revolution and that the students were used by him. They should not bear the full responsibility for what they had done, no matter how guilty they were—not to mention that many were totally innocent.

It was not difficult, however, to understand the feelings of the elders. "To err is human, to forgive, divine." My third uncle still bears malice toward his own daughter, my cousin Ping. During the height of the Cultural Revolution, many children and spouses of the targeted officials were urged to put pressures on their fathers or husbands to make confessions of "crimes" that they had never committed. The father of one of my sister's friends' collapsed under such pressure and killed himself. Cousin Ping also did some foolish things. Out of hatred for her stepmother, she joined the rebels in denouncing her father. Her father was so upset by this that he never forgave her.

Because of the Red Guard movement, senior Party leaders now linked people's resentment and anger against officials' power abuse and privileges to the earlier upheaval. They portrayed anyone bold enough to voice anger as somone who had been a thug in the Cultural Revolution. Democratic protesters were branded as hooligans. Survivors of the Cultural Revolution certainly were repulsed by such social upheaval. Their longing for peace and a quiet private life were used by the authorities to curtail any calls for democracy.

Things were complicated even further by Deng's call for a campaign against the so-called polluting influence of foreign bourgeois ideas. During the same meeting in October 1983, when the top Party leaders decided to launch the campaign to purify the Party, Deng delivered a speech calling for an anti–"spiritual pollution" campaign, casting a chill over academic and intellectual circles. Some prominent intellectuals were victimized, and many feared that another witch hunt was imminent. Fortunately, the anti–"spiritual pollution" campaign was called to a halt within a year. The Party's general secretary, Hu Yaobang, was believed to have been critical in persuading Deng that the campaign was counterproductive and that it was having a deleterious impact on economic reforms and on Westerners' willingness to do business with China.

The campaign to purify the Party, however, was carried out as planned for three years with almost no positive results and a remarkably negative impact. Like earlier political campaigns, it provided opportunities for those in power to crack down on those with different opinions and retaliate against those who voiced dissatisfaction. It also allowed for those who had such expertise to resort to all sorts of schemes and intrigues to remove political rivals. The less experienced often became victims of such personal politics and tricks. This happened to my third uncle.

When he was nominated the political commissar at the Army Academy in Nanjing in late 1983, another man was appointed as the military commander of the academy. As a team, their mission was to correct errors in the earlier leadership. Upon their arrival, my uncle heard many complaints about the old leadership that focused on two areas: the bureaucracy, and the power abuse and privileges of leaders. He tried to fight the latter by setting a good example, including letting my brother-in-law go to the front during the war. He also made an effort to break up the bureaucracy. An example was his effort to fix the problem of the shuttle buses between the campus and the city. Most faculty members' spouses worked and lived in the city. The academy had shuttle buses running on Wednesday evenings and Thursday mornings as well as Friday evenings and Monday mornings, so that the faculty members could join their families in the city twice a week. Those of higher rank, such as directors and department chairs, were provided with cars and chauffeurs. Because no important people depended on the shuttle bus service, the service was very poor. Buses often ran behind schedule, and sometimes few buses ran at all. When my uncle heard these complaints he tried to fix them through the normal bureaucratic channels. Seeing no results, he decided to take care of the matter in a more personal way. Every Wednesday and Friday afternoon he stood at the bus station at five o'clock to see if buses were running on schedule. Few high-level administrators ever went to the bus station. His presence created pressure on the supervisors of the shuttle bus service and sent a clear message to their supervisors as well. His effort was successful. The complaints about poor service soon disappeared and my uncle's popularity grew.

However, his growing popularity made some leaders agitated, especially the military commander. In the final phase of the "purifying the Party" campaign, he and others launched a surprise attack against my uncle. Leaders were asked to make self-criticism and invite constructive criticism. After my naive uncle finished his speech inviting criticism, he was bombarded with organized reprimands and reproaches. Someone even chided him for his involvement in the shuttle bus service. They argued that he must have overlooked more important issues by turning his attention to such trivial matters. Besieged by such orchestrated charges, he realized that he had been betrayed by his partner. The authorities of the Chinese military force took an unjustified action to resolve the split among the new leadership in the academy, removing both my uncle and the military commander from office.

As shown in this example, the campaign to purify the Party only proved the Party's incompetence. In retrospect, however, I believe the concept of purifying a political party is questionable in itself. Instead of an organization of people with the same or similar political ideology, the Communist Party was designed to consist of only those with the highest moral caliber. The Party charter explicitly highlighted this feature. How could a political party be formed in such a way that it became a "party of good men only"? Looking back, I cannot help wondering how such a myth could have deluded so many people for so long a time. Why had so few people foreseen its impossibility? Even politically experienced men such as my father and his brothers were unable to see this.

THE "RED," "BLACK," OR "GOLDEN" ROAD

In the mid-1980s, some new phrases describing different career paths became popular. If someone were following the traditional pattern of trying to join the Communist Party to become a government official, it was said that this person was taking the "red" road, because red was the color for communism. If someone tried to use education and training, especially that received abroad, as a vehicle to acquire a professional position and to be promoted, this person was described as taking the "black" road, because the graduation gown in the West was black. If a person tried to get rich first and then become influential, people called this "taking the golden road," because gold symbolized wealth. These phrases reflected the fact that a young person had more than one alternative. Until the end of the 1970s, this had not been the case. The economic reform in the 1980s encouraging entrepreneurship allowed a few individuals to earn much more than most of the rest in the society. Educated professionals became well respected and very active in the decision-making process. An ambitious youth no longer needed to join the Communist Party as a first step toward a successful career.

Even at home, my parents stopped urging me to join the Communist Party. In fact, after I graduated from the university and joined the faculty of a college in 1982, my father often commented that I was probably taking the right road. Before, he had always seen my sister as a role model for me and urged me to do whatever she did. She was taking the "red" road, joining the Party and holding administrative positions, and was now a dean of student affairs at a college in Nanjing.

I always admired my sister for her strong will and work ethic. It had been extremely difficult for her to take this "red" road, especially when my parents were under the shadow of being "public enemies." As a matter of fact, among all the cousins in my extended family, she was the only one who had managed to further her career so successfully. My father was very proud of her. Even Uncle Zhao, the long-time family friend who knew both my father and his brothers, had an almost paternal affection for her alone among all the second generation of our family.

By the end of the 1970s, however, my sister's model for success was challenged. Now, administrators and officials became less respected, and people had little confidence in the Communist Party. Instead, they loathed the corrupt Party members. As a Party member and the daughter of a high-ranking official, my sister often experienced malice she did not deserve.

Meanwhile, there was a growing respect for youths who took the "black" road. The comprehensive college entrance examination was a fair competition and people respected the winners. When the first examination was held in the end of 1977, my two cousins and I passed it. My second uncle's daughter, Liya, entered a college in Shanghai to major in computer science. My third uncle's elder son was accepted by China's best foreign language institute, which was located in Beijing. Now, even in the family circle, my sister was no longer the only success.

Her job was giving her more frustration than satisfaction. In her official position, she constantly found herself in conflict with colleagues whose sense of right and wrong was so out of step with that of ordinary people. At a time when people clearly had an affection for the late Premier Zhou and felt quite differently about the late Chairman Mao, these administrators disagreed. When Deng was much more popular than Mao's successor, Hua, these administrators were in favor of Hua. When the students voiced democratic concerns and the authorities cracked down on the students, these administrators showed no sympathy for the students. My sister was frustrated by these conflicts and was under a great deal of stress. To some extent, my father experienced the same stress, but he was a weathered politician and had either a better way of dealing with these officials or had more control over his feelings. My sister, however, poured out her frustrations at our dinner table and sought ways to cope with her difficulties at work. Each night her talk made the rest of the family uneasy and annoyed.

My father suggested that I was happier as a college faculty member and perhaps my sister should change her career. He talked more about his past as a student and teacher, and repeated that teaching was his favorite profession. From his talk I could see that he was also tired of his lifelong political career. Now he often talked about the road that he had not taken. He mentioned that if he had not become involved in the student movement early in his life he might have become a professor. Apparently, he had some regrets that too much of his life had been spent in less productive political work, although I suspected that if he had been given a second chance he would still have chosen the road he took, given his genuine social concerns. Seeing my relatively tranquil and seemingly productive academic life, he began to suggest that my sister change her career and take the "black" road by entering graduate school.

My sister took his advice and entered a graduate school in Nanjing in 1985 in the program of philosophy and ethics. Before the semester began, she helped other new students move luggage into their dorms. She felt sick that day and when she came home she looked tired and pale. My mother was very concerned and asked her what was going on. She said she didn't feel well in the morning and now after a day's work she felt even worse. My mother asked why she bothered to go in the first place. She said that the department asked the local students to help those from other places move in. "But you could tell them that you were sick, couldn't you?" My mother said in a chiding and concerned tone. "How could I, Mom? I'm a member of the Communist Party." "My poor silly girl," my mother sighed. "If only everyone were thinking like you!" My future wife, Meirong, whom I had just started to date, joined us for dinner for the first time. She was quite impressed by my sister's altruism. She never thought a Party member would make such a genuine effort to live up to the high moral standards of the Party charter. To her, all those high-sounding words were nothing but a joke, and all the Party members were power abusers and just as selfish as anyone else.

Even though the reputation of members of the Communist Party was not good, most powerful positions remained in their hands. Those who initially took the "black" road were often tempted to join the Party in the end. Many of the reformers inside the Party advocated that youths with better education should apply for Party membership and the Party should be more willing to accept them. Among these advocates was Professor Fang, who would later be expelled from the Party in 1987 and seek political asylum in the U.S. embassy in Beijing during the Tiananmen Incident in 1989. Because of the Party's skepticism toward intellectuals during the Maoist era, fewer well-educated people were accepted into the Party. It is not far from the truth to say that the country was actually run by a group of people whose educational background was worse than that of the general population. In that sense, I agreed with Fang and wished to see more well-educated people become Party members. However, at a personal level, I still believed that pledging to be a Party member meant devoting one's life to an idealistic cause. I did not feel ready for this. I did not want to be hypocritical, even in my own heart.

While the trend was for educated youths to join the Party, both my father and I were seriously considering the idea of my joining one of the other political parties. We knew that these so-called democratic parties were just like the ears of a deaf person and not really functioning. Yet it seemed politically healthier to us for these parties to have more strength and become a counterbalance. My father often told me stories of the 1930s and 1940s when Zhou Enlai persuaded some prominent progressive writers and intellectuals not to join the Communist Party. The argument was that they would be more influential in the society while remaining outside it. Under the circumstances, when a prominent non-Party member gave his or her support to the Communist Party, it carried more weight. Under the new circumstances in the 1980s, if more well-educated youths joined the other political parties, it might do the Communist Party good in the sense that a greater counterbalance might save the Communist Party from making big mistakes. I noticed my father's shifting attitude and the fact that he had stopped urging me to join the Communist Party since I graduated from the university in 1982. Was this because he had become disheartened by the Party and the cause to which he had devoted all his adult life, or because he thought this would be the best way to help the Party and the nation? I never asked, and I will never know.

IT'S TIME TO GO!

I was still hoping to go to Australia someday, although I lost my first chance. I knew it was a year-long exchange program and the woman who had gone instead of me was supposed to stay there for only one year. So I was looking forward to becoming the next candidate. However, news soon came that she refused to come back and had made arrangements to stay for another year. As a result, my college could not send anyone else abroad, because she used up the quota.

I was extremely annoyed and decided to try to change my job. It was ridiculous to be hurt again by such a manipulative person. If this institute could not treat us fairly, I had better find another place to work. Besides, other institutes seemed to offer better opportunities for their employees to study abroad. So I started a search and soon had several interviews. Five institutes wanted me, but my college wouldn't let me go! The rigid system in China at the time made it impossible for anyone to change jobs without approvals from all levels of officials involved. In my case, the main problem was the new chancellor, who saw me as a favorite of the previous chancellor and for personal reasons gave me a hard time.

During the Maoist era from the 1950s through the 1970s, the major means for control over ordinary citizens was through a system of "work units," the workplace where each individual worked. As a level of administration, the work unit controlled not only wages and bonuses, but also access to housing, education, medical benefits, certain consumer goods, and even marriage and divorce permits. Work units could thus easily use these resources to extract compliance from their members. In the 1980s, although far less powerful, work units still had control over their employees in many areas. They could refuse to let you leave, and few other work units could hire you without approval from your previous work unit.

For two years I tried in vain to change my job. My frustration made me very irritable at home. I often blamed my father for being responsible, at least for his part in bringing this ridiculous system into China. The society was still far from the egalitarian ideal that he had wished to see, and the people had also lost their rights to choose jobs. Who was to blame? He must have frequently asked himself similar questions. As a result, he lost his usual eloquence in debating with me.

I was not alone in having problems with the rigid system. By 1986, the demand from the people to reform the current system was really strong and growing very rapidly. Having survived the Cultural Revolution and witnessed the rapid changes brought by the economic reform beginning in the 1980s, most Chinese strongly believed that only further reform could lead their country forward. Many people, especially the young, became impatient with the tempo of the reform and less satisfied with the leadership of Deng Xiaoping.

Ironically, the Western world, especially its media, was still enthusiastically hailing the Chinese leader. *Time* magazine named him for the second time as the Man of the Year. Only eight others had been named more than once. In an article in *U.S. News & World Report* in its September 8, 1986, issue entitled "One Leads, A Billion Follow," the author wrote: "Deng Xiaoping is changing China and changing it by peaceful means. . . . The dramatic change in China shows what can be achieved by leadership. . . . Deng Xiaoping is awaking China." The American media was right in recognizing the achievements in China, but was praising the Chinese leader at perhaps the wrong time. It failed to see that now the leader was only "led" by the people's demand for further reform and changes. This was quite different from the late 1970s when the whole society was still frozen in extreme authoritarianism under the shadow of the late Chairman Mao. At that time, most people did not dare to say what they wanted to say, and they were happy to have a strong man like Deng voice their opinions. After half a decade of economic reform and more political freedom, people felt safer expressing their true thoughts. Now they wanted to push their reformist leader even further.

Unfortunately, the push forward backfired. At the end of 1986, some students in Shanghai went to the streets demanding further changes and the incident caused a great reversal in politics in China. Three prominent intellectuals, including Professor Fang, were expelled from the Communist Party. I was very surprised to see this development. Even though I disagreed with some of their political positions, I felt sympathetic with them, especially Professor Fang, who was an astrophysicist. I believed that he would not have been involved in politics if he had not had social concerns. Some in the West called him the Chinese Sakharov, and many youths in China wrote supporting and comforting letters to him after he was expelled from the Party. In fact, I also thought about sending him a copy of a poem by W. H. Auden, *A Dead Man*, which I deliberately selected for my students to read at the time, particularly because it points out that no tyrant ever fears his geologists or engineers.

The political setback did not stop here. To everyone's surprise, the Party general secretary, Hu Yaobang, was forced to resign. When the news was broadcast over radio and television, millions of families in China were shocked. Many lost their last measure of confidence in the system. That night the anchor on the national television news program appeared on screen in an old-fashioned Mao suit with stiff high collar instead of the Western-style suit he normally wore. Even before he opened his mouth, sensitive people began to spot that something serious must have happened. After the news my sister cried in her room. I knew she was extremely upset by the incident, too.

Meirong and I were planning to be married the next week. That night we were to visit a good friend of hers, a famous artist in our province. By the time we arrived at his house we had all heard the terrible news and were very disheartened. After a moment of painful silence, her friend spread out a painting on his desk and said that he was going to give it to us as a wedding gift. It was a beautiful scene in traditional Chinese style with mountains, streams, trees, and flowers. Without a word, the artist took out his brush-pen and added a pair of little birds flying in the air. We all understood his symbolism and wished that we could still have the freedom to go abroad. I had applied to several graduate schools in the United States and was hoping to be admitted with substantial financial aid. Now that the short-term political future of the country did not seem hopeful, my only wish was to get out of the country as soon as possible. It's time to go!

THE DEPARTURE

Meirong and I were married on January 24, 1987. When we returned from our honeymoon trip I found a letter from the United States sitting on my desk. It was just what I had been waiting for: a graduate school admission and a financial aid package covering both tuition and minimal living expenditure. I yelled the great news to everyone in the family, and we all rejoiced over the "good luck" that my marriage had brought me.

However, during the process of getting a visa and completing other paperwork, an unexpected misfortune befell my family. Early one morning my mother and sister were exercising in our little courtyard as usual. I was still lying in bed. Suddenly I heard my sister's frightened screaming. I jumped from my bed and rushed out of the house. There I saw my mother bending over, heavy in my sister's arms. When we moved her inside to an armchair, I found her mouth had twisted to one side. Instantly I knew she was having a stroke.

A month later, even though she was home from the hospital, she was still as much disabled as on the day she had the stroke. By that time I received my visa and had all the paperwork done. Yet, looking at her face distorted by pain and irritation, I really didn't know what to do. Part of me was saying that if I was going to leave her like that and go to America I would feel guilty for the rest of my life. But another part told me that if I canceled my trip, we would both regret it later on. Meantime, everybody was helping with my departure. Even my mother was reminding me of this and that and locating things that I could not find. The message seemed straight and clear; there was really only one choice.

The time of departure arrived so soon that suddenly I realized that I had fewer than thirteen hours left. My flight was on August 19, from the international airport in Shanghai. Passengers were required to verify their identifications at the airport in person a couple of days ahead of the flight. Therefore I had to take the early morning train to Shanghai on August 17.

It was dinner time on August 16. For a month, my mother had not joined us at the dinner table. That night she asked us to move her to the dining room. We had some wine and everybody gave me a toast. My parents were unusually quiet. My sister and her husband tried hard to keep the conversation going. Several times they mentioned that I would be coming back home in a few years as a learned man with lots of knowledge to build a better society in China. My mother kept her eyes on me almost all the time, while my father seldom looked my way at all. I knew they must have a lot to say, and yet they said nothing.

The next morning I had my last breakfast at home, and put all my luggage together in the sitting room. I looked around and found my mother sitting on her armchair in the front porch waiting for me to say good-bye. I gave her a hug, and she could no longer hold her tears. She mumbled a few words asking me to write as soon as I arrived in the United States.

My father and brother-in-law came with Meirong and me to the railway station. My sister stayed home to care for my mother. Meirong was coming with me to Shanghai to see me off at the airport. We arrived at the crowded station fairly early because my father was a cautious man and he never liked the idea of getting to the station at the last minute.

With a sick mother back at home I hardly thought about my father's health. Although it had deteriorated a great deal in the years since he retired in 1985, I never imagined that I might not see him again. He had been so strong. Even in his late sixties he was physically stronger than I was in my early twenties. How could I imagine that this was the last moment I would be with him and that I would never see him again?

My last words with him were about taking care of my mother. If I ever had the slightest sense that this might be our last meeting, I would have given him a long, long hug. At least I would have said something about his own health. Probably I would not even have left China. Now, all these speculations are too late. Within three years, I lost him forever, a man that not only gave me my life, but also had taught me why to live.

My wife accompanied me to Shanghai where we stayed at my second uncle's house. We had long conversations about the past and the future, and my wife was impressed by my uncle's open-mindedness, particularly his high expectations for our generation. Men of his age and achievement often tended to glorify their own youth and belittle the achievements of the contemporary youth. However, despite the ideological or philosophical difference, my uncle recognized the consistent patriotism in different generations.

His daughter had been in Japan for three years now, and was pursuing a Ph.D. degree in computer science. Soon we began discussing studying abroad. He said: "You know, those who have gone abroad and returned have played an important role in our recent history." Apparently he was referring to prominent figures such as Zhou Enlai and Deng Xiaoping, who went to study in France in 1920. In fact, many of the prominent Communist leaders were those who studied in France. They went abroad to improve their opportunities and lives. They were also strongly patriotic and felt it was their mission to find something abroad to save China, which was then under the double yoke of the wars among warlords and the oppression of international imperialism.

Our conversation was interrupted by some noises coming from the kitchen. My uncle's wife wanted to cook a duck dinner for us. While the housemaid was trying to kill the duck, it managed to escape from her hands and jump out the window. It flew over a wall and landed in the courtyard of a neighboring house. My goodness, I thought to myself: wasn't that the reserved historical site where Dr. Sun Yat-sen's widow, Madame Chiang's elder sister, had lived for many years? This timely incident just reminded me of the fact that Sun Yat-sen also went abroad, at the age of thirty-one. He stayed in Japan, England, and the United States, returned to China, and led the 1911 Revolution that overthrew the last emperor of China. I looked at my uncle, and felt more convinced that what he had told me was true. The youth who went abroad and returned did contribute a lot to each of the major social progress in China in this century. This reinforced my feeling of having a mission to help my motherland.

Many of the youth going abroad in the 1980s shared the same spirit and felt it was their mission to learn things that would be helpful to their beloved motherland China. Being a patriotic Chinese youth often meant searching for a medicine for China's disease. Those who went to France in 1920 helped to establish, almost thirty years later, a new China called the People's Republic of China. By the 1980s, about thirty years later, a new generation found themselves dissatisfied with what their parents or grandparents had found abroad and established at home. Many went abroad with the same sense of mission. It remains to be seen what they will find abroad and take back to their homeland, and what another generation will think of them thirty years later.

EPILOGUE

I could hardly believe my ears. I called my family in China from the MIT campus, only to learn that my father had died just a few hours earlier. It was August 4, 1990, and the clock on my desk said 10:29 a.m. Only two weeks before, when I had talked to him on the phone, he assured me that he was getting better. Although I knew he had lung cancer, I still hoped for the best.

The funeral was held in the city's public funeral home on August 10, 1990. I wish I could have been present, although later I heard almost every detail and saw a videotape of the service. At his funeral, government figures at various levels praised his achievements in public service. This was supposed to be a great comfort for the surviving family, but frankly, I was not very interested. What most touched me was the fact that more than 1,500 people attended his funeral, for no other reason than their simple desire to see him for the last time.

He was certainly not the last good man on earth. But the feeling that it was getting difficult to find such a man today was generally and genuinely shared by most of the people who attended the funeral. That is why they came, mostly on public transport, despite a temperature of 40° centigrade. The streets leading to the funeral home were jammed with the cars and shuttle buses provided for the event. The traffic jam lasted about fifteen minutes, a rare event in that part of town. The incident itself became newsworthy, quickly spreading by word of mouth.

The people at the funeral were from all walks of life. There were university and college professors, school teachers and principals, doctors and nurses, writers and journalists, musicians and artists, actors and actresses, businessmen and managers, engineers and factory workers, tailors and cooks, as well as administrators and high-ranking officials. They all came to pay their last tribute to a lifelong Communist, and the fact that this happened in August 1990, fourteen months after the brutal Tiananmen Incident, made it even more remarkable.

I didn't attend his funeral, nor did I visit him after he became sick, for both my wife and my mother did not want me to jeopardize my visa status. China might not let me out or the United States might not let me back in. Who knows what could happen in international politics? I hadn't yet finished my graduate study at MIT, and it was better that I complete it. Thus, these realistic fears prevented me from going back to China. It was a great comfort to me, however, to learn that a marble statue of my father was erected on the new campus of the technical school he had founded in the 1950s. The donations came from his former students at the school, mainly from those who live in Hong Kong and the prosperous neighboring Chinese cities today.

A few years passed before I visited China in the summer of 1994 and then again in the spring of 1996. China has changed dramatically. Some of the changes are probably even more shocking to former insiders like me than outsiders, for we know what it was like before.

For example, my wife comes from a typical peasant family in the countryside of eastern China, and until 1972 her village did not even have electricity. Even among city residents, to have a home telephone was a privilege less than five years ago. Now it has become unremarkable even in my wife's village. In fact, her father already has one, and his next-door neighbor had it even before him. In the cities, every day during my visits I encountered a great number of pedestrians talking on cellular phones. Also, no matter where I went, I could hardly avoid the annoying sounds of the beepers—at bars and restaurants, on buses and trains, in streets and friends' houses, and even in restrooms in public places. Indeed, I think I saw many more cellular phones and beepers in China during my two visits than I have seen in the ten years I've been in the United States.

The extravagant night life in the cities was another shock, although this only affects a small portion of the huge population. A private room equipped with MTV in a night club in Shanghai can charge an hourly rate of $50 to $100. Male patrons come here to be served by female evening escorts, whom they pay at least $25 each per hour. Sometimes these males have to wait their turn on the street because there are no rooms available.

Once I asked my taxi driver in Shanghai where I could enjoy a local opera, the type that my mother's theater group used to perform. He almost laughed in my face, and told me that nowadays people were only interested in having fun with girl escorts in night clubs. In Nanjing, a taxi driver even offered to take me to such a place. A comment by another taxi driver in Shanghai was both insightful and chilling. He said that the dirtier and more rotten society became, the better the business was. I didn't know if I should wish him good luck or bad!

Not all art disappeared, fortunately. In Nanjing, I found our artist friend had become a year-round guest in the five-star hotel named Jinlin, staying in an elegant suite normally reserved for a nation's vice-president or vice-premier. He has apparently benefited much from the buoyant economic boom in China. Dining with him in the hotel, I couldn't help thinking of the numerous poor artists I had encountered in New York. National borders are certainly not the lines to draw between rich and poor.

In our friend's elegant suite, my three-year-old son finally found a comfortable bathroom to use, the first one in Nanjing that he found as sanitary as ours in Boston. In fact, the unsanitary condition of public restrooms and private bathrooms in China is something that hasn't changed much. There were a few other unchanged phenomena, some of which surprised me. In shops I often saw three or four salesgirls chatting at a counter, and in a hospital I once found five nurses sitting in a room apparently doing nothing. In a business office I witnessed a man letting his phone ring ten times before picking it up. All these were familiar experiences that I had grown up with, but I could not reconcile their current presence with the reported economic boom and the new market system.

Maybe the picture wasn't as rosy as it was painted in the West in the mid-1990s. I had a revealing conversation in 1996 with a local entrepreneur in Nanjing named Gao, who appeared on the Sunday *New York Times Magazine* cover in the issue of February 18, 1996. The Gao family were old acquaintances of ours. He told me frankly that he had accumulated some capital in the past few years, but even with his ability and shrewdness he could hardly find a way to reinvest. All his money had been put in CD bank accounts to be safe.

Another story told by a cousin of mine on my mother's side is even painful. He is a successful businessman who owns a small telecommunications firm in Shanghai. In 1994, he purchased a cruiser to catch the booming market on the Yangtze River, but only a year later he had to sell it at a 30 percent loss due to the market bust. To both men, the future looks less promising and prosperous than it once did.

During my visit in 1994 I often encountered people with an extremely optimistic view of the nation's future. To them, the twenty-first century is surely China's. Yet, for each optimist I encountered I inevitably encountered a pessimist, whose view of China's future was as horrible as anyone could imagine. They would tell me that more than half of the state enterprises have not been making a profit. More recently I'd heard that even among the joint ventures between Chinese and foreign investors, a great portion were reporting a net loss. Both views seemed to have enough evidence to support them. The remarkable thing is that I could not find an income-based line dividing the opinions. Optimists and pessimists existed among both the rich and the poor.

On my most recent visit in 1996 I heard less of the conflicting outlooks. Yet it is not because the outlooks are less conflicting, but because there is less outlook at all. Today, few talk about the future or even about current events. My sister admitted that she rarely followed the news at all, either in newspapers or on television. As a professor of education and ethics, she is now concentrating fully on her narrow academic field. She still works very hard, often into the early hours of the morning, even though her income is pathetic compared with that of her husband's, who now works as a manager at a state-owned international trading firm. In today's prevailing materialism, she believes more in the philosophical value of her academic focus, the importance of moral and emotional development in education.

Morality is certainly an important issue and deserves greater attention. Nowadays there seem to be fewer complaints and less resentment against government corruption. Yet it is not because the corruption is less, but because it is much more diffused. When corruption is everywhere and bribes become a part of the daily life, people simply get used to it. A strange phenomenon stemming from this is that people are constantly consuming goods that they didn't purchase in the first place. Thus there is a current saying: Those who consume it didn't purchase it, and those who purchased it never consume it. One example is restaurant patronage. A decent twelve-course dinner for twelve people in a restaurant would cost an ordinary person's monthly salary. Yet restaurants are often crowded with such patronage, and apparently the folks enjoying the dinner are not paying for it. An unintentional justice or fairness came out of this disparity between purchasing and consuming. As people constantly gave and received gifts or bribes, sometimes even luxury goods may trickle down to the hands of ordinary people who could otherwise never afford to buy them. When I gave a friend a bottle of American-produced brandy, he didn't seem to be impressed by the brand, for he had just consumed a bottle of Remy Martin, which would have cost him his monthly salary if he had purchased it.

There is another paradox in China's life today that makes one look richer. While salary is still heavily regulated by the government, benefits are not. Therefore, a large quantity of consumer goods are distributed to employees as their benefits. For example, both my mother and my brother-in-law constantly received boxes of fresh apples, pears, and oranges as parts of their employment or retirement benefits. Often, they forgot about the fruit until it became rotten under the beds where they stored it.

Compared with the days in the early 1960s when my mother hoarded the hard-to-get eggs under her bed and no one in the family wanted to eat such luxurious food, life today is certainly much better. Yet my mother has never felt so poor, in relation to society at large and everyone else in the family. Many other elderly people in the city have become comparatively poor. Among them are retired professors and intellectuals. An old friend, Yang, celebrated her husband's eightieth birthday in November 1995. Her husband is a poet and a retired professor of Chinese and Western literature. A group of old friends wanted to get together and have a birthday party for the man, but none of them has a house big enough for such a party. If it had been ten or twenty years ago, they could have easily afforded to go dutch to a decent restaurant. But now it was almost impossible. Instead, they convened at a tea house in a little park. They each contributed some money to have tea together and buy a small gift for the old man.

At that party of more than thirty, a favorite topic of conversation was the wide-spread corruption of the current society. Yang told me that many at the event mentioned my father's name for they still remembered him as an official who was uncorruptible. Once again, a feeling about a-good-man-is-hard-to-find surfaces, just as it had at his funeral. Now more than five years have passed since my father's death, and the recent social changes have only made this consensus more deeply felt among some of his generation.

Here I unexpectedly found a ready and important link between past and present: I realized how I have actually acquired and expanded my knowledge of China through my father. He was a man whose life reflected his time, during which China modernized itself from a traditional kingdom into a state that is an emerging major economy in the world. The political party he belonged to, the Chinese Communist Party, played a very important role in the making of that history.

The changes China has undergone are certainly great, especially in the past few years. If these changes seem to be shocking to former insiders because we know the past so very well, they must also seem puzzling to outsiders because they don't know enough about the past. While the Tiananmen Incident certainly deserves attention, it should not be seen without a larger historical perspective. The changes in China thereafter might be thought puzzling to those who only remember the Tiananmen Incident. The regime remains the same, and the Communist Party is still the ruling party. How could the economic boom or miracles have happened? To better understand this, one has to take a historical view. After all, the twentieth century is only a comparatively brief period in which China has joined the modern world. The following story may help to provide that perspective.

Sixty years ago, there was a small tailor's shop near the campus of Beijing University in an area known as the Beach District. On the night of December 15, 1935, a couple of young men came in from the darkness to use the telephone. One of them was in his early twenties and the other was still a teenager. The elder one picked up the phone while the younger one stood by, watching.

The man on the phone kept his voice low as he didn't want to be overheard and he sometimes spoke in English, although his English wasn't fluent. He was a student leader at Qinghua University, a prestigious university in China. He was calling student leaders to discuss a student demonstration planned for the following day.

The previous week, there had been a large student demonstration in Beijing, demanding that the government concentrate on resisting the Japanese invasion and occupation rather than suppressing its political opponent, the Communist Party. Now the student leaders were organizing an even larger demonstration for the following morning. They exchanged information about the timing, routes, and passwords for internal communication.

When the man hung up the phone he smiled at his young companion, frankly admitting that his English wasn't as good as that of the latter's elder brother, a student leader at Beijing University. They left the tailor's shop and went back into the darkness outside. The following morning thousands of students in Beijing took to the streets; the demonstration was even larger and better organized than the one the week before.

The men in the tailor's shop were a man named Yao Keguang and my second uncle. The man they talked about, whose English was better, was my father. Yao and my father had been high school classmates in Shanghai and through my father Yao came to know my uncle. The student demonstrations they were organizing are remembered in China as the "December 9th Student Movement." The first breakout, on December 9, 1935, was followed by a larger demonstration on December 16. The movement was opposed by the authorities, and many demonstrators were badly beaten, injured, and jailed.

More than half a century later, in the spring of 1989, a much larger demonstration took place in Beijing, the participants including people from all walks of life. On June 4, the government cracked down on the demonstration, and hundreds of people were killed or wounded, including some soldiers. Among the authorities at the time was Deputy Premier Yao Yilin, one of the five highest-ranked officials in China. Fifty-four years before, his name was Yao Keguang, the older one of the two at the tailor's shop on that winter night. The man who had been a student leader was now confronted by another generation of student protesters. That's the bitter irony Chinese history holds. According to an article in a Chinese journal, *Xinhua Digest*, it also turns out that Mr. Jiang Zemin, the current Chinese leader handpicked by Deng Xiaoping, began his political career as a student activist in a university in Nanjing in 1943 under the influence of the underground Communist network, which was led by my father. Three years later Jiang was recruited into the Communist Party in Shanghai.

While the world seems indeed so small, history is never short of surprises. Only one thing is sure; youth is the future of a nation. No matter how debatable the outcome or value of the youths' actions, we should at least remember their efforts and respect their sincerity.

☆ • Di sees some of old ideas he hated in China surfacing here in U.S. + he feels most strongly about defending — perhaps more as a naturalized — U.S. freedoms ≈

☆ Interview with the citizen author at Harvard 1/15/02

• Di feels that—based on his visits back to China in the mid and late 90's — because of the deep entrenchment of corruption and "rot"— deterioration of moral values (widespread prostitution with police protection - as one example) he cannot see himself returning to live there — to raise his family - or to play a significant role in China's future.

• American business and businessmen are deeply involved also in this corruption as well.

• Younger generation in China is showing increasing anti-American sentiment! - A change from his generation Ex. Clinton's visit revealed this when he received abusive comments - Also U.S. bombing of Chinese embassy - as well as spy-plane incident.

• Li was shocked by levels of corruption but not so much by anti-American feelings because of U.S. policies

☆ VOA - Di misses old VOAmer. vs Rumsfeld on T.V. saying to people — I can't tell you. you don't need to know

INDEX

Accent (dialect), 41, 74, 108, 133, 136, 153, 171
Actor, actress, 16, 17, 56, 57, 171, 209, 216, 241
Acupuncture, 76–77, 88
Africa, 18, 134, 223
Albania, 134, 135
American civilization, xiii, 33, 202
American missionaries, 2, 35, 131, 137
American Revolution, 84
Anhui, 5, 60, 70, 71, 73, 74, 77, 88, 125, 150, 162, 164, 176, 180, 211
Anti-rightist campaign (drive), ix, 98, 173, 185, 197
Anti-"spiritual pollution" campaign, 230
Army Academy (Nanjing), 147, 209, 224, 230
Army Takeover Committee, 58
Art, 52, 53, 76, 77, 217, 237, 242
Asia, 18, 134
Australia, x, 134, 135, 213, 214, 216, 219, 235
Authoritarianism, 164, 168, 184, 207, 236

Bacon, Francis, 8
Bai Hua, 204, 206
Ba Jin, 206
Balzac, Honoré, 35, 163
Bankers, 5, 21, 149
Barbers, 15, 45, 123
Beauty, standards of, 15, 19
Beethoven, 207
Beijing, x, 3, 8, 36, 40, 41, 48, 53, 67, 76, 91, 93, 95, 97, 99, 102, 103, 134, 165, 166, 189, 190, 191, 195, 203, 205, 218, 222, 223, 225, 233, 246
Beijing University, 5, 34, 88, 246; Law and Business School, 5, 8

Bethune, Norman, 133
Bible, 153
Big-Character-Papers, 53
Bikes, 81, 152, 163, 166
Bitter Love (film), 204, 206
Black history, 31, 33
Boston, xi, xiv, 243
Bound feet, 5, 19–20, 121, 122, 123, 124, 151, 165
Brontës, the, 163
Buddhists, Buddhism, 59, 60, 151, 152, 153, 206, 224
Bulgaria, 187
Burns, Robert, 226

Cai Tingkai, 126
Cambodia, 134, 193
Capitalism, 32, 33, 187
Catholics, Catholicism, 59, 114, 151, 161
Central Party Academy (Beijing), 195, 196, 217, 220
Chaucer, 163
Chauffeurs, 66, 89, 114, 120, 197, 217, 221, 222, 231
Chen Boda, 108
Chen Yi, 29, 153
Chiang, Madame, 9, 240
Chiang Kai-shek, 6, 9, 24, 26, 31, 41, 45, 58, 60, 61, 62, 67, 73, 84, 94, 101, 121, 126, 157, 160, 201, 213, 216
China-U.S. relations, 54–55, 87
Chinese characters, 3, 20
Chinese checkers, 20
Chinese chess, 20
Chinese medicine, 141
Chinese names: family name, 3; given name, 3, 10
Chinese New Year, 17, 28, 74, 91, 140, 177, 220
Cinderella, 75

Nanjing, Army Academy at, 147, 209, 224, 230
Nanjing, Naval Academy at, 72
Nanjing Aeronautic Engineering University, 177, 203
Nanjing Agricultural University, 141, 204
Nanjing Foreign Languages School, 88
Nanjing Hotel, 18, 19
Nanjing Institute of Technology, 26
Nanjing Teachers' University, 179, 208
Nanjing University, 139, 165, 168, 186
Nankai High School, 6, 7, 8
Nankai University, 177
Nanny (author's nurse maid), 9–12, 80–83
Nantong, 148
Napoleon, 207
Nationalist government. *See* Chiang Kai-shek
Native Americans, 33
Naval Academy (Nanjing), 72
Neighborhood committees, 80, 81
New Fourth Army, 60, 61
Newspapers, 4, 7, 19, 20, 52, 53, 82, 83, 104, 108, 126, 132, 185, 191, 197, 244
New York, 212, 243
New York Times Magazine, 243
New Zealand, 134
1911 Revolution, the, 5, 19, 121, 202, 240
Ninth National Congress, 91
Nixon, Richard, 132, 135, 210
North Korea, 132
Nuclear attacks, 83

Olivier, Lawrence, *Hamlet* of, 209
Oxford University, 187

Pan Hannian, 175
Paradise Lost and *Paradise Regained* (John Milton), 202
Paris Commune, 107, 110

Pavlovian theory, 188
Peasants, 3, 42, 71, 75, 76, 86, 88, 123, 128, 142, 148, 157, 163, 169, 180, 201, 211, 242
Peking Review (magazine), 131
Peng, Marshal, 210, 211
People's commune, 75
People's Congress, 199
People's Government, 199
People's Liberation Army, 18, 31, 58, 63, 169
People's Political Advisory Conference, 199
People's Republic of China, 6, 35, 101, 240
Physicians, 3, 101
Picture books, 29–33
Police, policemen, 7, 8, 45, 63, 81, 121, 122, 131, 166, 176
Polo, Marco, 218
Population, ix, 26, 34, 84, 158, 159, 174, 201, 242
Population control, 2, 150
Pottier, Eugène, 107
Poverty, 5, 8, 24, 27–28, 75, 203, 204
Primary schools, 14, 23, 42, 72, 79, 88, 106, 107, 131, 134, 137, 138, 178, 200, 203
Principals, 36, 42, 109, 118, 119, 135, 161, 162, 177, 197, 241
Privacy, 79, 81
Prometheus, Promethean, ix, 191
Professors, xiii, 8, 11, 29, 33, 57, 151, 176, 177, 186, 204, 233, 234, 236, 241, 244, 245
Protestants, 59, 151
"Purifying the Party" campaign, 231

Qian, Professor, 204–5
Qinghua University, 34, 246

Racism, 32
Radicals, 39, 108, 116, 123, 133, 138, 140, 142, 144, 145, 146, 160, 163, 164, 165, 169, 170, 171, 173, 174, 175, 178, 181, 185, 191, 194, 204, 212, 227

Essay

Fathers. Famous Writers
Fathers celebrate bond
bet Father + Sons